주한미군지위협정(SOFA)

서명 및 발효 14

주한미군지위협정(SOFA)

서명 및 발효 14

한국학술정보

| 머리말

미국은 오래전부터 우리나라 외교에 있어서 가장 긴밀하고 실질적인 우호 · 협력관계를 맺어온 나라다. 6 · 25전쟁 정전 협정이 체결된 후 북한의 재침을 막기 위한 대책으로서 1953년 11월 한미 상호방위조약이 체결되었다. 이는 미군이 한국에 주둔하는 법적 근거였고, 그렇게 주둔하게 된 미군의 시설, 구역, 사업, 용역, 출입국, 통관과 관세, 재판권 등 포괄적인 법적 지위를 규정하는 것이 바로 주한미군지위협정(SOFA)이다. 그러나 이와 관련한 협상은 계속된 난항을 겪으며 한미 상호방위조약이 체결로부터 10년이 훌쩍 넘은 1967년이 돼서야 정식 발효에 이를 수 있었다. 그럼에도 당시 미군 범죄에 대한 한국의 재판권은 심한 제약을 받았으며, 1980년대 후반 민주화 운동과 함께 미군 범죄 문제가 사회적 이슈로 떠오르자 협정을 개정해야 한다는 목소리가 커지게 되었다. 이에 1991년 2월 주한미군지위협정 1차 개정이 진행되었고, 이후에도 여러 사건이 발생하며 2001년 4월 2차 개정이 진행되어 현재에 이르고 있다.

본 총서는 외교부에서 작성하여 최근 공개한 주한미군지위협정(SOFA) 관련 자료를 담고 있다. 1953년 한미 상호방위조약 체결 이후부터 1967년 발효가 이뤄지기까지의 자료와 더불어, 이후 한미 합동위원회을 비롯해 민 · 형사재판권, 시설, 노무, 교통 등 각 분과위원회의 회의록과 운영 자료, 한국인 고용인 문제와 관련한 자료, 기타 관련 분쟁 자료 등을 포함해 총 42권으로 구성되었다. 전체 분량은 약 2만 2천여 쪽에 이른다.

2024년 3월

한국학술정보(주)

| 일러두기

· 본 총서에 실린 자료는 2022년 4월과 2023년 4월에 각각 공개한 외교문서 4,827권, 76만 여 쪽 가운데 일부를 발췌한 것이다.

· 각 권의 제목과 순서는 공개된 원본을 최대한 반영하였으나, 주제에 따라 일부는 적절히 변경하였다.

· 원본 자료는 A4 판형에 맞게 축소하거나 원본 비율을 유지한 채 A4 페이지 안에 삽입하였다. 또한 현재 시점에선 공개되지 않아 '공란'이란 표기만 있는 페이지 역시 그대로 실었다.

· 외교부가 공개한 문서 각 권의 첫 페이지에는 '정리 보존 문서 목록'이란 이름으로 기록물 종류, 일자, 명칭, 간단한 내용 등의 정보가 수록되어 있으며, 이를 기준으로 0001번부터 번호가 매겨져 있다. 이는 삭제하지 않고 총서에 그대로 수록하였다.

· 보고서 내용에 관한 더 자세한 정보가 필요하다면, 외교부가 온라인상에 제공하는 『대한민국 외교사료요약집』 1991년과 1992년 자료를 참조할 수 있다.

| 차례

정/리/보/존/문/서/목/록					
기록물종류	문서-일반공문서철	등록번호	934 9607	등록일자	2006-07-27
분류번호	741.12	국가코드	US	주제	
문서철명	한.미국 간의 상호방위조약 제4조에 의한 시설과 구역 및 한국에서의 미국군대의 지위에 관한 협정 (SOFA) 전59권. 1966.7.9 서울에서 서명 : 1967.2.9 발효 (조약 232호) *원본				
생산과	미주과/조약과	생산년도	1952 - 1967	보존기간	영구
담당과(그룹)	조약	조약		서가번호	--
참조분류					
권차명	V.36 재교섭, 1966.2-7월				
내용목차	* 4.15 한국, 핵심내용의 일부 수정을 위한 재교섭 제의 6.9 한국, 수정안 수교 6.30 미국, 대안 제시 * 일지 : 1953.8.7 이승만 대통령-Dulles 미국 국무장관 공동성명 - 상호방위조약 발효 후 군대지위협정 교섭 약속 1954.12.2 정부, 주한 UN군의 관세업무협정 체결 제의 1955.1월, 5월 미국, 제의 거절 1955.4.28 정부, 군대지위협정 제의 (한국측 초안 제시) 1957.9.10 Hurter 미국 국무차관 방한 시 각서 수교 (한국측 제의 수락 요구) 1957.11.13, 26 정부, 개별 협정의 단계적 체결 제의 1958.9.18 Dawling 주한미국대사, 형사재판관할권 협정 제외 조건으로 행정협정 체결 의사 전달 1960.3.10 정부, 토지, 시설협정의 우선적 체결 강력 요구 1961.4.10 장면 국무총리-McConaughy 주한미국대사 공동성명으로 교섭 개시 합의 1961.4.15, 4.25 제1, 2차 한.미국 교섭회의 (서울) 1962.3.12 정부, 교섭 재개 촉구 공한 송부 1962.5.14 Burger 주한미국대사, 최규하 장관 면담 시 형사재판관할권 문제 제기 않는 조건으로 교섭 재개 통고 1962.9.6 한.미국 간 공동성명 발표 (9월 중 교섭 재개 합의) 1962.9.20~1965.6.7 제1-81차 실무 교섭회의 (서울) 1966.7.8 제82차 실무 교섭회의 (서울) 1966.7.9 서명 1967.2.9 발효 (조약 232호)					

마/이/크/로/필/름/사/항				
촬영연도	*롤 번호	화일 번호	후레임 번호	보관함 번호
2006-11-23	I-06-0070	04	1-235	

0001

기 안 지

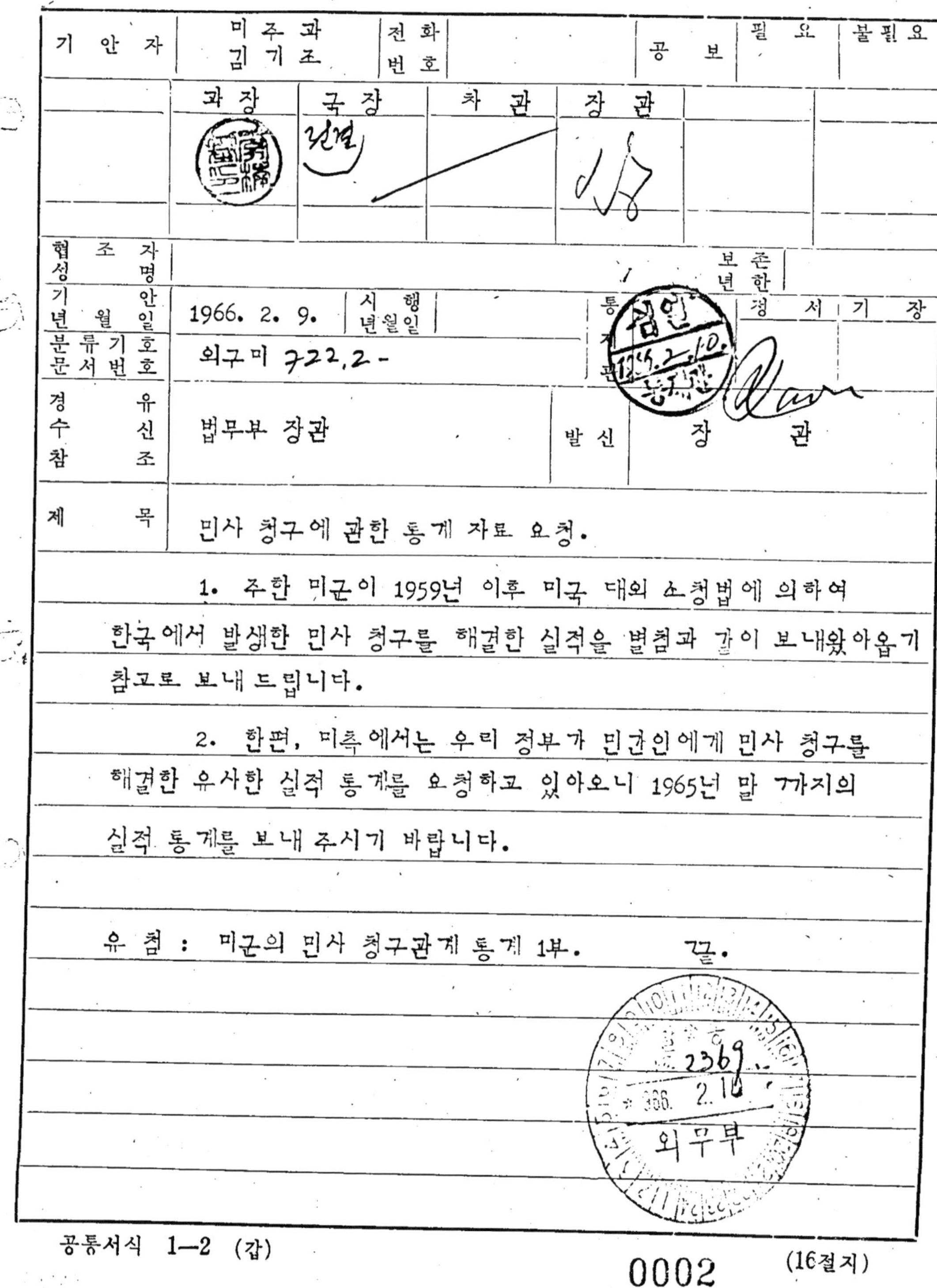

기 안 자	미주과 김기조	전화번호		공보	필요	불필요
	과장	국장	차관	장관		
협조자 성명				보존 년한		
기안 년월일	1966. 2. 9.	시행 년월일		통제관	정서기장	
분류기호 문서번호	외구미 722.2-					
경유 수신 참조	법무부 장관		발신	장관		
제목	민사 청구에 관한 통계 자료 요청.					

1. 주한 미군이 1959년 이후 미국 대외 소청법에 의하여 한국에서 발생한 민사 청구를 해결한 실적을 별첨과 같이 보내왔아옵기 참고로 보내 드립니다.

2. 한편, 미측에서는 우리 정부가 민간인에게 민사 청구를 해결한 유사한 실적 통계를 요청하고 있아오니 1965년 말 까지의 실적 통계를 보내 주시기 바랍니다.

유 첨 : 미군의 민사 청구관계 통계 1부. 끝.

외무부 2369 1966. 2. 10

공통서식 1—2 (갑)

0002 (16절지)

외 무 부

외구미 1966. 2. 10.

수 신 : 법무부 장관

제 목 : 민사 청구에 관한 통계자료 요청.

1. 주한 미군이 1959년 이후 미국 대외 소청법에 의하여 한국에서 발생한 민사 청구를 해결한 실적을 별첨과 같이 보내왔아옵기 참고로 보내 드립니다.

2. 한편, 미측에서는 우리 정부가 민간인에게 민사 청구를 해결한 유사한 실적 통계를 요청하고 있아오니 1965년 말 까지의 실적 통계를 보내 주시기 바랍니다.

유 첨 : 미군의 민사 청구관계 통계 1부. 끝.

외무부장관 이 동 원

0003

Claims Statistics

The number of Claims received by the U.S. Army Claims commission and amounts of compensation paid since the Claims Service began its operation on June 1, 1959 are shown as below: (As of Sept. 1. 1964)

	Nr. Received	Amount Paid
1959 (7 mos)	517	$282,688.28
1960	2,125	727,696.22
1961	1,163	361,801.26
1962	979	187,633.75
1963	839	148,185.86
1964 (8 mos)	911	101,433.52
Total	6,534	1,809,438.89

0004

외 무 부

처 리 전

1966. 2. 22.

1. 제 목 한·미간 주둔군 지위협정안에 대한 의견

2. 의 견

교통부에서는 한·미간 주둔군 지위협정안 중, 교통부 관계 조항을 검토후 별첨과 같이 협정안의 수정에 관한 의견을 제시하여 온바, 동 조항들은 :

1. 국제선례 (미.일협정)에 입각하고 있을뿐만 아니라,
2. 이미 한.미간에 합의를 본바 있음. (비고 참조)

따라서, 교섭 형편상 이 시점에서 미국측에 관계 조항의 수정을 제의하기는 곤란하다고 사료함.

3. 조치를 요하는 사항 (조치완료 예정일자)

4. 비 고

제 10 조 : 선박 및 항공기의귀착-1963. 1. 7. 합의
제 11 조 : 기상업무 - 1963. 4. 24. 합의
제 15조 : 초청계약자 (8항 제외) - 1964. 7. 8. 합의.

0005

고 흥 부

고기목722,2-ㅇ.　　　　　　　　　　　　　　　　　　　　　　　1966,2,17

수신 외무부장관

제목 한.미간 주둔군 지위협정(안)에 대한 의견 제출

외구미722,2-15로 송부하여 주신 표기 협정(안)을 검토한바 별첨과 같은 당부의견이 있아오니 적의 조치 하여주기 바랍니다.

유첨 한.미간 주둔군 지위협정(안)에 대한 의견 1부. 끝

첨부물에서 분리되면 일반문서로 재분류

고흥부장관　　　　안　　경　　모

1966, 10, 7,에 예고문에 의거 일반문서로 재분류됨

0006

협서로 자협정제

한·미간 주둔군 지위협정(안)에 대한 의견

1. 제10조 제1항중 "합중국에 의하여, 합중국을 위하여 또는 합중국 관리하에서 공용을 위하여 운항되는 합중국 및 외국의 항공기는"을 "합중국 군대를 위하여 운항되는 합중국 소속 군용항공기는"으로 수정이 필요함.

이 유

합중국 군용 항공기를 제외한 민간항공기는 합중국 군대에서 공용으로 사용한다 하드라도 항공기 소속회사에서는 상당한 임대료등을 수수하고 항공기를 제공하여 줄것이므로 그들에게 까지 착륙료 기타 과징금을 면제케 함은 부당하다고 사료됨.

2. 제10조 제2항중 "및 그들의 가족"을 삭제하고 "기타의 과징금을" 다음에 "공용에 한하여 이를"을 삽입토록 수정되어야 함.

이 유

군인 군속이라 하드라도 공용을 제외한 모든 사용일 경우에는 모든 과징금을 부과함은 당연할것이며 더욱이 그들의 가족까지도 그들과 동일한 대우로서 모든 과징금을 면제함은 타당치 못함.

3. 제11조 본문 말미의 "약속한다"를 약속하며"로 하고 다음과 같이 추가 함이 타당함.

"합중국군대가 대한민국 영역내에서 관측한 기상 자료도 또한 대한민국 정부에 제공할것을 약속한다.

이 유

현재 국내 기상관측에 있어서는 중앙관상대, 미공군, 한국공군등 세기관에서 기상자료를 수집하고 텔레타입으로 즉시즉시 그수집된 자료를 상호 교환하고 있으며 또한 교환하지 않으면 정확한 기상업무를 상호

0007

·수행 할수 없는데 한국정부에서만 기상자료를 미군에게 제공하고 한국 정부는 미군으로부터 자료를 제공받지 못하게되면 중앙관상대의 기상 업무는 수행이 곤란하게 될것이므로 이조항은 기필 수정되어야할것임.

4. 제15조의 내용은 초청 계약자에 관한것인바 동조 제3항에 의하면 초청계약자들에게도 본 협정상의 이익이 부여되어 있으나 이들은 자기자신을 위한 사업(영리)이므로 특권을 부여할 하등의 이유가 없으니 초청계약자에 대한 모든 특권은 삭제함이 타당함. 끝

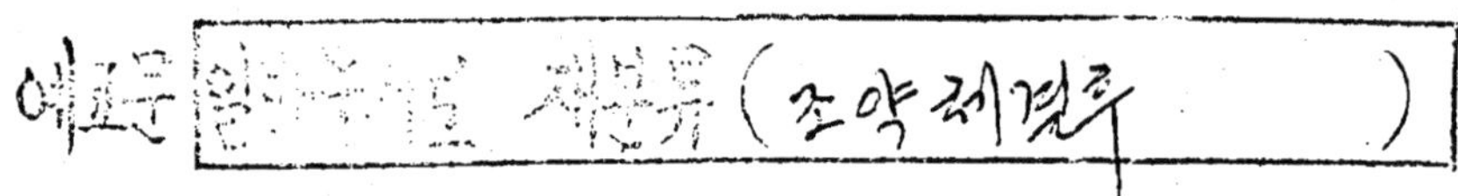

0008

한·미간 주둔군지위협정 체결 교섭에 대한 고찰

1. 서문

우리나라를 공산침략으로 부터 방위하기 위하여 미군이 주둔한지 어언 10여년이 지났다. 지금까지의 사정을 회고하건데 동두천 지구 미군부녀 2명에 대한 삭발 사건을 비롯하여 파주의 나무꾼 린치사건 및 최근의 운천리사건등 실로 열거하기 어려운 정도로 많는 사건이 돌발하였다. 이로 인하여 우리 국민의 감정은 격화되었고 여론은 불등하여 조속한 행정협정 체결을 갈구하는 마음 한이 없다. 그러나 한국동란이 발발하자 1950.7.12일 대전에서 각서교환 형식에 의하여 성립한 소위 대전협정은 잠정적으로 주한미군에 대한 배타적 형사재판관할권을 미군법회의에 부여하고 있는 형편으로서 이는 "전쟁이라는 긴박한 상태"를 전제로 한것임으로 휴전이된 현금에도 한미간의 행정협정이 체결되지 못하여 소위 대전협정이 폐기되지 못하고 있음은 심히 유감스러운 일이다. 물론 우리정부가 행정협정을 체결코저 10여년간 꾸준히 미군측에 교섭하여 온바를 모르는 바는 아니나 이제 1962년 9월부터 본격적인 교섭을 진행시켜서 최종적 협정체결을 안전에 두고 있는 이마당에 어째서 동교섭이 지연되는가를 한번 고찰하여 봄으로서 국민전체가 아직도 잘모르는 문제점을 밝혀 보고자 한다.

2. 교섭경위

우리정부가 국민의 염원에 호응하여 주한미군의 지위를 규제하는 주둔군지위협정 체결 교섭을 개시할 것을 미국측에 촉구한 것은 상당한 시일에 달하지만 한·미양국이 본격적으로 교섭을 시작한 것은 1962년 9월 20일 제 1차 실무자회의를 개최한 때라 하겠다.

13

0009

그후 양국실무자 대표단은 각기 자국의 조안을 고환하고 꾸준하게 회의를 거듭한 보람이 있어 지난 1964년 10월 16일까지 64회에 달하는 회의를 개최하였으며 그간 총 29개조항중 출입국관리, 관세, 소세, 현지조달 조항을 위시하여 20개조항에 완전합의를 보는 단계에 이르렀다. 그러나 상금 합의를 보지 못하고 있는 9개조항에는 형사재판관할권, 민사청구권, 노무조달등 몇몇 어려운 문제를 내포하고 있는 조항들이 있다.

3. 교섭 지연의 요인

이와 같이 교섭이 쉽사리 타결되지 않고 있는 이유는 여러가지 들을수 있겠으나 첫째로 우선 양국교섭단이 장기와 같은 어려운 문제를 위요하고 자국의 실리를 최대한으로 확보하려고 신중을 기하고 있다는데 있으리라고 보아야 하겠다. 둘째로는 상기한 미합의 9개조항중에서도 특히 쌍방교섭단간에 상당한 의견이 대립되어 있으며 본협정 체결의 "키"가 되는 조항은 형사재판관할권 이라고 할수 있으므로 이에 대해서는 문제점 별로 상세히 그내용을 검토해 보고자 하나, 그외에도 민사청구권 및 노무조항등에 대하여 간단히 문제점만을 제시하고 넘어 가고자 한다.

가. 민사청구권

이문제는 미·일협정, 나토협정, 또는 최근에 체결된 미국과 호주간의 협정문을 보드래도 모두 접수국의 법에 따라 공정한 보상액을 결정하여 사고를 낸 미군에게 부담을 시키도록 되어 있다. 우리나라에 있어서도 현재 국가배상법 및 동시행령에 따라 국가배상위원회가 있어서 신속하고도 공정한 심의를 거쳐 보상액을 결정하고 있음으로 전기 제협정의 선례에 따라 우리나라 법대로 해결한다 하여도 하등의 문제될 것이 없다고 본다. 다만

0010

구태여 문제되는 점이 있다면 우리나라의 국가배상 제도의 역사가 짧다는 점과 동일성질의 사건을 처리하는데 있어 미국인이 부담할 보상액을 한국인의 경우 보다 과중하게 책정하지나 않을까 하는 점에 대한 미국측의 의구심이 있지나 않을까 예상된다는 점이다.

그러나 우리나라 배상제도의 운영을 보건대 유능한 법관들이 공정한 법의 운영을 통하여 모든 사건을 신속히 처리하고 있으며 주권국가의 법의 존엄성과 양국간의 우호관계를 고찰할때, 미군에 대한 차별대우는 있을수도 없는 일임으로 전기와 같은 문제점은 본협정 체결지연의 요인이 된다고는 볼수 없다.

나. 노무조항

현재 미군에게 고용되고 있는 노무자는 3만여명에 달하고 있다. 따라서, 미군은 이들에 대한 모집, 임명, 급여, 해직등 고용조건 및 그들의 보호 및 복지를 위한 조건과 기타 노무자의 권리에 관하여 한국의 노동법 및 관계법규를 준수하여야만 될것이다. 이와같은 내용은 미국이 체결한 각국과의 협정에서도 그 예를 찾아 볼수 있는 것이다.

그러나 여기서 몇가지 문제될수 있는 점을 들어 보자면 첫째로 우리나라 노동관계 법규에 의하면 노동관계 당사자간에 분쟁이 야기될시 이를 해결하기 위하여 법정에 소송을 제기할수 있게 되어 있다. 그러나, 미군이 관련된 분쟁해결에 있어서도 미군이 피고로서 법정에 출도해야 될것이냐 하는 문제를 들수 있다. 그러나 각국의 선례를 보면 미군이 직접 법정에 출도하는 예는 찾아볼수 없음으로 국제선례에 따라 분쟁을 해결하는 방도가 마련되어야 할것이다. 둘째로 미군에 종사하는 노무자가 우리법에 규정된 모든 권리를 당연히 향유하여야 될것이나 미군이 우리나라의 방위를 위하여

0011

주둔하고 있는만큼, 동사명의 수행에 지장을 초래할 정도로 노무자의 파업권이 존중되어야 할것인가의 문제를 들수 있다. 그러나, 법적으로 인정된 권리는 원칙적으로 박탈될수 없다는 데에는 이론의 여지가 있을수 없으나 대만 군의 사명을 완수하는데 지장을 주는 결과가 초래된다면 이는 엄격히 방지되어야 할것이다. 따라서 미군당국과 한국의 노동관계 당국은 이와같은 곤난점을 실지운영을 통하여 해소하도록 상호 긴밀한 협조가 요망되는 것이다.

다. 형사재판 관할권

전기한 바와 같이 형사재판관할권 조항은 본협정을 체결하는데 있어서 가장 핵심이며 관건이 되는 조항이다. 본조항이 아직도 해결을 못보고 담보 상태에 있는 요인을 살펴보면 한마디로 말해서 형사재판관할권 행사에 대한 한국측의 태도 및 아량에 대하여 미국이 일종의 불신을 가지고 있는데 연유하고 있다고 볼수 있다.

(1) 전속적 관할권과 경합적 관할권

관할권이라면 전속적 관할권과 경합적 관할권 두가지를 들수 있는데 전자는 국가의 안전에 관한 범죄를 포함하여 일국가의 법에 의하면 범죄를 구성하나 타방국가의 법에서는 범죄가 구성되지 않는 범죄에 대한 관할권을 의미하는 것으로서 관할권 행사에 있어 한미양국간에 문제될 것이 별로 없는 것이다. 그러나 후자인 경합적 관할권이 문제가 되는 것으로서 좀 상세하게 기술하고저 한다. 경합적 관할권이라 함은 어떤 범죄가 파견국이나 접수국의 법에 의하여 다같이 범죄를 구성할 경우의 관할권을 의미하며 이때에는 양국중 어느편이 우선적으로 관할권을 행사할 것이냐 하는 것이 상당히 중요한 문제로서 일반적으로 공무집행중의 작위

0012

또는 부작위에 기인하는 범죄등의 경우는 파견국(미군)이 관할권을 행사하고 기타의 범죄에 대해서는 접수국(한국)이 관할권을 행사하게 되는 것이 대체적인 경향이다. 여기서 특기해야 할것은 우리나라에는 상당한 수의 미군이 주둔하고 있는 관계로 이런 범죄가 종종 발생하는데 미군인에 의한 범죄가 발항하였을 시 그범죄가 공무집행중에 발생하였는가의 여부를 어느편이 결정하느냐에 따라 관할권의 행사가 결정된 것인바 일본, 나토, 독일,기타 각국의 협정에서의 선례는 다같이 파견국 군인이 소속하고 있는 군대 지휘관이 발행하는 공무집행중 범죄증명서에 의거 파견국이 관할권을 행사하게 될 것이며 다만 일단 발행된 증명서에 대하여 접수국 당국이 이의를 제기할수 있는가에 약간의 정도차이는 있지만 이것 역시 각국의 실지운영 상황을 살펴보면 파견국 당국의 결정이 수락되는 것이 통례로 되어 있다. 참고로 1963년도 및 1964년도에 우리나라에서 일어난 미군관계 사건수는 다음과 같다.

년도	총건수
1963년도	215건
1964년도(10.9일현재)	169건

(상기 사건수에는 교통법규 위반사건은 포함되지 않음)

한.미간에 맺어질 협정의 형태가 어떻게 낙착될 것인가는 전혀 교섭의 결과에 달려 있지만 협정상 또는 실지운영에 관한 국제적 선례의 테두리를 벗어나지 않을 것으로 보며 그렇게 된다면 공무집행중 일어난 범죄에 대한 관할권 행사의 결정권은 미군당국에

0013

있게 될것이다. 이렇게 살펴볼때 과거 국민의 관심을 환기시킨길이 있는 어러사건(예를들면 운전사고사건)을 조사한 결과 공무집행중 범죄로 판정된 사건은 모다 파견국인 미군이 당연히 재판을 해야되는 것임으로 이러한 사실을 국민들이 사전에 알았다면 국민감정에만 호소하여 물의를 이르키지는 않었을 것으로 안다. 따라서 사건의 추세가 그러하다면 우리나라도 사건의 원만한 해결을 위하여 국제적 추세에 따라감에 있어서 조금도 인색함이 있어서는 안될 것이다.

(2) 관할권의 포기

위에서 말한바와 같은 절차에 따라 일단 접수국이 관할권을 행사하게 된 경우 파견국이 관할권의 포기를 요청하면 접수국은 특히 중대하다고 인정되는 범죄를 제외하고는 이요청에 응하여 상당올의 범죄를 파견국에 포기하는 제도가 발달되었다. 즉 일국의 관할권 행사를 포기하고 타국에 이양한다는 것은 그나라가 행사한다는 종래의 원칙에 대한 하나의 예외라고 할수 있는데 생각컨데 이것은 관할권 행사 그자체를 초월하여 그포기를 통하여 국제사회에 있어서 국가간의 우의를 증진하려는 점을 고려한데서 부터 연유한 것이 아닌가 한다. 각국 협정을 살펴보면 다음과 같은 포기에 관한 유형이 있음을 알수 있다.

ㄱ. 나토 협정, 미일협정, 미국-오스트리아 협정

만약 일방당사국으로 부터 관할권을 갖고 있는 국가에 관할권 포기요청이 있으면 타방당사국은 특히 중대하다고 인정하는 경우를 제외하고는 그러한 요청에 대하여 호의적인 고려를 하게 되어 있다.

0014

ㄴ. 희랍협정

희랍 당국은 미군법에 복하는 자에 관한한 질서와 기율을 유지할 주된 책임이 미국 당국에 있음을 인정하여 미국당국으로 부터 신청이 있으면 희랍당국이 관할권을 행사하는 것이 중대하다고 인정하는 경우를 제외하고는 미국당국에 관할권을 포기하게 되어 있다.

ㄷ. 독일 협정

파견국의 요청이 있으면 독일국은 독일국이 행사하게 되어 있는 관할권을 일단 파견국에 포기하며 그후 만약 독일국이 특정한 경우 특수한 이유로 독일국이 관할권을 행사하는 것이 불가결하다고 인정할 때에는 일정한 절차에 따라 포기를 철회하게 되어 있다.

이상 관할권 포기에 관한 3가지의 형태를 보건대 절차상 접수국이 일단 포기한 연후 중대하다고 인정되는 범죄를 파견국으로 부터 이양받는다는 독일협정의 내용과 접수국에서 중대하다고 인정하는 범죄 이외의 기타 사건만을 파견국에게 포기해주는 두가지 형태로대분할수 있갔으니 어떤 형태이든 간에 모두가 파견국에게 관할권을 포기한다는 점을 동일한 것이다. 그러면 이와 같은 포기제도 밑에서 여러나라들은 관할권을 어느 정도 포기하고 있는가를 다음과 같은 통계에서 보기로 하자.

ㄹ. 관할권 포기통계 (별표참조)

상기 통계로 보아 세계적인 포기의 경향을 알수 있거니와 1961년 12월 1일부터 1962년 11월 30일까지의 각국 총 포기율이 59 퍼센트였음에 비하여 1962년 12월 1일부터 1963년 11월 30일까지의 포기율은 70.45 퍼센트에

0015

달하여 점차적으로 증가하는 기세를 보이고
있다. 가장 포기율이 많은 국가는 미군이
많이 주둔하고 있는 일본, 독일, 불란서등
국가로서 보통 80 내지 90 퍼센트의 포기율을
보이고 있으며 특히 일본이 91.6 퍼센트 및
화란의 97.2 퍼센트 등은 주목할만한 고율이다.
따라서 실지 이러한 접수국들이 재판한 건수
는 얼마되지 않음을 알수있다. 물론 이와
같이 관할권의 포기율이 높은 것은 포기
건수의 대부분을 차지하고 있는 것이 교통
법규위반 사건인데 전세계에서 1962 년 12 월
1 일부터 1963 년 11 월 30 일까지 일어난 총
19,617 건의 사건중 고통법규위반사건이
12,713 건에 달하고 있으며 이는 총건수의
65 퍼센트에 해당한다. 따라서 남어지 35.2
퍼센트가 중대한 범죄로 들수 있으며 이중
90 퍼센트 이상의 포기가 이루워지고 있다는
것을 알수 있다. 이밖에 기타 종류의 범죄
의 경우도 상당히 포기되고 있다.

4. 결론

이상 형사재판관할권을 주심으로 한 관할권의 결정
절차, 공무집행중 범죄 및 관할권의 포기등 몇가지 문제
점을 고찰하였다. 양국실무자들이 각기 자국의 이익을
위하여 신중히 교섭에 임하고 있는 것은 이해할수는
있으나 여기서 한미 양당국에 부탁하고저 하는 것은 한국측은
특히 중대하다고 생각하는 경우를 제외하고는 타국의
선례에 따라 양보할 것은 양보하고 불충분한 점은 시정
하여 관대하게 미측에 협조하는데 추호라도 인색하지 않기
바라며 미국측도 한국의 주권국가로서의 법의 운영을
신뢰하고 국제선례를 토대로 하여 그 테두리 안에서
협정을 맺도록 교섭을 진행하기 바란다. 또 그렇게

0016

하드래도 협정의 실지운영에 있어서는 미측이 기대하는 이상으로 한국의 협조를 얻게 될것은 틀림없다.

재언하노니, 한·미양국은 양국간에 개재해 있는 전통적인 우호관계를 증진한다는 대국적 견지에서 자국의 주장만을 고집하지 말고 보앙의 정신으로 현안인 교섭을 하루바삐 타결할것을 촉구하는 바이다.

0017

각국의 관할권 포기에 관한 통계

기간 : 1962.12.1 – 1963.11.30
괄호내 수자는 전년도인
61.12.1 – 62.11.30까지의 통계

1. NATO 협정 제국

국가명	접수국의 관할권에 속하는 범죄건수		포기건수		관할권포기율 (퍼센트)	
Belgium	56	(42)	56	(20)	100	(47.6)
Canada	401	(415)	19	(21)	4.7	(5.0)
Denmark	5	(2)	3	(1)	60.0	(50.0)
France	4,625	(4,454)	3,928	(3,841)	84.9	(86.2)
Germany *	6,188		5,512		89.0	
Greece	45	(36)	36	(35)	80.0	(97.2)
Italy	271	(305)	163	(100)	60.1	(32.7)
Luxembourg	43	(26)	10	(3)	23.2	(11.5)
Netherlands	247	(119)	247	(119)	100.	(100.)
Norway	4	(1)	0	(1)	0.	(100.)
Portugal	0	(0)	0	(0)	-	-
Turkey	116	(95)	54	(6)	46.5	(6.3)
U. K.	1,640	(2,037)	144	(345)	8.7	(16.9)
Total	13,641	(7,532)	10,172	(4,492)	74.5	(59.6)

* 독일은 1963년 7월 1일에 NATO-SOFA 의 당사국이 되었음.

0018

2. 기타 협정제국

국가명	접수국의 관할권에 속하는 범죄건 수		포기건수		관할권포기율 (%)	
Australia	1	(0)	0	(0)	0	(-)
Iceland *	105	(0)	9	(0)	8.5	(-)
Japan	3,433	(3,191)	3,090	(2,906)	90.0	(91.6)
Morocco	42	(33)	20	(18)	47.6	(54.5)
New Zealand	29	(23)	28	(22)	96.5	(95.6)
Nicaragua	0	(1)	0	(0)	-	(0)
Philippines	67	(85)	52	(77)	77.7	(90.5)
Spain	122	(16)	99	(10)	81.1	(62.5)
West Indies	227	(172)	7	(4)	3.0	(2.3)
West Pakistan	1	(0)	1	(0)	100.	(-)
Total	4,027	(3,521)	3,306	(3,037)	82.0	(86.2)

* Iceland 는 NATO-SOFA 의 당사국이나 미군군대의 지위에 관한 협정은 별도로 있음.

3. 협정 미체결국

국가명	접수국의 관할권에 속하는 범죄건 수		포기건수		관할권포기율 (%)	
Ascension	1	(0)	0	(0)	0.	(-)
Hong Kong	13	(12)	2	(0)	15.3	(0)
Mexico	1,213	(772)	549	(143)	44.3	(18.5)
Panama	46	(140)	2	(22)	4.3	(15.7)
South Africa	0	(2)	0	(0)	-	(0)
Switzerland	0	(3)	0	(0)	-	(0)
Total	1,273	(929)	553	(165)	43.4	(17.7)

0019

법 무 부

법무송811.1- 4118 (23-1461) 1966. 2. 28.

수신 외무부장관

제목 통계자료 요청에 대한 회신

1. 외무미ㅋ 22.2-2369 (66.2.10)로 통계자료 요청한 것에 대하여 별첨과 같이 송부 합니다.

유첨 통계자료 1부. 끝

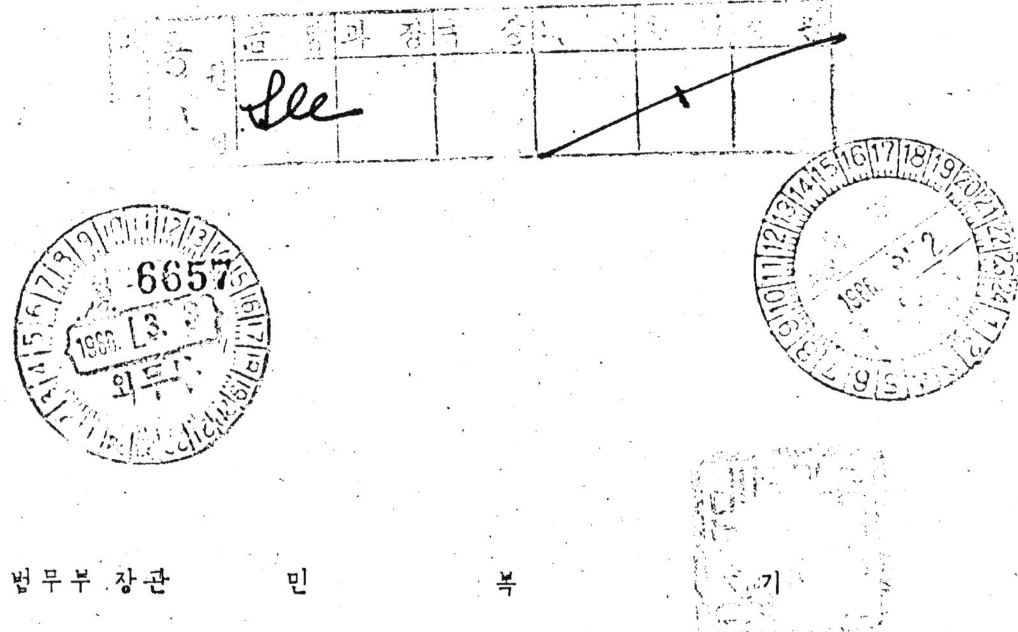

법무부 장관 민 복 기

0020

통 계 자 료

1. 법무부 배상금 심의 위원회 결정에 의한 지불

년 도	접수건수	지 불 액
1963 (5.1 이후)	194	11,996,925 50
1964	449	31,802,922 88
1965	303	22,487,260
합 계	946	66,287,108 38

"국가배상금 청구에 관한 절차법에 의거 63.5.1 부로 법무부에 배상금 심의위원회 재도설치 이후 접수처리 된것임"

2. 민사 재판에 의한 지불

년 도	접수건수	지 불 액
1963	233	44,402,603 40
1964	684	243,660,884 99
1965	1,554	391,217,757 〃
합 계	2,471	679,281,245 50

"63년 이전은 각부처별로 재판 지불 하였음"

0021

63rd Negotiating Session

Para.

7. Regarding the number of claims made against the U.S. armed forces, Lt. Colonel Thompson tabled the following data showing the number of claims processed during 1963 and up to September 1, 1964:

	Claims Adjudicated	Claims Allowed	Claims Disallowed	Claims Paid	Amount Paid Won	Amount Paid Dollars
1963	839	680	159	649	19,264, 162	148,185,86
1964 (as of Sept 1)	911	589	322	576	25,865, 548	101,433.52

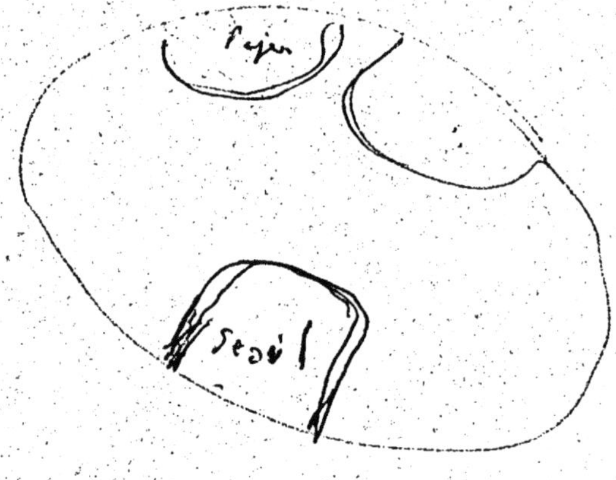

0022

62nd SOFA Negotiating Session

ROK Claims Service

Para 2.c.

c. Claims Processed in the Years 1963 and 1964

In 1963, 283 cases had been received and processed during the period from May 1 to December 31, 1963.

As of 30 June 1964, 207 cases had been received and 139 cases had been processed thus far in 1964. Sixty eight cases were under consideration on 30 June 1964.

In other words, during the past 14 months, 490 claims cases have been received and processing of 422 has been completed. Detailed tabulation of the claims which have been received and considered by the Committee are as shown on the table.

Number of Claims Processed in 1963 and 1964

YEAR	NO. OF CLAIMS RECEIVED	AWARDED	DISPOSITION REJECTED	WITHDREW	TOTAL	PENDING
1963 (1 May—31 Dec)	283	189	81	13	283	-
1964 (1 Jan-30 Jun)	207	91	27	21	139	68
TOTAL	490	280	108	34	422	68

d. ... .

e. Appropriations for awards in 1963 and 1964

In the 1963 and 1964 budgets, 30,390,000 Won and 25,910,200 Won, respectively, were appropriated for awards. Although the amount of the budget for fiscal year 1964 is a little less than that for 1963, this will not affect the payment of claims awards. If additional appropriations should be necessary, the Korean authorities would take appropriate measures.

Incl 2

0023

Para 2.c. (contd)

f. Number of Claims Offices

As had been explained at the 39th session, there is one central office in the Ministry of Justice. However, as the Korean negotiators pointed out at the 61st session, actions designed to improve the central office as well as enlarge the system are now being taken by the Korean authorities.

駐韓美軍訴請当局의 請求权 処理 統計
(1959年6月1日부터 1964年9月10까지)

7. Claims Statistics

The number of claims received by Claims Commissions and amounts of compensation paid since the Claims Service began its operations on 1 June 1959 are shown below:

年度	請求权 受付件数 ~~Nr. Received~~:	支拂額 ~~Amount Paid~~:
1959 (7個月內)	517	$282,688.28
1960	2,125	$727,696.22
1961	1,163	$361,801.26
1962	979	$187,633.75
1963 ~~(6 mos)~~	~~378~~ 839	~~$ 77,032.16~~ $148,185.86
1964 (9月10日現在)	911	$101,433.52

~~Total claims received since 1 June 1959: 5,162 cases.~~

~~Total compensation paid since 1 June 1959: $1,636,851.67~~

~~(12,639,775 Won)~~

計	6,534	$1,809,438.89

주: 미군이 지불한 배상총액을 277대 1로 환산하면 다음과 같음며, ~~년간 약 1억원 이상을 지불한 것이 됨.~~

~~$1,636,851.67 × ₩277 = ₩453,638,935.69~~

$1,809,438.89 × ₩277 = ₩501,214,572.53

0025

ROK Claims Service

1. Claims processed and paid on the decision by the National Compensation Council of the Ministry of Justice.

Year	No. of Claims Received	Amount Paid (Won)
1963 *	194	11,996,925.50
1964	449	31,802,922.88
1965	303	22,487,260.
Total	946	66,287,108.38

* This tabulation denotes; those claims received and processed since the Compensation Council began its operations on May 1, 1963 under Law Concerning Procedures on Claims for Damages by the State (Law No. 1223, promalgated on December 24, 1962)

2. Claims processed by Civil Courts

Year	No. of Claims Received	Amount Paid (Won)
1963 *	233	44,402,603.40
1964	684	243,660,884.99
1965	1,554	391,217,757.11
Total	2,471	679,281,245.50

* Those claims submitted prior to year of 1963 were settled and paid individually by the central governmental agency concerned.

0026

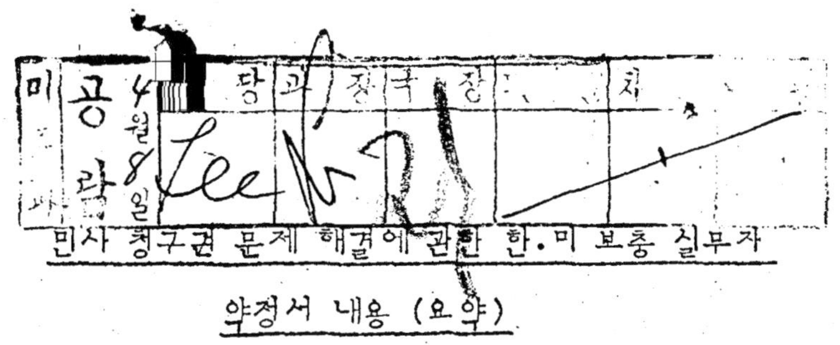

민사 청구권 문제 해결에 관한 한.미 보충 실무자

약정서 내용 (요약)

1. 목 적 : 주월 한국군의 군인, 군속 및 고용원의 비전투 행위로 인한 모든 재산상의 손해, 신체상의 상해 및 사망에 대한 배상 처리.

2. 재원 및절차 :

다음과 같은 절차에 따라 주월 한국군이 청구를 접수, 판정, 배상금을 지불하며, 주월 미군이 이 금액을 한국군에 상환.

1) 청구를 접수한 주월 한국군 소청사무소는 조사후 판정, 주월 미군 소청사무소의 소청담당 법무관의 확인 (certification)을 받은후 주월 한국군 사령관의 허가 (approval)를 얻어 배상금을 지불하고 관계 서류를 미군사령부 (법무관 참조)로 송부.

2) 미군사령부 법무관은 동 일건 서류를 미군사령부 감사관에 송부.

3) 미군 사령부 감사관은 서류접수후, 한국군이 지불한 배상금액 상환에 충분한 월남 화페를 한국군 관계 장교에 지불.

3. 단, 다음 사항은 별도로 처리한다.

1) 한국인에 대한 손해 배상은 제외 (국내법에 의거 처리)

2) 한.미 양국 군대간의 민사 청구권은 별도로 처리 (전부 포기)

3) 전투 행위로인한 민사 청구는 월남 지방 당국이 신청을 접수 처리 (Military Civil Assistance Program 에 의거 별도 처리).

0027

협 조 전	응신기일
분류기호 외방조 410	제 목 민사청구권 문제 해결에 관한 한.미 보충 실무자약정서(안) 사본 송부
수신 구미국장	발신일자 1966. 4. 4. (협조제의)

방 고 국 장 (발신명의) 이 문 용

(제1의견)

별첨과 같이 민사청구권 문제 해결에 관한 한.미 보충 실무 약정서(안) 사본을 송부하오니 참고하시기 바랍니다.

유첨: 민사청구권 문제 해결에 관한 한.미 보충 실무 약정서(안) 사본 1통 끝.

(제2의견)

예고문에서 분리되면 보통문서로 재분류

공통서식 1-23 (16절지)

0028

(안)

SUPPLEMENTAL WORKING ARRANGEMENT

BETWEEN

COMROKFV AND COMUSMACV

Article 1. COMROKFV and COMUSMACV signed a MILITARY WORKING ARRANGEMENT on 6 September 1965. Article 15 of that arrangement provides that the subject of non-combat tort claims asserted against ROKFV would be the subject of a separate working arrangement. Accordingly, the following working arrangement is agreed upon for the handling of non-combat claims arising in Vietnam against ROKFV.

Article 2. In order to process all claims asserted against ROKFV in Vietnam, COMROKFV will, within existing personnel ceilings, establish a ROKFV Claims Service at Headquarters ROKFV and will provide all information and statistics on ROK claim activities in Vietnam requested by COMUSMACV. Implementing procedures for the Claims Service shall be provided in APPENDIX A.

Article 3. In accordance with the implementing procedures prescribed in APPENDIX A, COMROKFV and COMUSMACV will provide for mutual assistance between the officers concerned from both parties on legal and technical matters involved in non-combat tort claims asserted against ROKFV. COMUSMACV will:

a. Provide sufficient legal and technical guidance as explained in Article 8 of APPENDIX A to the ROKFV Claims Service for the proper processing and disposition of claims, and

b. Provide financial support for the payment of meritorious non-combat claims as adjudicated by the ROKFV Claims Service, certified by the Claims Judge Advocate USMACV and approved by COMROKFV.

0023

Certification will constitute for the Claims Judge Advocate USMACV approval of the claimant as the proper party, liability under the criterior set out in Article 5, and approval for payment in the amount certified.

Article 4. COMROKFV and COMUSMACV agree that the provisions of Article 15, MILITARY WORKING ARRANGEMENT between COMROKFV and COMUSMACV, dated, on 6 September 1965, relating to waiver of claims between COMROKFV and COMUSMACV, remain unchanged by this SUPPLEMENTAL WORKING ARRANGEMENT.

Article 5. Those civil laws, decrees, customs and precedents which relate to tort claims in the Republic of Vietnam and the regulations and customs which are applied in Vietnam by the United States Foreign Claims Commission, USMACV, shall be applied, as legal basis, by the ROKFV Claims Service in determining whether the claims are payable or in adjudicating whether the amount of awards are legall sufficient.

Article 6. This SUPPLEMENTAL WORKING ARRANGEMENT shall be retroactively effective to September 6, 1965.

Article 7. Upon signature by COMROKFV and COMUSMACV this SUPPLEMENTAL WORKING ARRANGEMENT constitutes a general military working arrangement agreed to by both parties. Either party may request renegotiation of all or any part of this arrangement. This arrangement is signed on ________ 1966.

0030

APPENDIX "A"

The prompt and timely settlement of meritorious claims fosters good will on the part of host country and its populace toward visiting forces. The necessity for such compenpensation is particularly heightened in areas where even small losses can be disastrous to its victims, such as in the Republic of Vietnam. In order to insure the proper implementation of the SUPPLEMENTAL WORKING ARRANGEMENT, the following procedures are mutually agreed upon by COMROKFV and COMUSMACV.

Article 1. COMROKFV will staff the ROKFV Claims Service, established in the Article 2, SUPPLEMENTAL WORKING ARRANGE- ment, with sufficient personnel to handle the expected volume of claims to be asserted against ROKFV.

Article 2. A Claims Officer in the Claims Service will conduct investigation of each non-combat claims asserted against ROKFV under the supervision of Chief, ROKFV Claims Service.

Article 3. Claims by nationals of the Republic of Korea are not payable under the SUPPLEMENTAL WORKING ARRANGEMENT or these procedures.

Article 4. Combat claims are not payable under the SUPPLE- MENTAL WORKING ARRANGEMENT or these procedures. Claimants who wish to file claims for property damage, personal injury, or death resulting from combat situations will be referred to the Village Chief, District Chief or Province Chief where the claim originated. Claims that have been received and upon investigation found to be of combat origin will be forwarded to the Province Chief of the province where the claims originated or to the Psychological Warfare Director, RVNAF, for procedsing under the MILCAP program.

0031

Article 5. To determine whether claims asserted aross out of a combat activity, the following definition will be used as a guideline:

COMBAT CLAIM: A Claim for property damage, personal injury or death arising from action by the enemy or directly or indirectly from an act or omission of the ROKFV personnel while engaged in combat, in preparation for combat, or a combat operation or return therefrom.

Article 6. To determine whether a claim asserted arose out of a non-combat activity, the following definition will be used as a guideline:

NON-COMBAT CLAIM: A claim other than a combat claim for property damage, personal injury or death, caused in Vietnam, by the negligence, misconduct or other act or omission involving fault on the part of a military or civilian member of the ROKFV, while on duty or off-duty, or by an indigenous employee of ROKFV while acting within scope of his employment.

Article 7. COMUSMACV will provide to the ROKFV Claims Service all claims forms, settlement agreements, payment vouchers, and other forms necessary to process claims asserted against ROKFV.

Article 8. The legal and technical matters required by Article 3a of the SUPPLEMENTAL WORKING ARRANGEMENT shall be furnished to the ROKFV Claims Service through the Office of the Staff Judge Advocate, USMACV. It shall include, but not be limited to, furnishing guidance on criteria used by the United States forces in determing whether the claims are preoperly payable, standards employed in determining amount of awards, procedures for disposition of disputed claims and accounting procedures, and advice on similar administrative and legal matters.

0032

Article 9. a. All claims certified by the Claims Judge Advocate, USMACV, and subsequently approved by the COMROKFV to be meritorious and payable in a specific amount, either by approval of amount claimed or as the result of obtaining a settlement agreement from the claimant, shall be sent, with the required copies of the claims file, to the COMUSMACV, Attention: SJA.

b. Upon receipt of such certificate, document of approval, and requisite copies of the claims files from COMROKFV, the Staff Judge Advocate, USMACV, will forward them to Comtroller, USMACV,

Article 10. Upon receipt of properly executed payment vouchers, the Comptroller, USMACV, will furnish to the ROK officer who has been authorized by the Ministry of National Defense, Republic of Korea, to receive monies on behalf of the Republic of Korea, sufficient piasters to reimburse the payment of these claims.

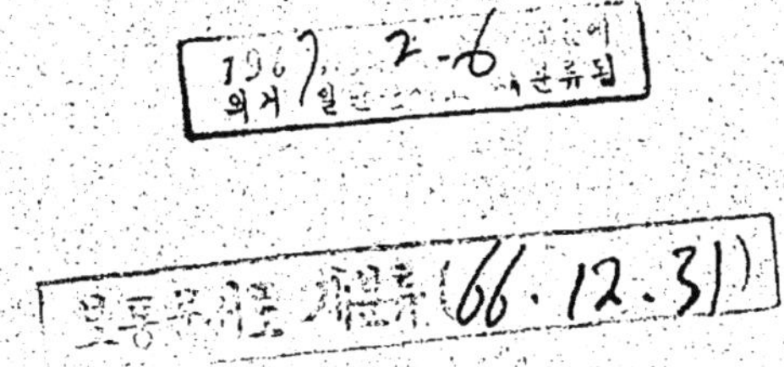

0033

AGREED MINUTE 1 TO ARTICLE XXIII: CLAIMS

(Proposal by U.S. side)

June 30, 1966

1. Unless otherwise provided, the provisions of paragraphs 5, 6, 7 and 8 of this Article will become effective six months from the date of entry into force of this Agreement with respect to claims arising from incidents in the Seoul Special City area, and one year from that date with respect to claims arising elsewhere in the Republic of Korea.

0034

ARTICLE XXIII CLAIMS

Agreed Minutes

1. Unless otherwise provided,

(a) The provisions of paragraphs 5,6,7 and 8 of this Article will become effective six months from the date of entry into force of this Agreement as to claims arising from incidents in the Seoul Special City Area.

(b) The provisions of paragraph 5, 6, 7 and 8 will be extended, at the earliest date practicable, to other areas of the Republic of Korea and determined by the Joint Committee.

1. Delete

(To be consistent with the above revision, the ensuing Agreed Minutes #2 and 3 shall also be deleted.)

0035

ARTICLE XXIII CLAIMS

proposed on June 9, 16
to Amb. Brown

Agreed Minutes

1. Unless otherwise provided,

(a) The provisions of paragraphs 5,6,7 and 8 of this Article will become effective six months from the date of entry into force of this Agreement as to claims arising from incidents in the Seoul Special City Area.

(b) The provisions of paragraph 5, 6, 7 and 8 will be extended, at the earliest date practicable, to other areas of the Republic of Korea and determined by the Joint Committee.

1. Delete

(To be consistent with the above revision, the ensuing Agreed Minutes #2 and 3 shall also be deleted.)

0036

ARTICLE XXIII CLAIMS

Agreed Minutes

1. Unless otherwise provided, (a) The provisions of paragraphs 5,6,7 and 8 of this Article will become effective six mo months from the date of entry into force of this Agreement as to claims arising from incidents in the Seoul Special City area. (b) The provisions of paragraph 5,6,7 and 8 will be extended, at the earliest date practicable, to other areas of the Republic of Korea as determined by the Joint Committee.	1. Delete (To be consistent with the above revision, the ensuing Agreed Minutes #2 and 3 shall also be deleted.)

0037

韓美間 駐屯軍地位協定
締結 交涉

1966. 4. 16.

1. 交涉經緯

가. 韓美兩側은 朴大統領 訪美時 兩國 大統領이 協定의 早期締結原則을 確認한바에 立脚하여 實務者級會議를 積極 推進한 結果 그간 停頓狀態에 있던 交涉은 急進展을 보게되어 1965年 6月7日 開催된 第81次會議까지 協定의 前文과 31個條項中 前文및 25個條項에 完全合意를 보게 되었음.

나. 그러나 81次會議에서도 完全히 解決을 보지 못한 刑事裁判權, 勞務, 請求權을 비롯하여 6個條項에 關하여 그後 우리側은 銳意 美國側과 非公式交涉을 繼續하여 全般的인 合意에 到達하였음. 따라서 外務部長官은 1966年 1月 本協定을 締結코저 建議코저

하였으나 共和党의 要請에 依하여 同協定의 締結을 現在까지 保留하여 왔음.

다. 韓美間에 合意된 同協定의 內容은 現在 美國이 NATO加盟國이나 其他 各國 特히 日本과 締結한 協定과 比較하여 볼때 條文上으로는 多少 差異가 있으나 実地運営에 있어서는 우리가 맺은 同協定의 內容과 別다른 差異가 없는 것으로 봄. 더욱이 本協定中 刑事裁判權의 第一次裁判權의 抛棄形態는 美國이 西獨과 맺은 補充協定에 規定된 刑事裁判權條項中 第一次裁判權의 抛棄形態를 우리나라에 有利하도록 補完한 것으로서 그 內容이 더욱 充実하게 되었다고 할수 있으며 日本은 協定文에도 不拘하고 実際로는 第一次裁判權을 9割以上이나 抛棄하고 있음.

공통서식 1—1 (을)

0039 (16절지)

—2—

라. 한편 協定의 締結交涉의 妥結이 지금까지 遲延되어 온 것은 主로 美國側의 頑强한 態度에 依한 것이며

1953年 韓美相互防衛條約 假調印 以來 우리 政府가 協定의 早速한 締結을 促求하였음에도 不拘하고 美側은 이를 繼續 拒否하여 왔으며 民主黨執權時 交涉을 始作한 일은 있으나 實質的인 內容檢討에는 이르지 못하고, 5.16 革命으로 中斷狀態에 있던 것인바 政府는 繼續 美側을 說得시켜 協定全般에 關하여 合意를 보게된 것은 하나의 成功이라고 할수 있음.

마. 當部에서는 協定締結에 앞서 1965年末부터 今年 1月까지 數次에 걸쳐 法曹界, 學界 및 言論界 著名人士들을 招請하여 合意된 內容을 中心으로 意見交換 및 對國民 "피·알" 活動을 爲한 모임을 가졌든 結果 協定의 重要條項인 刑事裁判權條項의

공통서식 1—2 (을) (16절지)

0040

第一次裁判權의 抛棄條項, 民事請求權의 発効時期, 및 労務條項의 軍事上必要에 依하여 美軍이 우리나라의 労動法令을 지키지 않을수 있는 範囲, 罷業權을 行使할수 없는 者의 範囲等 問題에 있어서 反響이 좋지 않았음에 鑑하여 이미 合意된 内容대로 締結하는 境遇, 國会同意要請時期를 前后하여 野党이 政治的目的을 為하여 最大로 悪用하면 一部 國民이 煽動되며 次期選挙에 悪影響을 미칠 可能性이 있음.

바. 따라서 지금까지 合意된 刑事裁判權, 民事請求權 및 労務條項을 中心으로 한 本協定 内容이 政治的으로 利用되는 것을 막기 為하여는

첫째로, 再交涉을 美側에 提議하여 問題된 條項의 内容을 우리에게 有利하도록 修正하여 協定을 締結하는 方法,

둘째로, 万一 再交涉結果가 우리에게 滿足스러운 內容이 되지 못할 境遇에는 協定締結을 送峯할때까지 遲延시키는 方法等

여러가지 方法을 考慮할수 있는바, 當部에서는 可能한 限 送峯前에 合意된 刑事裁判權, 民事請求權, 및 勞務條項을 一部修正코저 于先 再交涉可能性 与否에 對한 美側意向을 非公式으로 打診中에 있음.

공통서식 1—1 (을)

0042 (16절지)

2. 重要合意內容의 問題点

가. 合意된 內容中 修正할것을 檢討하고 있는 條項의 內容은 大略 다음과 같다.

(1) 刑事裁判權

우리나라가 가지는 第一次裁判权을 一旦 美国에 抛棄하고 個々事件이 発生하였을 境遇에 우리나라가

裁判权을 行使하는 것이 重要하다고 決定하는 때에는 抛棄를 撤回하여 裁判权을 行使한다.

(2) 民事請求權

民事請求权條項은 実質的으로 서울에 있어서는 協定発効 6個月後, 地方에 있어서는 合同委員会가 決定하는 可能한 限 빠른 時期에 発効한다.

(3) 労務條項

(가) 労動條件, 補償 및 労使関係는 美軍의 軍事上必要에 背馳되지

않는限 韓國의 勞動關係法令에
따라야 한다.

(나) 勞動爭議調整期間 70日後에도
그 爭議가 解決되지 않을 境遇,
合同委員會에서 定하는 必要한
雇傭員은 團体行動(罷業)을
하지 못한다.

보통문서로 재분류(1967. 12. 31.)

공통서식 1—2 (을)

0044 (16절지)

6.

第一次裁判權의 抛棄條項, 民事請求權의 発効時期 및 労務條項

의 軍事上必要로 因하여 美軍이 우리나라의 労動法令을 지키지 않을수 있는 範囲, 罷業權을 行使할수

없는 者의 範囲等 問題에 있어서 反響이 좋지 않았음에 鑑하여 이미 合意된 内容대로 締結하는 境遇

~~國会同意 要請 時期를 前後하여 野党이 一部 国民들로부터의 反対가 있을 것으로 豫想됨.~~

바. 따라서 지금까지 合意된 刑事裁判權, 民事請求權 및 労務條項을 中心으로한 本協定内容~~에 있어서~~ 이 政治的으로 利用되는 것을 ~~野党과 一部 国民의 反対를~~ 막기 為하여는

첫째로, 再交涉을 美側에 提議하여 問題된 條項의 内容을 우리에게 有利하도록 修正하여 協定을 締結하는 方法,

 0045 (16절지)

결 번

넘버링 오류

한•미간 주둔군 지위협정 체결교섭

1966. 4. 16.

1. 교섭 경위

가. 한.미 양측은 박 대통령 방미시 양국 대통령이 협정의 조기 타결 원칙을 확인한바에 입각하여 실무자급 회의를 적극 추진한 결과 그간 정돈상태에 있던 교섭은 급진전을 보게 되어 1965년 6월 7일 개최된 제 81차 회의까지 협정의 전문과 31개 조항중 전문 및 25개 조항에 완전 합의를 보게 되었음.

나. 그러나 81차 회의에서도 완전히 해결을 보지 못한 형사 재판권, 노무, 청구권을 비롯하여 6개 조항에 관하여 그후 우리측은 미국측과 비공식 교섭을 계속하여 전반적인 합의에 도달하였음. 따라서, 외무부 장관은 1966년 1월 본 협정을 체결코저 건의코저 하였으나, 공화당의 요청에 의하여 동 협정의 체결을 현재까지 보류하여 왔음.

다. 한.미간에 합의된 동 협정의 내용은 현재, 미국이 "나토" 가맹국이나 기타 각국 특히 일본과 체결한 협정과 비교할때 조문상으로는 다소 차이가 있으나 실지 운영에 있어서는 우리가 맺은 협정의 내용은 별다른 차이가 없을 것으로 봄.

0047

더욱이 본 협정 형사재판권의 제1차 재판권의 포기형태는 미국이 서독과 맺은 보충협정에 규정된 형사 재판권 조항중 제1차 재판권의 포기형태를 우리나라에 유리하도록 보완한 것으로서 그 내용이 더욱 충실하게 되었다고 할수 있으며, 일본은 협정문에도 불구하고 실제로는 제1차 재판권을 9할 이상이나 포기하고 있음.

다. 한편, 협정의 체결교섭의 타결이 지금까지 지연되어 온것은 주로 미국측의 완강한 태도에 의한 것이며 1953년 한.미 상호 방위조약 가조인 이래 우리정부가 협정의 조속한 체결을 촉구하였음에도 불구하고 미측은 이를 계속 거부하여 왔으며 민주당 집권시 교섭을 시작한 일은 있으나 실질적인 내용 검토에는 이르지 못하고 5. 16 혁명으로 중단 상태에 있던 것인바, 정부는 계속 미측을 설득시켜 협정 전반에 합의를 보게된 것은 하나의 성공이라고 할수 있음.

마. 당부에서는 협정 체결에 앞서 1965년 말부터 금년 1월까지 수차에 걸쳐 법조계, 학계 및 언론계 저명 인사들을 초청하여 합의된 내용을 중심으로 의견교환 및 대국민 피.알 활동을 위한 모임을 가졌던 결과 협정의 중요조항인 형사재판권 조항의 제1차 재판권의 포기조항, 민사청구권의 발효시기 및 노무조항의 군사상 필요로 인하여 미군이 우리나라의 노동관계 법령을 지키지 않을수 있는 범위, 파업권을 행사할수 없는자의 범위등 문제에 있어서

0048

반향이 좋지 않았음에 감하여 이미 합의된 내용대로 체결하는 경우, 국회동의 요청 시기를 전후하여 야당이 정치적 목적을 위하여, 최대로 악용하면 일부 국민이 선동되어 선거에 악영향을 미칠 가능성이 있음.

바. 따라서, 지금까지 합의된 형사 재판권, 민사청구권 및 노무 조항을 중심으로 한 본 협정 내용이 정치적으로 이용되는 것을 막기 위하여서는, 첫째로, 재교섭을 미측에 제의하여 문제된 조항의 내용을 우리에게 유리하도록 수정하여 협정을 체결하는 방법. 둘째로, 만일 재교섭 결과가 우리에게 만족스러운 내용이 되지 못할 경우에는 협정 체결을 선거후 까지 지연시키는 방법등, 여러방법을 고려할수 있는바, 당부에서는 가능한 한, 선거전에 합의된 형사 재판권, 민사 청구권 및 노무 조항을 일부 수정코저 우선 재교섭 가능성 여부에 대한 미측 의향을 비공식으로 타진중에 있음.

2. 중요합의 내용의 문제점

가. 합의된 내용중 수정할 것을 검토하고 있는 조항의 내용은 대략 다음과 같다.

(1) 형사 재판권

우리나라가 가지는 제1차 재판권을 일단 미국에 포기하고, 개개 사건이 발생하였을 경우에 우리나라가 재판권을 행사

0049

하는것이 중요하다고 결정하는 때에는 포기를 철회하여 재판권을 행사한다.

(2) 민사 청구권

민사 청구권 조항은 실질적으로 서울에 있어서는 협정 발효 6개월후, 지방은 합동위원회가 결정하는 가능한 한 빠른 시기에 발효한다.

(3) 노무조항

(가) 노동조건, 보상 및 노사관계는 미군의 군사상 필요에 배치되지 않는한 한국의 노동관계 법령에 따라야 한다.

(나) 노동쟁의 조정 기간 70일후에도 그 쟁의가 해결되지 않을 경우 합동위원회에서 정하는 긴요한 고용원은 단체행동(파업)을 하지 못한다. 끝.

협정 종료후 자진으로 재분류

- 4 -

0050

한·미간 주둔군 지위협정 체결교섭

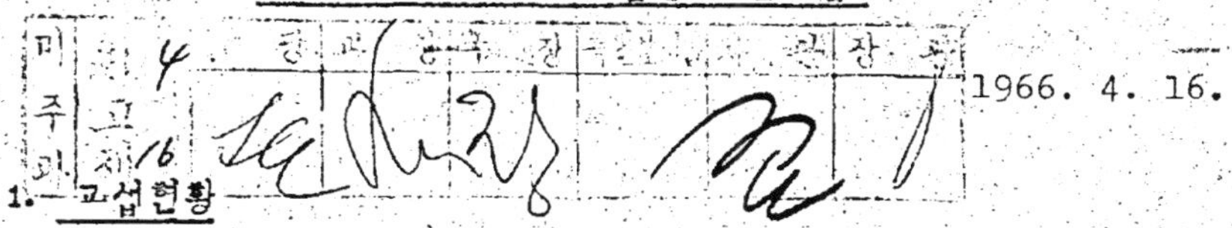

1966. 4. 16.

1. 교섭현황

가. 한·미 양측은 박 대통령 방미시 양국 대통령이 협정의 조기 타결 원칙을 확인한바에 입각하여 실무자급 회의를 적극 추진한 결과 그간 정돈 상태에 있던 교섭은 급진전을 보이게 되어 1965년 6월 5일 개최된 제 81차 회의가지 협정의 전문과 31개 조항중 전문 및 25개 조항에 완전 합의를 보게 되었음.

나. 그러나, 81차 회의에서도 완전히 해결을 보지 못한 형사 재판권, 노무, 청구권등 각 조항에 관하여 그후 우리측은 여의 미국측과 비공식 교섭을 계속하여 전반적인 합의에 도달하였음.

다. 그후, 금년 1월 말경 협정을 체결할 계획하에 1965년말부터 금년 1월 가지 수차에 걸쳐 법조계 및 학계, 언론계 저명인사들을 초청하여 합의된 내용을 중심으로 의견교환 및 대국민 피.알 활동을 위한 모임을 가졌던 결과 중요조항인 형사 재판권 조항의 제 1 차 재판권의 포기조항, 민사청구권의 발효시기 및 노무 조항의 군사상 필요로 인하여 미군이 우리나라 법을 지키지 않을수 있는 범위, 파업권을 행사 할수 없는 자의 범위 결정등 문제에 있어서 반향이 좋지 아니하였음에 감하여, 본 협정의 국회 동의 요청시를 중심으로 하여 국회와 국민으로 부터의 반배가 있을 것으로 예상됨.

라. 따라서, 당부에서는 지금가지 합 의된 협정안중 형사 재판권, 민사청구권 및 노무조항의 합의내용을 일부 수정코저 재교섭 가능성 여부에 대한 미측의향을 타진중에 있음.

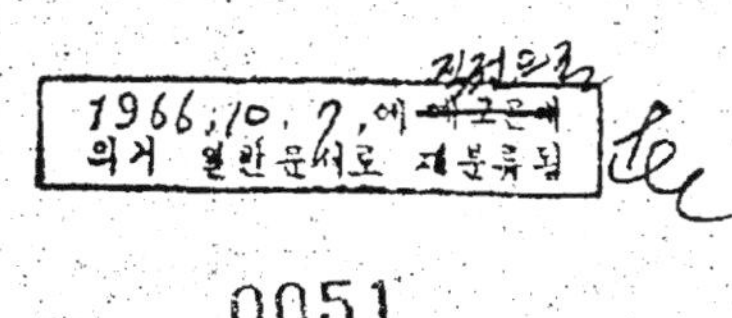

0051

2. 중요합의내용의 문제점

가. 합의된 내용중 수정할 것을 검토하고 있는 조항의 내용은 대략 다음과 같음.

(1) 형사 재판권

우리나라가 가지는 제1차 재판권을 일단 미국당국에 포기하고, 개개 사건이 발생하였을 경우에 우리나라가 재판권을 행사하는 것이 중요하다고 결정하는때에는 포기를 철회하여 재판권을 행사한다.

(2) 민사 청구권

민사청구권 조항중, 공무집행중 제 3자에 대한 손해와, 비공무중 손해 배상조항은 서울특별시는 협정발효 6개월후, 기타 지역은 합동위원회가 결정하는 가장빠른 시기에 발효한다.

(3) 노무조항

(가) 노무조항의 규정과 미군의 군사상의 필요에 배치되지 아니하는한 노동조건 보상 및 노사관계는 한국 노동법령의 제규정을 따라야 한다.

(나) 일정한 쟁의 해결절차에 따라 쟁의의 해결을 시도하되 쟁의 발생후 70일이 경과하여도 해결되지 아니할 때에는 그 이상 쟁의를 할수 있는자와 할수없는 자를 결정한다.

0052

66-5-4 (1)

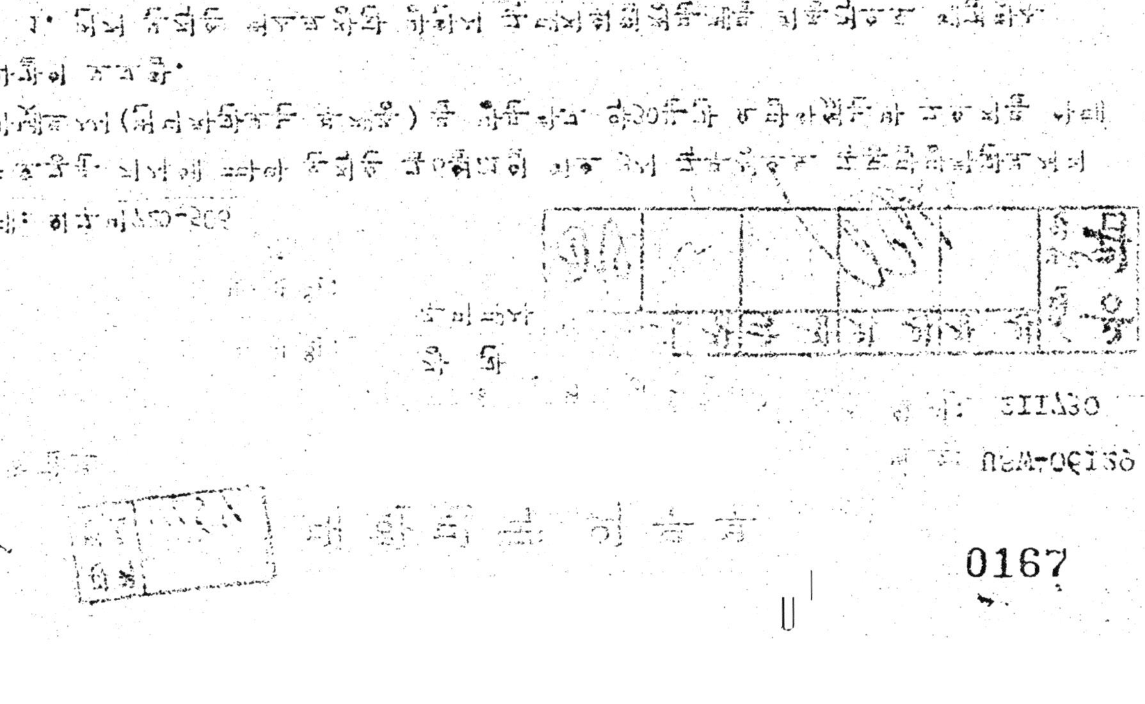

0167

when they determine that it is of particular importance that jurisdiction be exercised by the Greek authorities.

(3) West Germany

(a) Article 19:

1. At the request of a sending state, the Federal Republic shall, within the framework of sub-paragraph (c) of paragraph 3 of Article VII of the NATO Status of Forces Agreement, waive in favour of that State the primary right granted to the German authorities under sub-paragraph (b) of paragraph 3 of that Article in cases of concurrent jurisdiction, in accordance with paragraph 2, 3, 4 and 7 of this Article.

3. Where the competent German authorities hold the view that, by reason of special circumstances in a specific case major interests of German administration of justice make imperative the exercise of German jurisdiction, they may recall the waiver granted under paragraph 1 of this Article by a statement to the competent military authorities within a period of twenty-one days after receipt of the notification ....

4. If, pursuant to paragraph 3 of this Article, the competent German authorities have recalled the waiver in a specific case and in such case an understanding cannot be reached in discussions between the authorities concerned, the diplomatic mission in the Federal Republic of the sending State concerned may make representations to the Federal Government. The Federal Government, giving due consideration to the interests of German administration of Justice and to the interests of the sending State, shall resolve the disagreement in the exercise of its authority in the field of foreign affairs.

(b) Protocol Re Article 19:

2(a). Subject to a careful examination of each specific case and to the results of such examination, major interests of German administration of justice.

0054

within the meaning of paragraph 3 of Article 19 may make imperative the exercise of German jurisdiction, in particular in the following cases:

(ii) offenses causing the death of a human being, robbery, rape, except where these offenses are directed against a member of a force or of a civilian component or a dependent:

(iii) attempt to commit such offenses or participation therein. (외구미)

관할권 포기요청에 관한 한·미 양측의 입장은 제67차 및 70차 실무자회의록을 참조하시기 바람. 끝

장 관

0055

발신전보

대한민국외무부

지급

종별

번호: WUS-0479

일시: 201810

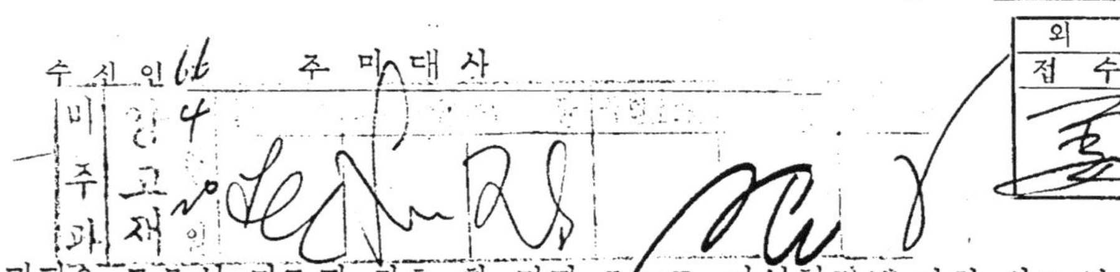

수신인 주미대사

귀관은 국무성 당국과 접촉 한.미간 주둔군 지위협정에 관한 아국의 입장을 다음과 같이 설명 하시고 그 결과를 지급 회시 바람.

1. 현재 동 협정은 실무자간에 비공식으로 합의된바 있으나 그간 언론계, 학자등에 대한 "부리핑" 을 통하여 현재 합의된 내용으로 동 협정을 체결할시는 동 협정의 국회 비준 동의에 있어 상당한 곤난이 야기될 것으로 예상되고 있음.

2. 따라서, 정부로서는 가장 문제점인 형사재판관할권, 노무, 민사청구권의 3개 조항은 가능한 한 미측과의 재교섭을 통하여 이러한 곤난을 배제할수 있는 내용으로 동 협정을 수정할 것을 희망하고 있음.

3. 특히, 형사재판관할권의 제1차 관할권 표기형태는 미국이 일본 특히 비율빈과 맺은 형태에 비하여 우리에게 불리한것임으로 일반국민들 에게 정치적이나 비정치적인 견지에서 국가적인 차별을 당하였다는 인상을 줌으로서 대미감정에 좋지 않은 영향을 줄것임.

또한 이는 심각한 여론의 반발을 초래할것으로 예상되며 특히 오는 총선거를 앞두고 정치적으로 이용 당할 가능성이 다대한것으로봄.

0056

송신시간:

장관

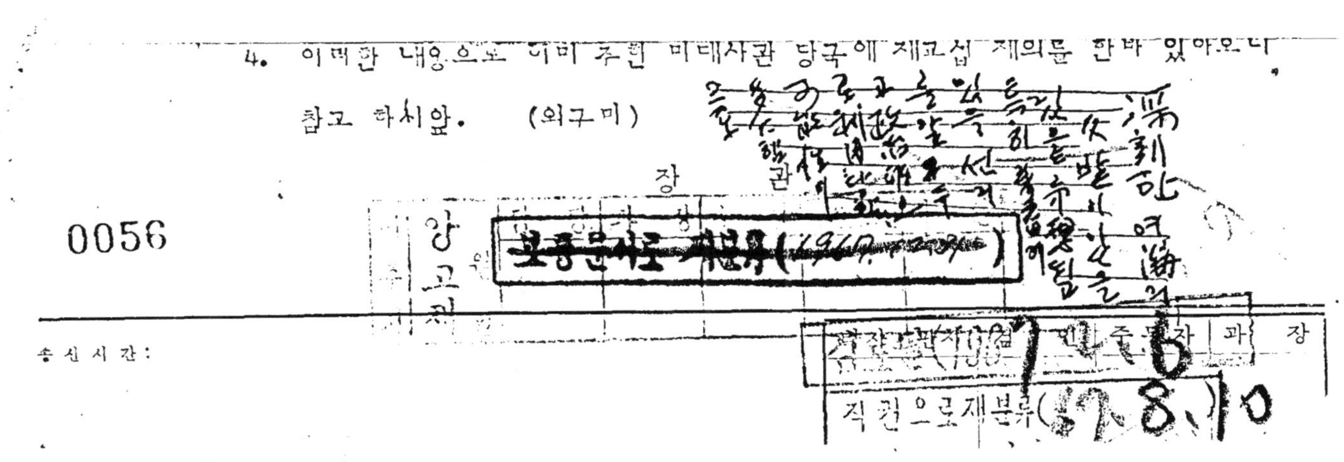
4. 이러한 내용으로 이미 주한 미대사관 당국에 재교섭 제의를 한바 있아오니

참고 하시압. (외구미)

0056

송신시간:

직권으로재분류(1978.8.10)

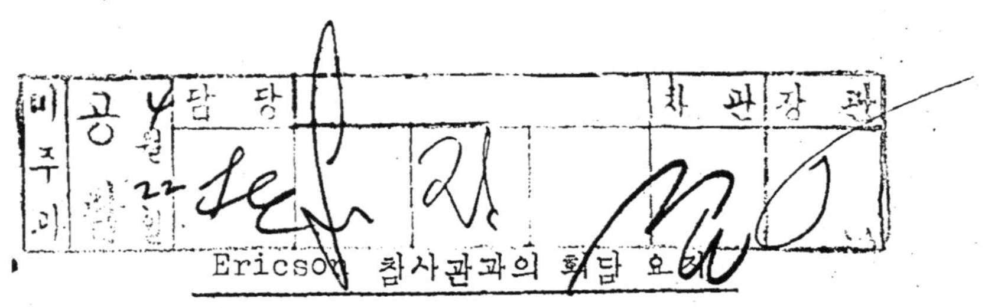

Ericson 참사관과의 회담 요지

1. 제 목 : 주둔군 지위협정 체결교섭

2. 일 시 : 1966년 4월 15일 (금)

3. 장 소 : 구미국장 실

4. 참석자 : 외무부 장상문 구미국장

미대사관 Richard A. Ericson Jr. 정치담당 참사관

5. 회담요지 :

Chang: Under instructions of the Minister, I would like to present to your side our position on the long-pending problem of the SOFA negotiations. We want to renegotiate some of the articles of the agreement, the contents of which have been agreed upon by both sides through the course of informal meetings.

I would not dwell upon the reasons for our proposal for reopening the negotiations since I understand that essential part of them have been intimated to your side by the Vice Minister to Minister Doherty the other day.

Ericson: May I take it that you are making a formal proposal to reopen the negotiation?

Chang: That is correct. I am making a formal proposal for reopening of the negotiation. We are aware that formal response of your side to our proposal

0058

would be available only after your consultation with Washington, D.C. Nevertheless, we would appreciate an early response from your side. This brings to an end to my presentation this afternoon, as far as formal part of the presentation is concerned. However, I would be at your disposal if you wish to know more about our position for your own information. I would answer whatever questions you may have on a strictly informal basis.

Ericson: Could you name "some of the Articles" you have just mentioned?

Chang : They are Articles on Criminal Jurisdiction, Labor, and Claims.

Ericson: Could you indicate specific points of the Articles your side would like to renegotiate?

Chang : With regard to Criminal Jurisdiction article, our main concern is on the waiver formula. We feel very strongly that the waiver formula should be improved to the level of, at least, Philippine formula or Greek formula. As to labor Article, we like to eliminate the "restriction on the further right to exercise collective actions" to be applied to "certain categories of essential employees". As to the Claims Article, we would like to have the new principle applied throughout Korea, while the presently agreed text limits Seoul City as the area of application. These are major points of our concern in proposing renegotiation

0059

of the agreement, but points of renegotiation will not necessarily be limited to those I have just mentioned.

Ericson: I will report to Ambassador Brown what you have told me and act upon his advice. For my own information, I should like to know reasons for making such a proposal for renegotiations and what has prompted your side to propose such a proposal at this junctune, I mean, in terms of timing of the proposal.

Chang : As far as reasons and motives of our proposal are concerned, I believe that they have been dealt with by my superiors and I doubt whether it would be appropriate for me to elaborate them. Since you seems to be curious, I would venture to express my own personal view. As you are aware, we have had several briefings on the contents of agreement for the leading figures in academic and press circles. Their response was generally of negative nature, not to speak of their inherent tendency to be critical toward any achievement of the administration. In particular, the response of the opposition party has been far more serious than we had expected. I feel the contents of the agreement, rather, the principles we agreed upon. nearly one year ago would be hardly accepted by our National Assembly.

Ericson: You mean, you would have certain difficulties in getting the agreement approved by the Assembly rather than the agreement would not be approved by the National Assembly.

Chang : Let me put it this way. We would certainly face a great deal of difficulties which would

0060

place the Government in a very difficult position and no one can rule out the possibility that the National Assembly may disapprove the agreement depending upon the political climate that may develop at the time of the congressional action.

Ericson: With regard to some of the negative or critical responses you have just referred to, we feel that everyone of them does not necessarily reflect truthfully the reality of the situation we have to face together in Korea. We have our own difficulties in meeting the requirements of the military side.

Chang: Well, the difficulty of your side is the matter which we have to tackle in the future discussions at the meeting if and when the proposed renegotiation starts.

Note(1): After the meeting, Mr. Ericson indicated that there has been an inquiry by U.S. Embassy in Seoul to State Dept on this particular question sometime in the last January when the pre-heralded signing of the agreement was indefinitely postponed.
Mr. Ericson said "this state of afair is not totally unexpected by our side. As a matter of fact, when your side failed to sign the agreement last January, we asked for instructions of Washington, in anticipation of new development on this problem. I would not speculate the response of Washington on your response. According to the instructions,

0061

we received, we may respond to your side similary, that is, we may go along with your proposal with a proviso that we would propose to retract some of the important concessions we made through the negotiations."

Note (2): On April 16, (Sat.) Mr. Ericson asked for a clarification on the remarks of Mr. Chang made on April 15, (over the phone)

Ericson: Could you say that the proposal you made yesterday was made on behalf of your government?

Chang : It's rather an unusual question Mr. Ericson. As I told you, I made the proposal under instructions of the Foreign Minister. When we act upon the instructions of the Minister with regard to a question of this nature it could not be anything else, but a government presentation.

Ericson: I am sorry, Mr. Chang, for asking this sort of question. I am drafting a report and I merely wanted to clarify a point which was not so sure myself. Would you say, then, the proposal was made with the knowledge of the highest authority of the Government.

Chang : I do not think it is an appropriate question to answer. I can only repeat that I made the presentation upon instructions of my superiors.

Ericson: I understand. Sorry to troubling you.

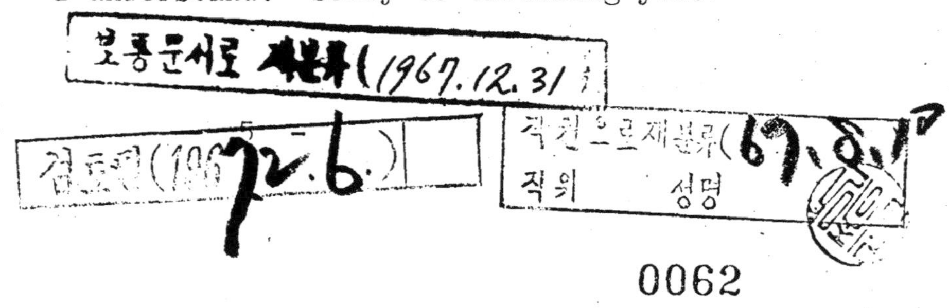

0062

기 안 지

기 안 자	미주과 이근팔	전화 번호		공 보	필 요	불필요
	과 장	국 장	차 관	장 관		
협조자 성 명					보존 년한	
기 안 년 월 일	66. 4. 21.	시 행 년월일		통 제	정 서	기 장
분류기호 문서번호	외구미 722.2-					
경 유 수 신 참 조	주 미 대 사			발 신	장 관	
제 목	주둔군 지위협정 체결교섭					

1. 1966. 4. 20 일자 WUS-0479 호 전문지시에 관련된 사항입니다.

2. 지금까지 한.미간에 비공식으로 실무자간에 합의된바 있는 주둔군 지위협정안의 해설서 1부를 송부 하오니 앞으로있을 합의된 내용의 일부 수정 재교섭을 위한 국무성 당국과의 교섭에 참고 하시기 바랍니다.

3. 귀관은 연 WUS-0479 호 전문 지시에 포함된 본부의 입장을 참작하여 적어도 다음과 같은 3개 조항의 문제점이 반드시 시정되어야 한다는 정부의 입장을 반영시키도록 미측에 교섭 하시기 바랍니다.

가. 형사 재판권 조항 (제22조)

(1) 합의내용

우리나라가 가지는 제1차적 재판권을 일단 미국에 포기하고 개개 사건이 발생하였을 경우에 우리나라

공통서식 1—2 (갑) (16절지)

0063

66-5-1

가 재판권을 행사하는 것이 중요하다고 결정하는 때에는 포기를 철회하여 재판권을 행사한다. (Agreed Minute Re Paragraph 3(b) P. 263-266)

(2) 해결방안

독일 보충협정 형태에 입각한 상기와 같은 합의 내용대신 미국이 "그리스" 또는 비율빈과 체결한 다음과 같은 포기형태에 따라 접수국인 우리나라가 제1차 재판권의 포기여부를 자주적으로 결정할수 있는 권리를 확보코저 하는 것임.

"대한민국 당국은 미군 당국의 포기요청이 있을 경우에는 대한민국이 재판권을 행사함이 중요하다고 결정하는 경우를 제외하고 대한민국이 가지는 제1차적 재판권을 미군당국에 포기한다."

나. 청구권 (제23조)

(1) 합의내용

민사 청구권 조항은 실질적으로 서울에 있어서는 협정 발효 6개월후, 지방은 합동위원회가 결정하는 가능한 한, 빠른 시기에 발효한다.

(Agreed Minute Paragraph 1(a) & (b), P. 274)

(2) 해결방안

민사 청구권의 핵심인 제3자에 대한 손해 배상 규정을 비롯한 본 조항은 서울은 물론 기타 지역에 있어서도

0064

그 발효시기를 합동위원회가 결정하는 가장 빠른 시기로 막연하게 규정할 것이 아니라 협정 발효즉시 또는 그후 일정한 시기로 명확하게 규정하여야 한다.

다. 노무조항 (제17조)

(1) 합의내용

(가) 노동조건, 보상 및 노사관계는 미군의 군사상 필요에 배치되지 아니하는한, 한국의 노동관계 법령에 따라야 한다. (Paragraph 3, P 225)

(나) 노동쟁의 조정기간 70일 후에도 그 쟁의가 해결되지 않을 경우 합동위원회에서 결정하는 긴요한 고용원은 단체행동 (파업)을 하지 못한다. (Paragraph 4(b), P. 226)

(2) 해결방안

(가) 미군은 "군사상의 필요"를 이유로 우리나라 법을 지키지 아니할수 있는 애매한 것인바 우리는 군사상 필요를 이유로 할때에도 사전에 쌍방이 합의하여야 하며,

(나) 쟁의 조정기간 70일 후에도 해결되지 아니할 경우에 파업을 할수 없는자의 범위는 우리나라 헌법과 노동법에 따라 제한할수 있는 최소한도의 범위로 한정하여야 한다.

4. 교섭결과에 따라서는 상기 문제점 외에도 몇 가지 문제를 수정하여야 할 것으로 사료합니다.

유 첨 : 1. 대한민국과 미합중국간의 주한 미합중국 군대의 지위에 관한 협정 해설서 1부. (관리번호 4085)

2. 집무자료 외구미 65/3 호, Agreements concerning Status of Forces 1부. 끝.

66-1 (16절지)

66-5-1 (3)

보존문서 78-7(2)

0066

교통부의 협정안 수정 요청 요지

1966. 4. 25.

1. 교통부는 협정안 제10조 "선박 및 항공기의 기착" 조항의 내용을 다음과 같이 수정할 것을 요청하고 있음.

제1항 : 착륙료를 면제하는 항공기의 범위를 "합중국을 위하여 운행되는 합중국 소속 군용 항공기"로 한정하여 공용을 위한 민간 항공기를 제외할 것.

제2항 : 과징금을 면제하는 인적 범위를 "공용을 위하여 출입하는 군인, 군속"으로 한정하여, 비공용 출입자 및 가족과 초청계약자를 제외할것.

2. 협정안의 제1항 및 제2항은 미일협정과 동일한 내용이며, 교통부의 제1항에 대한 수정안은 미.비 협정 제4조 1항에 선례가 있음.

3. 장차, 미국측이 재교섭에 응하는 경우에도 우리측은,

가. 재교섭 타결지연에 상관없이 협정안을 전면적으로 수정코져 하는 경우에만 상기 수정안을 미국측에 재의할수 있을 것이며,

나. 만일, 상기와 같은 수정안을 제안하는 경우, 우리가 수정코져 하는 중요조항의 재교섭에도 영향이 있을 것으로 사료됨. 끝.

0067

구미과

교 통 부

교항정1554

1966,4,19

수신 외무부장관

제목 한미간 주문군 지위 협정 개정(안)

한미주둔군 지위 협정 개정(안)을 다음과 같이 제출하오니 관계 조치를 취하여 주시기 바랍니다.

1. 동 제10조 (선박과 항공기의 기착) 제1항중 "합중국에 의하여 합중국을 위하여 또는 합중국 관리하에서 공용을 위하여 운항되는 합중국및 외국의 항공기는"을 수정하여 "합중국 군을 위하여 운항되는 합중국 소속 군용항공기는"으로함.

이유 : 공용일 경우 민간항공용 항공기 일지라도 착륙료를 부담하지 않게되어 있는바 이는 군을 위해서 사용되어 진다하도라도 동 항공기 소속회사에서는 이에 상당한 대절료 또는 항공기 임대료를 수수하고 제공될것이므로 착륙료및 기타 과징금을 부담함은 당연한것으로 보아야함.

2. 동 제10조 제2항중 5—7행의 "시설과 구역에의 출입및 이들 시설과 구역간의 이동에는 기타의 과징금을 과하지 아니한다"의 적용대상을 "합중국 군대의 구성원및 군속"에 한하도록 할것이며 이도 공용을 위한 목적에만 적용 하도록함.

이유 : 군인및 군속일지라도 공용의 목적 이외의 출입및 이동에 따른 기타의 과징금을 과하지 않음을 부당하다고 사료되며 (사적 목적일 경우 이는 신분을 떠난 자연인으로 봄이 타당) 더우기 그들의 가족까지 이에 포함하여야 할것은 없는 것으로 사료됨 또한 동 제15조(초청계약자)의 규정에 해당하는자도 이에 해당(동제3항 가) 토록 하였는데 이들은 당사자 자신을 위한 사업가(군

0068

(관계) 이므로 조문 내용과 같은 이익을 부여할 하등의 이유가 없음. 끝.

교통부장관 안 경 모

0069

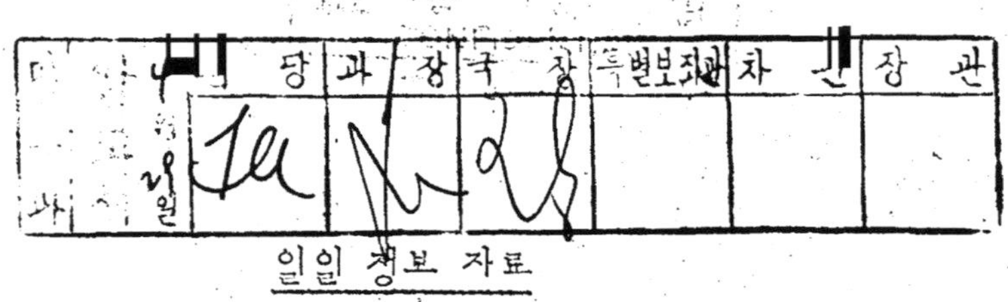

일일 정보 자료

1966. 4. 29.

수 신 : 정보문화국장

발 신 : 구 미 국 장

제 목 : 한.미간 주둔군 지위협정 체결교섭

당부에서는 그간 실무자간에 비공식으로 합의된 미주둔군 지위협정안을 언론계, 학계 및 법조계 저명 인사들에게 부리핑하고 그 반향을 타진하였던 결과 현재 합의된 내용대로 협정을 체결할시에는 협정의 국회 비준동의에 있어 상당한 곤난이 야기될 것으로 예상하고 협정안의 일부 내용의 수정을 위한 재교섭을 주한 미국 대사관에 제의하는 한편, 주미대사관에 미국정부의 의향을 타진케 하였던바 1966. 4. 29. 주미대사관으로부터 다음과 같은 중간 보고에 접하였음.으니 업무상에 참고하시압.

1. 형사 재관권, 노무조항, 청구권등 가장 문제된 조항에 대한 재교섭을 통하여 아국이 당면하고 있는 곤난한 문제점을 배제할수 있는 내용으로 수정할 것을 강력히 희망하고 우리측의 재교섭 제의에 응하여 줄것을 요청하였음.

2. 국무성 관계관은 우리 정부의 재교섭 제의에 관하여 서울 주재 미국 대사관으로 부터 상세한 보고를 접수하였다고 말하고 현재

0070

국무성 당국에서는 아국의 재교섭 제의에 대하여 Serious consideration 을 하고 있으며 그 결과가 있는대로 통지하여 주겠다고 언약하였음.

3. 또한 주미대사는 가까운 시일내에 국무성 고위층과 재차 접촉하여 미측 견해를 타진할 예정임. 끝.

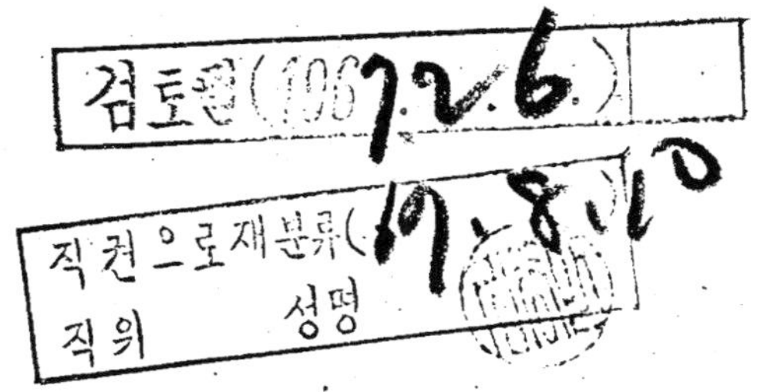

0071

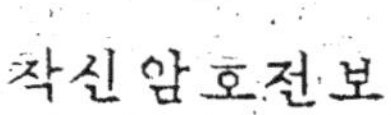

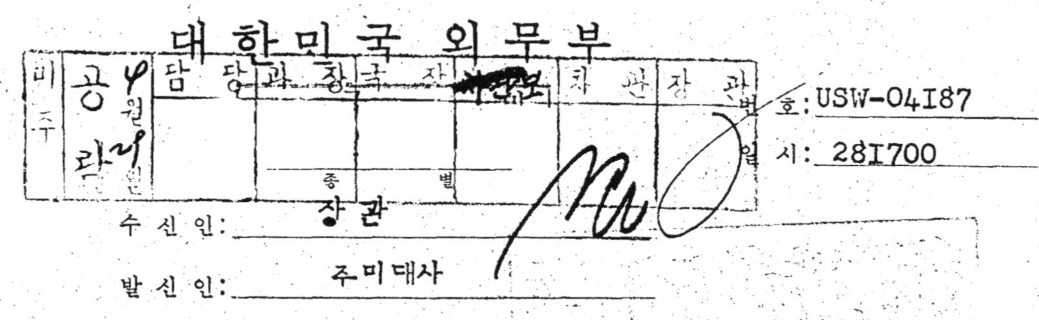

번호: USW-04187

일시: 281700

수신인: 장관

발신인: 주미대사

대: WUS-0479

대호로 지시하신건 국무성관계관과 접촉한결과를 아래와 같이 보고함.

1. 대호전문에서 지적한 제반사정을 설명하고 아국정부로서는 가장문제점인 형사재판관할권 노무민사청구권의 3가지 조항은 재교섭을 통하여 아국이 당면하고 있는 곤란한 문제점을 배제할수있는 내용으로 동협정을 수정할것을 강력히 희망하며 우리측의 재교섭제의에 응하여줄것을 요청하였음.

2. 국무성관계관은 이러한 우리정부의 재교섭제의에 관하여 서울주재 미국대사관으로부터 상세한 보고를 접수하였다고 말하면서 이미 국내절차에 따라 국회상하원 외교국방분과위원회에 합의된 협정내용을 설명하고 양해를 얻었으며 만일 동협정을 수정한다면 다시 국회에 수정내용을 설명하여야되는바 국무성으로는 매우 곤란한입장에 있다고 말하였음. 그러나 현재 국무성당국에서는 아국의 재교섭 제의에 대하여 SERIOUS CONSIDERATION 를 하고있으며 그결과가 있는대로 통지하여 주겠다고 언약하였음.

3. 본직은 가까운 시일내에 국무성 고위층과 접촉하여 본건에 관한 미측견해 및 태도를 타진코저 예정하고있음을 첨언함. (방조.구미.정공)

예고: 1966.12.31 재분류

수신시간:

비서	✓	아주		통상		상공		청와대	
총무		구미	O	경기		농림		총리실	
의전		정문	✓	정공		조달		수산	
여권		방교	✓	중정		외연		공보부	
육군		해군		공군		해병		합참	

외신과

검인

1966 ... 29	주무자	과장
AM 10 53		

0072

대한민국 외무부

착신암호전보

번호: USW-0548
일시: 061700

발신인: 주미대사

당관에서 금 5.6. 국무성관계관과 접촉한결과를 아래와같이 보고함.

1. 국무성 극동담당부차관보 버거씨는 오는 6.9. 당지를출발하여 한국을방문할예정이며 약 2일간 체류하게될것이라고함. 동씨의 금번한국방문은 특별한 목적이있는것은 아니고 극동국의 관할국가인 비율빈, 태국, 대만 일본등을 방문하는기회를 이용하여 한국도 방문하는것이라고함.

2. 동남아 외상회담에관하여 미국으로서는 최선을 다하여 지지하여줄것이나 다만 첫째 동외상회담이 미국이 뒷받침하는회의라는 인상을 주지않기위하여 표면에는 나올수가없으며 둘째로 정치 및 안전보장문제를 한국이 너무 조급하게 토의를추진하는경우 오히려 역효과를 가져올수있을것이므로 서서히 다루는것이 좋을것이라고말함.

SOFA. 3. 한미군대지위협정문제에관하여 아직도 아국의 재교섭제의를 신중검토하고있다고 말하면서 한미고위층에서 완전합의를보고 국회해당분과위원회에 설명한후 동의를얻어 국내절차를 끝났으므로 재교섭제게는 미측에대하여 상당한 곤난을조성하고있다고말하였음. 동관계관이주는 인상으로서는 매우 미국측 태도가 경화해진것같으며 아측의 재교섭제의에 대하여 좋은반응을 보이는것같지는않음.

4. 동관계관이 사견으로서 언급한바에의하면 만일 한국정부가 현재월남정부와 교섭협의하고있는방식의 행정협정을 체결할의사가있든가 또는 주한미군이 철수한후가아니면 군대지위협정의 조인가능성은 없을것같다고 지나는말로 시사한점은 극히 주목되는것임.

(외구미)

예고: 일반문서로 재분류 (66.12.31)

1966 MAY 7 AM 10 39

수신시간:

비서	✓	아주		통상		상공		청와대	
총무		구미	○	경기		농림		총리실	
의전		정문	✓	정공		조달		수산	
여권		방교	✓	중정		외연		공보부	
육군		해군		공군		해병		합참	

외신과

검인

담당	주무자	과장

0073

66-5-2 (6)

예문 118-6(1)

[illegible]

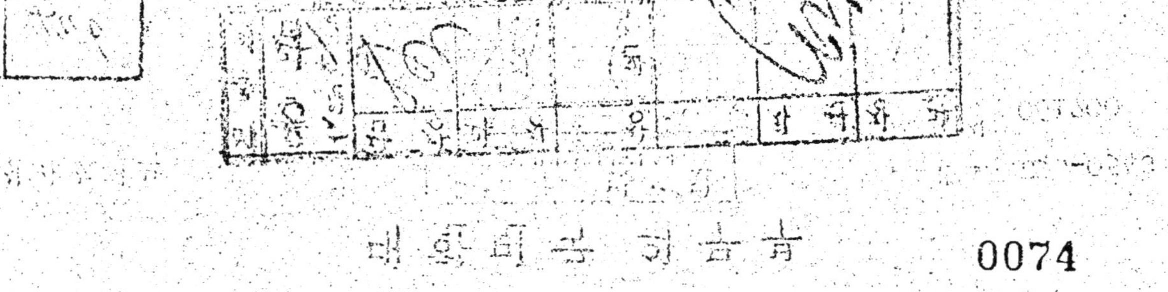

0074

1. If either Government desires to request a waiver of the other government's primary right to exercise jurisdiction, a written request shall be made within ten days of receipt of notification of the commission of an offense. A Philippine request for waiver will be delivered to the United States commander concerned, and a United States request for waiver will be delivered to the city or provincial fiscal concerned.

If either Government is not advised by the other Government within fifteen days of the date of receipt by such other Government of a request for a waiver of jurisdiction that jurisdiction will be exercised by such other Government (the criteria for waiver requests and retention of primary jurisdiction are set forth in paragraph 3(c) and Agreed Official Minute No. 4), the requesting Government shall be free to exercise jurisdiction.

If either Government, however, notifies the other Government that for special reasons it desires to reserve decision with respect to the exercise of jurisdiction, the requesting Government will not be free to exercise its jurisdiction until notice is received that the other Government will not exercise jurisdiction or until the expiration of an additional period of fifteen days, whichever is sooner.

0075

대 한 민 국 외 무 부

발신전보

번 호: WUS-0560

일 시: 121520

종 별

외 신 과	
접 수	암 호
+	

수 신 인 : 주 미 대 사

대: USW-04187 및 USW-0548

대호 전문 보고서등에서 언급된, 귀관이 면담한 국무성 관계관의 직위 및 성명을 회보 바라며, 차후 보고시에는 면담관계관의 직위 및 성명을 명기 하시기 바람. (외구미)

장 관

미주과	66 5월 12일 양고재	담 당	과 장	국 장	특별보좌관	차 관	장 관

송신시간:

타자 • 판치	검 인	주무자	과 장

0076

미주과	양5월16일 고재	담 당	과 장	국 장	차관보	차 관	장 관

한.미간 주둔군 지위협정 체결교섭

(1966. 5. 18자 국회외무, 국방위원회 보고자료)

1966. 5. 16.

1. 교섭경위

가. 한.미양국은 박 대통령 방미시 양국 대통령이 조기 타결원칙을 확인한바에 입각하여 교섭을 적극 추진한 결과 그간 정돈상태에 있던 교섭은 진척을 보게되어 1965. 6. 7. 개최된 제81차 회의 까지 협정의 전문과 31개 조항중 25개 조항에 합의를 보게 되었음.

나. 그러나 미측의 완강한 태도로 말미아마 81차 회의까지도 완전히 해결을 보지 못한 형사 재판권, 노무, 청구권을 비롯하여 6개 조항에 관하여 그후 우리측은 미국측과 비공식 교섭을 계속하여 전반적인 합의에 도달하였던 것임.

2. 합의내용과 각 국 협정과의 비교

가. 한.미간에 합의된 협정안의 내용은 나토협정, 미.일협정등과 비교 할때 조문상으로는 다소 차이가 있으나 실지 운영에 있어서는 우리 협정안의내용은 타국의 협정과 별다른 차이가 없을 것임.

나. 특히 협정안중 형사 재판권의 제1차 재판권의 포기형태는 미국이 서독 과 맺은 보충협정에 규정된 형사 재판권 조항중 제1차 재판권

0077

1966. 7. 20. [signature]

의 표기형태를 우리나라에 유리하도록 보완한 것으로서 그 내용이 더욱 충실하게 되었다고 할수 있으며, 나토 각국이나, 일본은 협정의 실지 운영에 있어서는 협정문의 차이에도 불구하고 80-90 퍼센트 까지 그들의 재판권을 포기하고 있는 실정임.

3. 합의내용과 여론

그러나 정부에서는 신중을 기하기 위하여 협정체결에 앞서 1965년 말경부터 금년 1월 까지 수차에 걸쳐 법조계, 학계 및 언론계등 각계 저명 인사들을 초청하여 합의된 내용을 중심으로 의견을 교환한 결과 협정의 중요조항인 형사 재판권, 조항의 제1차 재판권의 포기형태, 청구권의 발효시기 및 노무조항의 군사상 필요로 인하여 미군이 우리나라의 노동관계 법령을 지키지 않을수 있는 범위등 문제를 수정하는 것이 좋겠다는 요망이 있었으며 그후 국내 여론 또한 대체적으로 이를 뒷받침 한바 있음.

4. 재교섭 제의

정부에서는 이와같은 사계의 권위자들의 의견과 국민의 여론을 기초로 협정안을 예의 검토한 끝에 지난 4월초에 이미 합의된 협정안의 내용중 형사재판권, 청구권, 노무등 중요조항의 내용을 일부 수정하기 위한 재교섭을 미측에 제의하고 미측의 의향을 타진중에 있음.

5. 미국측 비공식 반향

지금까지의 주미대사로 부터의 보고에 의하면 미국 당국에서는 현재 우리의 제의를 신중히 검토하고 있으며 동 검토가 끝나는 대로

0078

정식으로 회답할 것이라고 하는바 주미대사가 타진한 미국무성 관계당국의 비공식적인 반향은 대체적으로 다음과 같은 이유로 우리측의 재교섭 제의는 미측에 대하여 상당한 곤난이 있음을 시사하고 있음.

가. 미국이 이미 국회상원 외교, 국방위원회에 합의된 협정 내용을 보고하여 동의를 얻어 필요한 국내절차를 끝냈으므로 만일 동 협정을 수정한다면 다시 국회에 수정내용을 보고하여야 되며,

나. 동 내용은 한.미간 고위층간에 완전 합의를 본바 있음.

다. 비율빈 및 기타 국가와 비교할때 각기 국가 마다 사정이 다름.

6. 전 망

(가) 상기와 같은 미측의 비공식적인 시사로 보아 우리측 재교섭 제의에는 앞으로 상당한 난관이 있을 것으로 예측됨.

(나) 그러나, 정부로서는 이와같은 미측의 곤난점을 예기치 아니한 것은 아니며, 따라서 앞으로 기회있을 때 마다 한.미간의 고위회담 등을 통하여 우리정부와 국민의 요망을 반영코저 계속 노력 할것임.

7. 중요합의 내용의 문제점과 해결방안

그런데, 합의된 협정안의 중요내용과 재교섭을 통하여 수정코저 하는 해결방안은 다음과 같음.

0079

가. 형사 재판권조항

(1) 합의내용

우리나라가 가지는 제1차적 재판권을 일단 미국에 포기하고 개개사건이 발생하였을 경우에 우리나라가 재판권을 행사하는 것이 중요하다고 결정하는 때에는 포기를 철회하여 재판권을 행사한다.

(2) 해결방안

독일 보충협정 형태에 입각한 상기와 같은 합의내용 대신 미국이 "그리스" 또는 비율빈과 체결한 다음과 같은 포기형태에 따라 접수국인 우리나라가 제1차 재판권의 포기여부를 자주적으로 결정할수 있는 권리를 확보토저 하는 것임.

"대한민국 당국은 미군 당국의 포기요청이 있을 경우에는 대한민국이 재판권을 행사함이 중요하다고 결정하는 경우를 제외하고 대한민국이 가지는 제1차적 재판권을 미군당국에 포기한다."

나. 청구권

(1) 합의내용

민사 청구권 조항은 실질적으로 서울에 있어서는 협정발효 6개월후, 지방은 합동위원회가 결정하는 가능한 한, 빠른 시기에 발효한다.

0080

(2) 해결방안

민사 청구권의 핵심인 제3자에 대한 손해 배상 규정을 비롯한 본 조항은 서울은 물론 기타 지역에 있어서도 그 발효시기를 합동위원회가 결정하는 가장 빠른 시기로(막연하게)규정할 것이 아니라 협정 발효즉시 또는 그후 일정한 시기로 명확하게 규정하여야 한다.

다. 노무조항

(1) 합의내용

(가) 노동조건, 보상 및 노사관계는 미군의 군사상 필요에 배치되지 아니하는한, 한국의 노동관계 법령에 따라야 한다.

(나) 노동쟁의 조정기간 70일 후에도 그 쟁의가 해결되지 않을 경우 합 동위원회에서 결정하는 긴요한 고용원은 단체 행동 (파업)을 하지 못한다.

(2) 해결방안

(가) 미군은 "군사상의 필요"를 이유로 우리나라 법을 지키지 아니할수 있는 애매한 것인바 우리는 군사상 필요를 이유로 할때에도 사전에 쌍방이 합의하여야 하며,

(나) 쟁의 조정기간 70일 후에도 해결되지 아니할 경우에 파업을 할수 없는자의 범위는 우리나라 헌법과 노동법에 따라 제한할수 있는 최소한도의 범위로 한정하여야 한다. 끝

0081

미주과	앙고재	담당	과장	국장		차관	장관

이와같은 문제점에도 불구하고 수락한 이유

1. 우리측은 교섭당초 부터 교섭의 목표를 미.일 협정이나, 나토 협정에 두고 교섭하여 왔음.

2. 그러나 외교에는 상대방이 있으니 만큼, 쌍방의 의견을 절충 하지아니할수 없으며,

3. 무협정 상태를 무작정 지연시키는 것보다 다소 우리에게 불만스러운 점이 있음에도 불구하고 우리가 타협할수 있는 선에서 우선 협정을 체결하여 무협정 상태를 지양하여 실리를 도모하는 한편,

4. 협정을 실지 운영하여 결점이 들어나면 장차 수정을 제의코저 하였던 것이며,

5. 문제된 조항에 있어서도

(1) 형사재판권에 있어서는 독일 보충협정의 포기형태를 우리에게 유리하게 강화하여 우리나라가 재판권을 행사하는 것이 필요하다고 결정하는 경우에는 우리나라가 권리포기를 철회할수 있으며 이때에 철회의 효과는 최종적이며 확정적인 것으로 하였으며,

(2) 노무에 있어서 미군의 군사상 필요로 우리나라의 법을 지키지 못할 경우는 가능한 한 사전에 그렇지 못하면 사후에라도

0082

우리나라의 동의를 얻도록 하였음. 또한,

(3) 청구권에 있어서는 발효시기를 우선 서울지구만이라도 6개월후로 확정하여 우리나라의 운영 실적을 통하여 기타지역에서도 가능한 빠른 시일내에 적용토록 보강하는데 노력하였던 것임.

0083

<u>한·미간 주둔군지위협정 체결 교섭</u>

<u>~~국무~~총리의 Samuel D. Berger 미국무성 극동담당 부차관보와의 면담자료)</u>

1966. 6. 4.

1. 그간 주한미군의 지위에 관한 협정은 한미간의 교섭을 통하여 일단 비공식 합의에 도달한바 있으나 동 합의 내용에 대한 법조계, 학계, 및 언론계를 비롯한 국민들의 반대의 대상이 되고 있는 형사재판권, 청구권, 및 노무조항의 일부 내용을 협정 체결 전에 수정코저 정부에서는 지난 4월중순에 미측에 재교섭을 제의한바 있음.

2. 물론, 미측으로서도 일단 합의된 내용을 수정한다는 것은 상당한 애로가 있을 줄 짐작하는 바이지만 우리측 제의에 대하여 특별한 정치적 고려를 하여 주기 바람.

3. 특히, 내년초의 대통령 및 국회의원 선거를 맞이하게 되는 정부의 입장을 참작하여 동 협정 내용의 일부 수정이 절실히 요망되는 바이니 이러한 정부의 입장을 충분히 고려하여 주기 바람.

0084

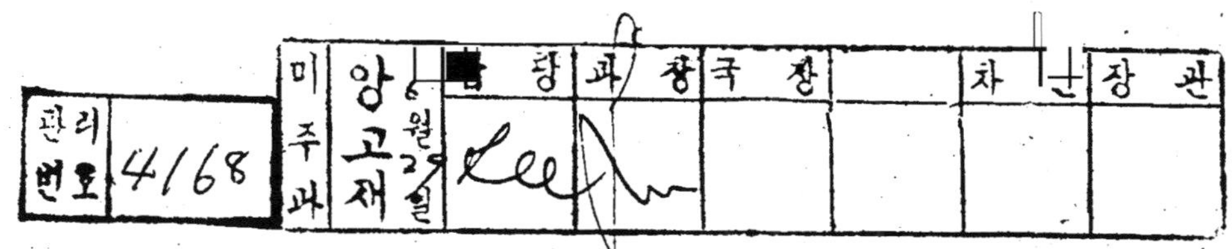

한.미간 주둔군 지위협정 체결교섭

(타스크 미국무장관과의 회담 자료)

1966. 6. 29.

1. 교섭경위

가. 한.미 양국은 1962년 9월 20일 주한 미군의 지위를 규제하기 위하여 협정체결교섭을 제시한 이래 예의 노력하여 왔으나 교섭의 조기타결을 보지 못하여 오던중 1965년 5월의 박대통령 방미시 양국 대통령이 조기타결 원칙을 확인한바에 입각하여 교섭을 적극 추진한 결과 현저한 진척을 보게되어 1965. 6. 7. 개최된 제 81차 회의까지 협정의 전문과 31개 조항중 25개 조항에 완전 합의를 보게 되었음.

나. 그러나 미측의 완강한 태도로 말미아마 81차 회의 까지도 완전히 해결을 보지 못한 형사 재판권, 노무, 청구권을 비롯하여 6개 조항에 관하여 그후 우리측은 미측과 비공식 교섭을 계속하여 일단 전반적인 합의에 도달하였으며 제82차 회의에서 비공식으로 합의된 내용을 정식으로 확인한다음 서울에서 조인코저 하였던 것임.

2. 합의내용과 여론

그러나 정부에서는 협정을 체결하기에 앞서 신중을 기하기 위하여 1965년 말경 부터 금년 초에 걸쳐 수차에 걸쳐 법조계, 학계 및 언론계등 각계 저명인사들을 초청하여 합의된 내용을 중심으로

0085

의견을 교환한 결과 협정의 중요조항인 형사 재판권, 조항의 제1차 재판권의 포기형태, 청구권의 발효시기 및 노무조항의 군사상 필요로 인한 미군의 우리나라 노동관계 법령을 지키지 않을수 있는 범위등 몇가지 문제를 수정하는 것이 좋겠다는 요망이 있었으며 그후 국내 여론 또한 대체적으로 이를 뒷받침 한바 있음.

3. 재교섭 제의

가. 정부에서는 이와같은 사계의 권위자들의 요망과 국민의 여론을 존중하는 한편,

나. 우리 정부가 당초의 교섭 목표를 미.일협정이나 나토협정에 두고 교섭하여 왔으나 미측의 고집으로 협정안이 조문상으로 보아 이들 협정과 다소 차이가 나게 되고 따라서 우리 정부나 국민에 만족할 만한 것이 못되었던것이니 만큼,

다. 한.미간에 체결될 협정이 결코 나토제국, 일본 또는 비율빈등 미국이 여러나라와 체결한 협정과 차이가 있어서는 아니되겠다는 결론에 도달, 협정안을 예의 검토한 끝에 지난 4월 15일 협정안의 핵심인 형사 재판권, 청구권, 노무조항의 중요내용을 일부 수정하기 위한 재교섭을 미측에 제의하는 한편, 6월 9일에는 본국 정부와의 정무 연락차 귀국하는 "부라운" 주한 미국대사에게 수정안 수교와 더불어 우리측의 재교섭 제의에 대한 입장을 밝히고 미국 정부의 성의를 촉구하고 계속 미측의 의향을 타진중에 있음. (별첨 참조)

0086

4. 미국측 반향

가. 지금까지의 주미대사로 부터의 보고와 주한 미국 대사관과의 접촉 결과에 의하면, 미국 당국에서는 현재 우리의 제의를 신중히 검토하고 있으며 동 검토가 끝나는대로 정식으로 회답할 것이라고 하는바, 미국무성 관계당국의 비공식적인 반향은 대체적으로 다음과 같은 이유로 우리측의 재교섭 제의는 미측에 대하여 상당한 곤난이 있음을 시사하고 있음. 6월 26일 귀임한 "부라운" 대사의 의견도 대체적으로 동일한 것임.

(1) 미국이 이미 국회 상원, 외교, 국방위원회에 합의된 내용을 보고하여 동의를 얻어 필요한 국내 절차를 끝냈으므로 동 협정안을 수정하려는 경우에는 재차 국회에 수정내용을 보고하여야 되며,

(2) 동 내용은 한.미 고위층간에 완전합의를 본바 있음.

(3) 비율빈 및 기타 국가와 비교할때 각기 국가 마다 사정이 다름.

(4) 특히 1965년 8월 10일 미.비 간에 체결, 발효된 형사 재판권의 수정조항의 운영 결과가 미측이 만족할 만큼 제1차 재판권의 포기를 얻지 못하고 있는 실정에 비추어 우리측이 비율빈식 포기형태를 요구하고 있는데 대하여 미국 국방성이 특히 난색을 표명하고 있음.

0087

5. 전 망

가. "머스크" 미국무장관의 방한을 계기로 미측이 우리측의 재교섭 제의 자체에는 응하여 올 것으로 보나,

상기와 같은 미측의 비공식적인 반향으로 보아 미측이 우리측 수정안대로 수락하는데에는 상당한 난관이 예측됨.

나. 그러나 정부로서는 이와같은 미측의 곤난점을 예기치 아니한 것은 아니므로 우리측 입장을 강경하게 주장할 필요가 있음.

다. 특히 미측은 재교섭 제의를 수락한후 타결을 지연 시킬 가능성도 없지 않음으로 우리측으로서는 단시일내에 (예를 들어 내년초의 선거에 임할 정부의 입장을 이유로) 타결토록 미측의 성의를 촉구함이 필요할 것으로 사료됨.

6. 중요합의 내용의 문제점과 해결방안

그런데, 합의된 협정안의 중요내용과 재교섭을 통하여 수정코저 하는 해결 방안은 다음과 같음.

가. 형사재판권 조항

(1) 합의내용

(가) 미군당국은, 미국군대의 구성원, 군속 및 그들의 가족에 대하여, 형사재판권을 행사할 권리를 가진다.

(나) 대한민국은 미국당국이 대한민국의 전속적 재판권의 포기를 요청하는 경우에는 호의적인 고려를 한다.

0088

(다) 대한민국이 가지는 제1차적 재판권을 일단 미국에 포기하고 개개 사건이 발생하였을 경우에 대한민국이 재판권을 행사하는 것이 중요하다고 결정하는 때에는 포기를 철회하여 재판권을 행사한다.

(2) 해결방안

(가) 미군당국은 미국 군법에 복하는 모든자에 대하여 형사 재판권을 행사할 권리를 가지며, "미국 군법에 복하는 모든자" 라함은 미군당국에 효과적인 재판권이 없는 군속 및 가족이 포함되지 아니함을 말한다.

(나) 미군당국이 재판권을 행사할수 있는 법적 근거가 없는 우리나라의 전속적 재판권은 포기할수 없다.

(다) 독일 보충협정 형태에 입각한 합의내용 대신 미국이 "그리스", "네델란드" 또는 비율빈과 체결한 다음과 같은 포기형태에 따라 접수국인 우리나라가 제1차적 재판권의 포기여부를 자주적으로 결정할수 있는 권리를 확보하여야 한다.

"대한민국 당국은 미군당국의 포기요청이 있을 경우에는 대한민국이 재판권을 행사함이 중요하다고 결정하는 경우를 제외하고 대한민국이 가지는 제1차적 재판권을 미군당국에 포기한다".

나. 청구권조항

(1) 합의내용

청구권 조항의 핵심인 제3자에 대한 손해 배상구절을 0089

서울에 있어서는 협정발효 6개월후, 지방은 합동위원회가 결정하는 가능한 한 빠른 시기에 발효한다.

(2) 해결방안
(2) 청구권의 핵심인 제3자에 대한 손해 배상규정을 비롯한 본 조항의 발효시기를 서울은 물론 기타 지역에 있어서도 협정 발효즉시 또는 그후 일정한 확정된 시기로 명확하게 규정하여야 한다.

다. 노무조항

(1) 합의내용

(가) 노동조건, 보상 및 노사관계는 미군의 군사상 필요에 배치되지 아니하는한, 한국의 노동관계 법령에 따라야 한다.

(나) 노동쟁의 조정기간 70일후에도 그 쟁의가 해결되지 않을 경우 합동위원회에서 결정하는 긴요한 고용원은 단체행동 (파업)을 하지 못한다.

(2) 해결방안

(가) 미군은 "군사상의 필요"를 이유로 우리나라 법을 지키지 아니할수 있을 경우에는 사전에 상호 합의하여야 하며,

(나) 쟁의 조정기간 70일후에도 해결되지 아니할 경우에 파업을 할수 없는자의 범위는 우리나라 헌법과

0090

노동관계 법령에 따라 제한할수 있는 최소한도의 범위로 한정하여야 한다.

유 첨 : "부라운" 주한 미국대사에게 수교한 우리측의 수정안 및 입장.

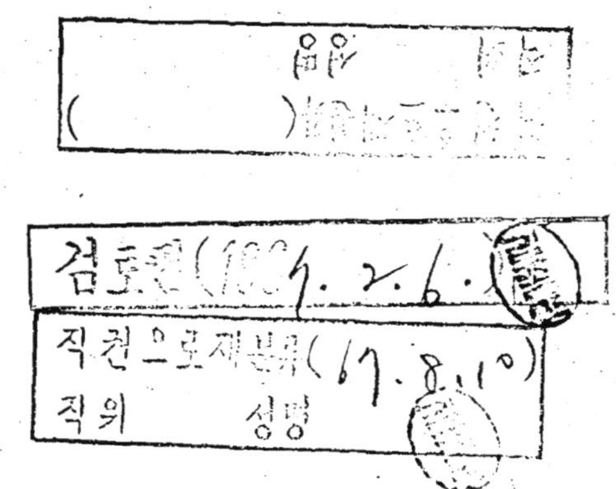

0091

ARTICLE XXIII CLAIMS

1966.6.2.

Agreed Minutes

1. Unless otherwise provided, (a) The provisions of paragraphs 5,6,7 and 8 of this Article will become effective six months from the date of entry into force of this Agreement as to claims arising from incidents in the Seoul Special City area. (b) The provisions of paragraph 5,6,7 and 8 will be extended, at the earliest date practicable, to other areas of the Republic of Korea as determined by the Joint Committee.	1. (Delete)
2. Until such time as the provisions of paragraphs 5,6,7 and 8 become effective in any given area. (a) The United States shall process and settle claims (other than contractual claims) arising out of the acts or omissions of members or employees of the United States armed forces done in the performance of official duty or out of any other act, omission or occurrence for which the United States armed forces are legally responsible, which	2. (Delete)

0092

the United States armed forces are legally responsible, which cause damage in the Republic of Korea to Parties other than the two Governments.

(b) The United States shall entertain other non-contractual claims against members or employees of the armed forces and may offer an ex gratia payment in such cases and in such amounts as is determined by the appropriate United States authorities; and

(c) Each Party shall have the right to determine whether a member or employee of its armed forces was engaged in the performance of official duties and whether property owned by it was being used by its armed forces for official purposes.

3. For the purposes of subparagraph 2(d), subparagraph 5(e) shall be effective throughout the Republic of Korea from the date of entry into force of this Agreement.	3. (Delete)

0093

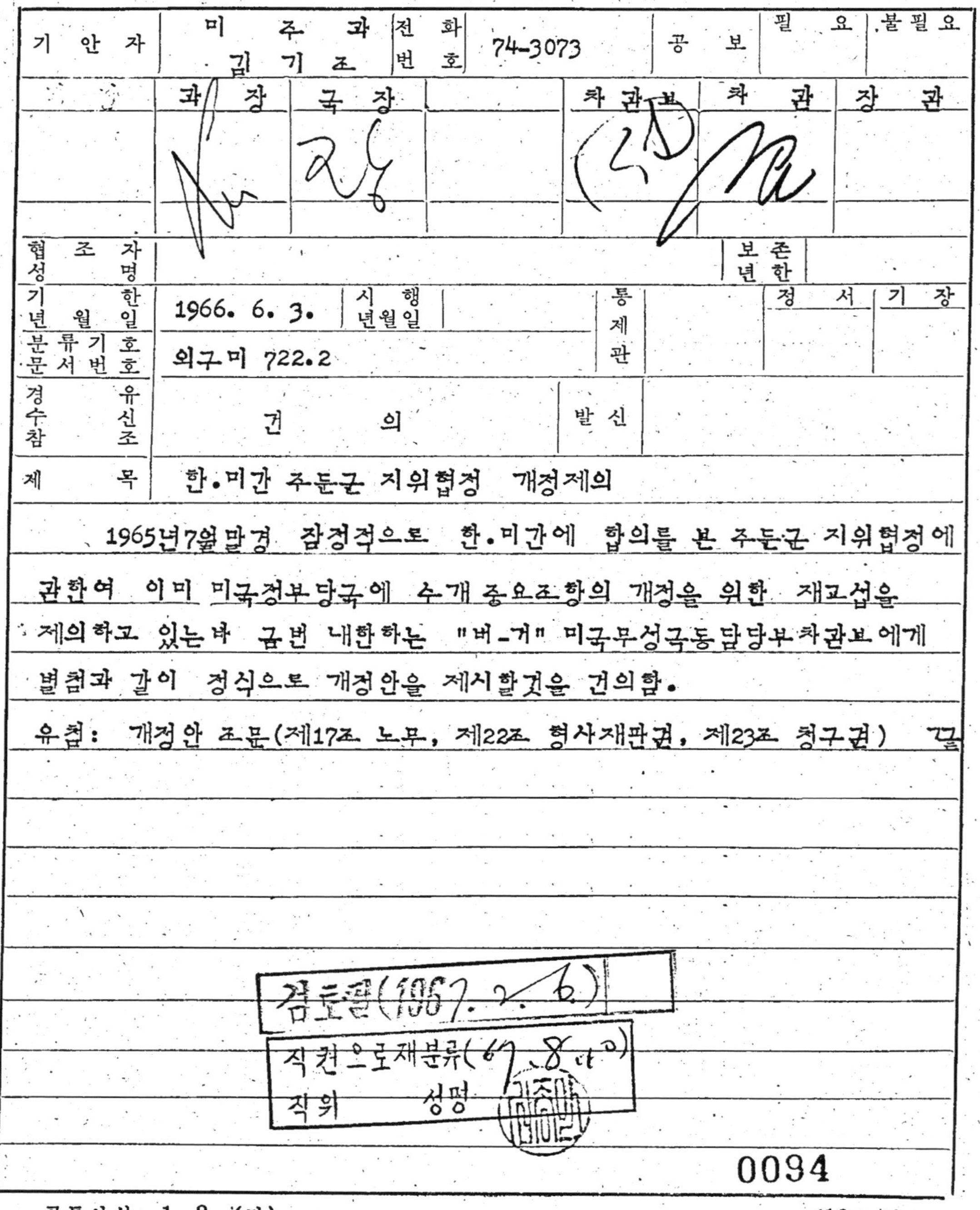

기 안 지

기 안 자	미 주 과 김 기 조	전 화 번 호	74-3073	공 보	필 요	불필요

	과 장	국 장		차관보	차 관	장 관

협 조 자 성 명		보 존 년 한	
기 한 년 월 일	1966. 6. 3.	시 행 년월일	
분류기호 문서번호	외구미 722.2	통 제 관	
경 유 수 신 참 조	건 의	발 신	
제 목	한.미간 주둔군 지위협정 개정제의		

정 서 | 기 장

1965년7월말경 잠정적으로 한.미간에 합의를 본 주둔군 지위협정에 관한여 이미 미국정부당국에 수개 중요조항의 개정을 위한 재교섭을 제의하고 있는바 금번 내한하는 "버-거" 미국무성극동담당부차관보에게 별첨과 같이 정식으로 개정안을 제시할것을 건의함.

유첨: 개정안 조문(제17조 노무, 제22조 형사재판권, 제23조 청구권) 끝

검토필(1967. 2. 6)

직권으로재분류(67. 8. 10)
직위 성명

0094

공통서식 1-2 (갑) (16절지)

ARTICLE XVII LABOR

(Underlined parts are modifications.)

Present Draft	New Draft
4. (b) The Joint Committee, taking into consideration the role of the employees of the United States armed forces in the defense of the Republic of Korea and pertinent provisions of legislation of the Republic of Korea, shall determine those categories of essential employees who shall not exercise the right of further collective action in the event a labor dispute is not resolved by the foregoing procedures. In the event an agreement cannot be reached on this question in the Joint Committee, it may be made the subject of review through discussions between appropriate officials of the Government of the Republic of Korea and the diplomatic mission of the United States of America.	4. Employees or any employee organization shall have the right of further collective action in the event a labor dispute is not resolved by the foregoing procedures except in cases where the Joint Committee determines such action seriously hampers military operations of the United States armed forces for the joint defense of the Republic of Korea. In the event an agreement cannot be reached on this question in the Joint Committee, it may be made the subject of review through discussions between appropriate officials of the Government of the Republic of Korea and the diplomatic mission of the United States of America.

AGREED MINUTES

4. When employers cannot conform with provisions of labor legislation of the Republic of Korea applicable	4. When employers cannot conform with provisions of labor legislation of the Republic of

0095

under this Article on account of the military requirements of the United States armed forces, the matter shall be referred, in advance <u>whenever possible</u>, to the Joint Committee for consideration and appropriate action. In the event mutual agreement can not be reached in the Joint Committee regarding appropriate action, the issue may be made the subject of review through discussions between appropriate officials of the Government of the Republic of Korea and the diplomatic mission of the United States of America.	Korea applicable under this Article on account of the military requirements of the United States armed forces, the matter shall be referred, <u>in advance</u>, to the Joint Committee <u>for mutual agreement</u>. In the event mutual agreement cannot be reached in the Joint Committee regarding appropriate action, the issue may be made the subject of review through discussions between appropriate officials of the Government of the Republic of Korea and the diplomatic mission of the United States of America.

0096

ARTICLE XXII CRIMINAL JURISDICTION

Present Draft	New Draft 3(a)
1. Subject to the provisions of this Article.	1. Subject to the provisions of this Article.
(a) the military authorities of the United States shall have the right to exercise within the Republic of Korea all criminal and disciplinary jurisdiction conferred on them by the law of the United States over members of the United States armed forces or civilian component, and their dependents;	(a) the military authorities of the United States shall have the right to exercise within the Republic of Korea all criminal and disciplinary jurisdiction conferred on them by the law of the United States over all persons subject to the military law of the United States;
	(To be consistent with the above revision, the following relevant portions in this Article and these Agreed Minutes shall also be revised: 1. Article : Paragraphs 2(a), 3(a). 2. Agreed Minutes: Re Paragraph 1(b), Re Paragraph 3(a))
None	Re Paragraph 1(a) The term "all persons subject to the military law of the United States" as referred to in this Article and in these Agreed Minutes does not apply to members of the

0097

civilian component or dependents, with respect to whom there is no effective military jurisdiction at the time this agreement enters into force. If the scope of U.S. military jurisdiction changes as a result of subsequent legislation, constitutional amendment or decision by appropriate authorities of the United States, the Government of the United States shall inform the Government of the Republic of Korea through diplomatic channels.

Re Paragraph 2

The Republic of Korea, recognizing the effectiveness in appropriate cases of the administrative and disciplinary sanctions which may be imposed by the United States authorities over members of the United States armed forces or civilian component, and their dependents, will give sympathetic consideration in such cases to requests in the Joint Committee for waivers of its right to exercise jurisdiction under paragraph 2.	Delete
Re Paragraph 3(b)	Re Paragraph 3(b)
1. The Government of the Republic of Korea waives in favor of the United States the primary	1. The authorities of the Republic of Korea, recognizing that it is the primary responsibility

-32-

0098

right granted to the authorities of the Republic of Korea under subparagraph (b) of paragraph 3 of this Article in cases of concurrent jurisdiction, in accordance with paragraphs 2,3,4,5,6, and 7 of this Minute.

of the United States military authorities to maintain good order and discipline where persons subject to the military law of the United States are concerned, will, upon the request of the military authorities of the United States pursuant to paragraph 3(c), waive their primary right to exercise jurisdiction under paragraph 3(b), except where they determine that it is of particular importance that jurisdiction be exercised by the authorities of the Republic of Korea.

(In accordance with the above proposal regarding waiver formula, changes shall be made in the Paragraphs 2,3,4,6(a), and 7 of this Minute.)

0099

ARTICLE XXIII. CLAIMS

Agreed Minutes

1. Unless otherwise provided,	1. Delete
(a) The provisions of paragraphs 5,6,7 and 8 of this Article will become effective six months from the date of entry into force of this Agreement as to claims arising from incidents in the Seoul Special City Area.	(To be consistent with the above revision, the ensuing Agreed Minutes #2 and 3 shall also be deleted.)
(b) The provisions of paragraph 5, 6, 7 and 8 will be extended, at the earliest date practicable, to other areas of the Republic of Korea and determined the Joint Committee.	

0100

ARTICLE XXII CRIMINAL JURISDICTION

Present Draft	New Draft
1. Subject to the provisions of this Article.	1. Subject to the provisions of this Article.
(a) the military authorities of the United States shall have the right to exercise within the Republic of Korea all criminal and disciplinary jurisdiction conferred on them by the law of the United States over members of the United States armed forces or civilian component, and their dependents;	(a) the military authorities of the United States shall have the right to exercise within the Republic of Korea all criminal and disciplinary jurisdiction conferred on them by the law of the United States over all persons subject to the military law of the United States;
	(To be consistent with the above revision, the following relevant portions in this Article and these Agreed Minutes shall also be revised: 1. Article : Paragraphs 2(a), 3(a). 2. Agreed Minutes : Re Paragraph 1(b), Re Paragraph 3(a)
None	Re Paragraph 1(a)
	The term "all persons subject to the military law of the United States" as referred to in this Article and in these Agreed Minutes does not apply to members of the

0101

1-2

civilian component or dependents, with respect to whom there is no effective military jurisdiction at the time this agreement enters into force. If the scope of U.S. military jurisdiction Changes as a result of subsequent legislation, constitutional amendment or decision by appropriate authorities of the United States, the Government of the United States shall inform the Government of the Republic of Korea through diplomatic channels.

Re Paragraph 2

The Republic of Korea, recognizing the effectiveness in appropriate cases of the administrative and disciplinary sanctions which may be imposed by the United States authorities over members of the United States armed forces or civilian component, and their dependents, will give sympathetic consideration in such cases to requests in the Joint Committee for waivers of its right to exercise jurisdiction under paragraph 2.	Delete

0102

Re Paragraph 3(b)

1. The Government of the Republic of Korea waives in favor of the United States the primary right granted to the authorities of the Republic of Korea under paragraph (b) of paragraph 3 of this Article in cases of concurrent jurisdiction, in accordance with paragraphs 2,3,4,5,6, and 7 of this Minute.

Re Paragraph 3(b)

1. The authroities of the Republic of Korea, recognizing that it is the primary responsibilit of the United States military authorities to maintain good order and discipline where persons subject to the military law of the United States are concerned, will, upon the request of the military authorities of the United States pursuant to paragraph 3(c), waive their primary right to exercise jurisdiction under paragraph 3(b), except where they determine that it is of particular importance that jurisdiction be exercised by the authorities of the Republic of Korea.

(In accordance with the above proposal regarding waiver formula, changes shall be made in the Paragraphs 2,3,4,6(a), and 7 of this Minute.)

2. Subject to any particular arrangements which may be made under paragraph 7 of this Minute, the military authorities of the United States shall notify the competent authorities of the Republic of Korea

Delete

of individual cases falling under the waiver provided in paragraph 1 of this Minute.

3. Where the competent authorities of the Republic of Korea hold the view that, by reason of special circumstances in a specific case, major interests of Korean administration of justice make imperative the exercise of jurisdiction by the Republic of Korea, they may recall the waiver granted under paragraph 1 of this Minute by a statement to the competent military authorities of the United States within a period of twenty-one days after receipt of the notification envisaged in paragraph 2 of this Minute or any shorter period which may be provided in arrangements made under paragraph 7 of this Minute. The authorities of the Republic of Korea may also submit the statement prior to receipt of such notification.

Delete

(a) Subject to a careful examination of each specific case and to the results of such examination, major interests of Korean administration of justice within the meaning of paragraph 3 above may make imperative the exercise of jurisdiction by the Republic of Korea, in particular, in the following cases:

— 4 —

0104

75

(i) security offenses against the Republic of Korea;

(ii) offenses causing the death of a human being, robbery, and rape, except where the offenses are directed against a member of the United States armed forces or the civilian component, or a dependent and

(iii) attempts to commit such offenses or participation therein.

(b) In respect of the offenses r==rred to in subparagraph (a) of this paragraph, the authorities concerned shall proceed in particularly close cooperation from t|_ beginning of the preliminary investigation in order to provide the mutual assistance envisaged in paragraph 6 of this Article.

4. If, pursuant to paragraph 3 of this Minute, the competent authorities of the Republic of Korea have recalled the waiver in a specific case and in such case an understanding cannot be reached in discussions between the authorities concerned, the Government of the United States may make representations to the Government of the Republic of Korea through diplomatic channels.

Delete

The Government of the Republic of Korea, giving due consideration to the interests of Korean administration of justice and to the interests of the Government of the United States, shall resolve the disagreement in the exercise 出 its authority in the field of foreign affairs. In case the Government of the Republic of Korea, in resolving the disagreement in accordance with the foregoing provisions, determines that it is imperative that jurisdiction be exercised by the authorities of the Republic of Korea, the recall of waiver shall be final and conclusive.

5. With the consent of the competent authorities of the Republic of Korea, the military authorities of the United States may transfer to the courts or authorities of the Republic of Korea for investigation, trial and decision, particular criminal cases in which jurisdiction rests with the United States.

With the consent of the military authorities of the United States, the competent authorities of the Republic of Korea may transfer to the military authorities of the United States for investigation, trial and

0106

decision, particular criminal cases in which jurisdiction rests with the Republic of Korea.

6 (a) Where a member of the United States armed forces or civilian component, or a dependent, is arraigned before a court of the United States, for an offense committed in the Republic of Korea against Korean interests, the trial shall be held within the Republic of Korea.

(i) except where the law of the United States requires otherwise, or

(ii) except where, in cases of military exigency or in the interests of justice, the military authorities of the United States intend to hold the trial outside the Republic of Korea. In this event they shall afford the authorities of the Republic of Korea timely opportunity to comment on such intention and shall give due consideration to any comments the later may make.

(b) Where the trial is held outside of the Republic of Korea the military authorities of the United States shall inform the authorities of the Republic of Korea of the place and date of the trial. A representative of the Republic of Korea shall be entitled to be present at the trial. The authorities of the United States shall inform the authorities of the Republic of Korea of the judgment and the final outcome of the proceedings.

7. In the implementation of the provisions of this Article and this Agreed Minute, and to facilitate the expeditious disposal of offenses of minor importance, arrangements may be made between the competent authorities of the Republic of Korea and the military authorities of the United States. These arrangements may also extend to dispending with notification and to the period of time referred to in paragraph 3 of this Minute, within which the waiver may be recalled.

In the implementation of the provisions of this Article and this Agreed Minute, and to facilitate the expeditous disposal of offenses of minor importance, arrangements may be made between the competent authorities of the Republic of Korea and the military authorities of the United States. These arrangements may also extend to dispending with the necessity for a request for a waiver of jurisdiction to be made in each particular case.

Re Paragraph 3(c)

Where either Government, in accordance with paragraph 3(c) and Agreed Minute Re Paragraph 3(b) of this Article, desires to request a waiver of the other Government's primary right to exercise jurisdiction, a written request shall be made within ten days or receipt of notification of the commission of an offense.

0108

A request from the Republic of Korea for waiver shall be delivered to the competent authorities of the United States, and a request from the military authorities of the United States for waiver shall be delivered to the competent authorities of the Republic of Korea.

Where either Government is not advised by the other Government within fifteen days of the date of receipt by such other Government of a request for a waiver of jurisdiction that jurisdiction will be exercised by such other Government, the requesting Government shall be free to exercise jurisdiction.

Where either Government, howeve notifies the other Government that for special reasons to reserve decision with respect to the exercise of jurisdiction, the requesting Government will not be free to exercise its jurisdiction until notice is received that the other Government will not exercise jurisdiction or until the expiration of an additional period of fifteen days, whichever is sooner.

Status of Forces Agreement

1. Subject to the provisions of this Article,

(a) the authorities of the Republic ofKrea shall have jurisdiction over the members of the United States armed forces or civilian component, and their dependents, with respect to offenses committed within the territory of the Republic of Korea and punishable by the law of the Republic of Korea.

(b) the military authorities of the United States shall have the right to exercise within the Republic of Korea all criminal and disciplinary jurisdiction conferred on them by the law of the United States over over all persons subject to the military law of the United States.

2. (a) The authorities of the Republic of Korea shall have the right to exercise exclusive jurisdiction over members of the United States armed forces or civilian component, and their dependents, with respect to offenses, including offenses relating to the security of the Republic of Korea, punishable by its law but not by the law of the United States.

(b) The military authorities of the United States shall have the right to exercise exclusive jurisdiction over persons subject to the military law of the United States with respect to offenses, including offenses relating to its security, punishable by the law of the United States, but not by the law of the Republic of Korea.

(c) For the purpose of this paragraph and of paragraph 3 of this Article, a security offense against a State shall include:

(i) treason against the State;

(ii) sabotage, espionage or violation of any law relting to official secrets of that State, or secrets relating to the national defense of that State.

-1-

0110

3. In cases where the right to exercise jurisdiction is concurrent the following rules shall apply:

(a) the authorities of the Republic of Korea shall have the primary right to exercise jurisdiction in all offenses except as enumerated in paragraph (b) hereof.

(b) the military authorities of the United States shall have the primary right to exercise jurisdiction over all persons subject to the military law of the United States in relation to:

(i) offenses solely against the property or security of the United States, or offenses solely against the person or property of another member of the United States armed forces or civilian civilian component or of a dependent;

(ii) offenses arising out of any act or omission done in the performance of official duty.

(c) If the State having the primary right decides not to exercise jurisdiction, it shall notify the authorities of the other State as soon as practicable. The authorities of the State having the primary right shall give sympathetic consideration to a request from the authorities of the other State for a waiver of its right in cases where that other State considers such waiver to be of particular importance.

4. The foregoing provisions of this Article shall not imply any right for the military authorities of the United States to exercise jurisdiction over persons, who are ordinarily resident in the Republic of Korea, unless they are members of the United States armed forces, or who are nationals of the Republic of Korea.

military authorities of the United States shall assist each other in the arrest of members of the United States armed forces, the civilian component, or their dependents in the territory of the Republic of Korea and in handing them over to the authority which is to have custody in accordance with the following provisions.

(b) The authorities of the Republic of Kofea shall notify promptly the military authorities of the United States of the arrest of any member of the United States armed forces, or civilian component, or a dependent. The military authorities of the United States shall promptly notify the authorities of the Republic of Korea of the arrest of a member of the United States armed forces, the civilian component, or a dependent in any case in which the Republic of Korea has the primary right to exercise jurisdiction.

(c) The custody of an accused member of the United States armed forces or civilian component, or of a dependent, over whom the Republic of Korea is to exercise jurisdiction shall, if he is in the hands of the military authorities of the United States, remain with the military authorities of the United States pending the conclusion of all judicial proceedings and until custody is requested by the authorities of the Republic of Korea. If he is in the hands of the Republic of Korea, he shall, on request, be handed over to the military authorities of the United States and remain in their custody pending completion of all judicial proceedings and until custody is requested by the authorities of the Republic of Korea. When an accused has been in the custody of the military authorities of the United States, the military authorities of the United States may transfer custody to the authorities of the Republic of Korea at any time, and shall give sympathetic consideration to any request for the transfer of custody which may be made by the authorities of the Republic of Korea in specific cases. The military authorities of the United States shall promptly make any such accused available to the authorities of the Republic of Korea upon their request for purposes of investigation and trial, and shall take all appropriate measures to that end and to prevent any prejudice to the course of justice. They shall take full account of any special request regarding custody made by the authorities of the Republic of Korea. The authorities of the Republic of Korea shall give sympathetic consideration to a request from the military authorities of the United States for assistance in maintaining custody of an accused member of the United States armed forces, the civilian component, or a dependent.

-3

0112

(d) In respect of offenses solely against the security of the Republic of Korea provided in paragraph 2(c), an accused shall be in the custody of the authorities of the Republic of Korea.

6. (a) The authorities of the Republic of Korea and the military authorities of the United States shall assist each other in the carrying out of all necessary investigations into offenses, and in the collection and production of evidence, including the seizure and, in proper cases, the handing over of objects connected with an offense. The handing over of such objects may, however, be made subject to their return within the time specified by the authority delivering them.

(b) The authorities of the Republic of Korea and the military authorities of the United States shall notify each other of the disposition of all cases in which there are concurrent rights to exercise jurisdiction.

7. (a) A death sentence shall not be carried out in the Republic of Korea by the military authorities of the United States if the legislation of the Republic of Korea does not provide for such punishment in a similar case.

(b) The authorities of the Republic of Korea shall give sympathetic consideration to a request from the military authorities of the United States for assistance in carrying out a sentence of imprisonment prnounced by the military authorities of the United States under the provisions of this Article within the territory of the Republic of Korea. The authorities of the Republic of Korea shall also give sympathetic consideration to a request from the authorities of the United States for the custody of any member of the United States armed forces or civilian component or a dependent, who is serving a sentence of confinement imposed by a court of the Republic of Korea. If such custody is released to the military authorities of the United States, the United States shall be obligated to continue the confinement of the individual in an appropriate confinement facility of the United States until the sentence to confinement shall have been served in full or until release from such confinement shall be approved by competent authorities of the Republic of Korea. In such cases, the authorities of the United States shall furnish relevant information on a routine basis to the authorities of the Republic of Korea, and a representative of the Government of the Republic of Korea shall have the right to have access to a member of the United States armed forces, the civilian component, or a dependent who is serving a sentence imposed by a court of the Republic of Korea in confinement facilities of the United States.

8. Where an accused has been tried in accordance with the provisions of this Article either by the authorities of the Republic of Korea or the military authorities of the United States and has been acquitted, or has been convicted and is serving, or has served, his sentence, or his sentence has been remitted or suspended, or he has been pardoned, he may not be tried again for the same offense within the territory of the Republic of Korea by the authorities of the other State. However, nothing in this paragraph shall prevent the military authorities of the United States from trying a member of its armed forces for any violation of rules of discipline arising from an act or omission which constituted an offense for which he was tried by the authorities of the Republic of Korea.

9. Whenever a member of the United States armed forces or civilian component or a dependent is prosecuted under the jurisdiction of the Replic of Korea he shall be ended:

(a) to a prompt and speedy trial;

(b) to be informed, in advance of trial, of the specific charge or charges made against him;

(c) to be confronted with the witnesses against him;

(d) to have compulsory process for obtaining witnesses in his favor, if they are within the jurisdiction of the Republic of Korea;

0114

(e) to have legal representation of his own choice for his defense or to have free or assisted legal representation under the conditions prevailing for the time being in the Republic of Korea;

(f) if he considers it necessary, to have the services of a competent interpreter; and

(g) to communicate with a representative of the Government of the United States and to have such a representative present at his trial.

10. (a) Regularly constituted military units or formations of the United States armed forces shall have the right to police any facilities or areas which they use under Article II of this Agreement. The military police of such forces may take all appropriate measures to ensure the maintenance of order and security within such facilities and areas.

(b) Outside these facilities and areas, such military police shall be employed only subject to arrangements with the authorities of the Republic of Korea and in liaison with those authorities, and in so far as such employment is necessary to maintain discipline and order among the members of the United States armed forces, or ensure their security.

11. In the event of hostilities to which the provisions of Article II of the Mutual Defense Treaty apply, the provisions of this Agreement pertaining to criminal jurisdiction shall be immediately suspended and the military authorities of the United States shall have the right to exercise exclusive jurisdiction over (members of the United States armed forces, the civilian component, and their dependents.) (all offenses which may be committed by persons subject to the military law of the United States.)

12. The provisions of this Article shall not apply to any offenses committed before the entry into force of this Agreement. Such cases shall be governed by the provisions of the Agreement between the Republic of Korea and the United States of America effected by an exchange of notes at Taejon on July 12, 1950.

Agreed Minutes

Article XXII

The provisions of this Article shall not affect existing Agreements, arrangements, or practices, relating to the exercise of jurisdiction over personnel of the United Nations forces present in the Republic of Korea other than forces of the United States.

Re Paragraph 1(b)

The term "all persons subject to the military law of the United States" as referred to in this Article and in these Agreed Minutes does not apply to members of the civilian component or dependents, with respect to whom there is no effective military jurisdiction at the time this arrangement enters into force. If the scope of U.S. military jurisdiction changes as a result of subsequent legislation, constitutional amendment or decision by appropriate authorities of the United States, the Government of the United States shall inform the Government of the Republic of Korea through diplomatic channels.

Re Paragraph 1(a)

1. In the event that martial law is declared by the Republic of Korea, the provisions of this Article shall be immediately suspended in the part of the Republic of Korea under martial law, and the military authorities of the United States shall have the right to exercise exclusive jurisdiction over all persons subject to the military law of the United States in such part until martial law is ended.

2. The jurisdiction of the authorities of the Republic of Korea over members of the United States armed forces or civilian component, and their dependents, shall not extend to any offenses committed outside the Republic of Korea.

Re Paragraph 2(c)

Each Government shall inform the other of the details of all security offenses mentioned in this subparagraph, and of the provisions regarding such offenses in its legislation.

0116

-7

Re Paragraph 3(b)

1. ~~Where a member of the United States armed forces or civilian component is charged with an offense,~~ Whenever it is necessary to determine whether an alleged offense arose out of an act or omission done in the performance of official duty, a certificate issued by competent military authorities of the United States, only upon the advice of a Staff Judge Advocate, stating that the alleged offens, if committed by him, arose out of an act or omission done in the performance of official duty shall be sufficient evidence of the fact for the purpose of determining primary jurisdiction. The term "official duty" as used in this Article and Agreed Minute is not meant to include all acts by the individuals ~~members of the United States armed forces and the civilian component~~ during periods when they are on duty, but is meant to apply only to acts which are required to be done as functions of those duties which the individuals are performing.

2. In those exceptional cases where the Chief Prosecutor for the Republic of Korea considers that there is proof contrary to a certificate of official duty, it shall be made the subject of review through discussions between appropriate officials of the Government of the Republic of Korea and the diplomatic mission of the United States in the Republic of Korea.

Re Paragraph 3(c)

The authorities of the Republic of Korea, recognizing that it is the primary responsibility of the United States military authorities to maintain good order and discipline where persons subject to the military law of the United States are concerned, will, upon the request of the military authorities of the United States pursuant to paragraph 3(c), waive their primary right to exercise jurisdiction under paragraph 3(a) (b), except where they determine that it is of particular importance that jurisdiction be exercised by the authorities of the Republic of Korea.

Where either Government desires to request a waiver of the other Government's primary right to exercise jurisdiction, a written request shall be made within ten days of receipt of notification of the commission of an offense. A request from the Republic of Korea for waiver will be delivered to the United States commander concerned, and a United States request for waiver will be delivered to the District Prosecutor concerned.

Where either Government is not advised by the other Government within fifteen days of the date of receipt by such other Government of a request for a waiver of jurisdiction that jurisdiction will be exercised by such other Government, the requesting G;vernment shall be free to exercise jurisdiction.

Where either Government, however, notifies the other Government that for special reasons it desires to reserve decision with respect to the exercise of jurisdiction, the requesting Government will not be free to exercise its jurisdiction until notice is received that the other Government will not exercise jurisdiction or until the expiration of an additional period of fifteen days, whichever is sooner.

Trials of cases in which the authorities of the Republic of Korea waive the primary right to exercise jurisdiction, and trials of cases involving offenses described in paragraph 3(a)(ii) committed against the state or nationals of the Republic of Korea will be held within a reasonable distance from the place where the offenses are alleged to have takne place unless other arrangements are mutually agreed upon. Representatives of the Republic of Korea may be present at such trials.

In the implementation of the provisions of this Article and this Agreed Minute, and to facilitate the expeditious disposal of offenses of minor importance, arrangements may be made between the competent authorities of the Republic of Korea and the military authorities of the United States. These arrangements may also extend to dispensing with the necessity for a request for a waiver of jurisdiction to be made in each particular case.

Re Paragraph 4

For the purpose of this paragraph, dual nationals, Korean and United States, and Korean nationals, who are members of the United States and are brought to the Republic of Korea by the United States shall not be considered as nationals of the Republic of Korea, but shall be considered as United States nationals.

39

0118

Re Paragraph 3(b)

1. Where a member of the United States armed forces or civilian component is charged with an offense, a certificate issued by competent military authorities of the United States stating that the alleged offense, if committed by him, arose out of an act or omission done in the performance of official duty shall be sufficient evidence of the fact for the purpose of determining primary jurisdiction. The term "official duty" as used in this Article and Agreed Minute is not meant to include all acts by members of the United States armed forces and the civilian component during periods when they are on duty, but is meant to apply only to acts which are ~~requ~~ required to be done as functions of those duties which the individuals are performing.

2. In those exceptional cases where the Chief Prosecutor for the Republic of Korea considers that there is proof contrary to a certificate of official duty, it shall be made the subject of review through discussions between appropriate officials of the Government of the Republic of Korea and the diplomatic mission of the United States in the Republic of Korea.

Re Paragraph 3(c)

The authorities of the Republic of Korea, recognizing that it is the primary responsibility of the United States military authorities to maintain good order and discipline where persons subject to United States military law are concerned, will, upon the request of the military authorities of the United States pursuant to paragraph 3(c), waive their primary right to exercise jurisdiction under paragraph 3(a) except when they determine that it is of particular importance that jurisdiction be exercised by the authorities of the Republic of Korea. In case where any question arises concerning such determination as may be made by the authorities of the Republic of Korea in accordance with the foregoing provisions, the United States diplomatic mission will be afforded an opportunity to confer with the proper authorities of the Republic of Korea.

Trials of cases in which the authorities of the Republic of Korea waive the primary right to exercise jurisdiction, and trials of cases involving offenses described in paragraph 3(a)(ii) committed against the state or nationsla of the Republic of Korea will be held within a reasonable distance from the place where the offenses are alleged to have taken place unless other arrangements are mutually agreed upon. Representatives of the Republic of Korea may be present at such trials.

In the implementation of the provisions of this Article and this Agreed Minute, and to facilitate the expeditious disposal of offenses of minor importance, arrangements may be made between the competent authorities of the Republic of Korea and the military authorities of the United States. These arrangements may also extend to dispensing with the necessity for a request for a waiver of jurisdiction to be made in each particular case.

Re Paragraph 6

1. The authorities of the Republic of KOrea and the military authorities of the United States shall assist each other in obtaining the appearance of witnesses necessary for the proceedings conducted by such authorities within the Republic of Korea.

When a member of the United States armed forces in the Republic of Korea is summoned to appear before a court of the Republic of Korea, as a witness or a defendant, United States military authorities shall, unless military exigency requires otherwise, secure his attendance provided such attendance is compulsory under the law of the Republic of Korea. If military exigency prevents such attendance, the military authorities of the United States shall furnish a certificate stating the estimated duration of such disability.

Service of process upon a member of the United States armed forces or civilian component, or a dependent required as a witness or a defendant must be personal service in the English language. Where the service of process os tp be effected by a process server of the Republic of Korea upon any person who is inside a military

77 0120

installation or area, the military authorities of the United States shall take all measures necessary to enable the process server to effect such service.

In addition, the authorities of the Republic of Korea shall promptly give copies of all criminal writs(including warrants, summonses, indictments, and subpoenas) to an agent designated by the United States military authorities to receive them in all cases of criminal proceedings of the Republic of Korea involving a member of the United States armed forces or civilian component, or a dependent.

When citizens or residents of the Republic of Korea are required as witnesses or experts by the military authorities of the United States, the courts and authorities of the Republic of Korea shall, in accordance with the law of the Republic of Korea, secure the attendance of such persons. In these cases the military authorities of the United States shall act through the Attorney General of the Republic of Korea, or such other agency as is designated by the authorities of the Republic of Korea.

Fees and other payments for witnesses shall be determined by the Joint Committee established under Article XXVIII.

2. The privileges and immunities of witnesses shall be those accorded by the law of the court, tribunal or authority before which they appear. In no event shall a witness be required to provide testimony which may tend to incriminate him.

3. If, in the course of criminal proceedings before authorities of the Republic of Korea or the United States, the disclosure of an official secret or either of these States or the disclosure of any information which may prejudice the security of either appears necessary for the just disposition of the proceedings, the authorities concerned shall seek written permission to make such disclosure from the appropriate authority of the State concerned.

72

0121

Re Paragraph 9(a)

The right to a prompt and speedy trial by the courts of the Republic of Korea shall include public trial, except when the court decrees otherwise in accordance with the law 6f the Republic of Korea, and trial by an impartial tribunal composed exclusively of judges who have completed their probationary period. A member of the United States armed forces, or civilian component, or a dependent, shall not be tried by a military tribunal of the Republic of Korea.

Re Paragraph 9(g)

The right to communicate with a representative of the Government of the United States shall exist from the moment of arrest or detention. Such representative shall be entitled to be present at all preliminary investigations, examinations, pretrial hearings, the trial itself, and subsequent proceedings, at which the accused is present.

13 0122

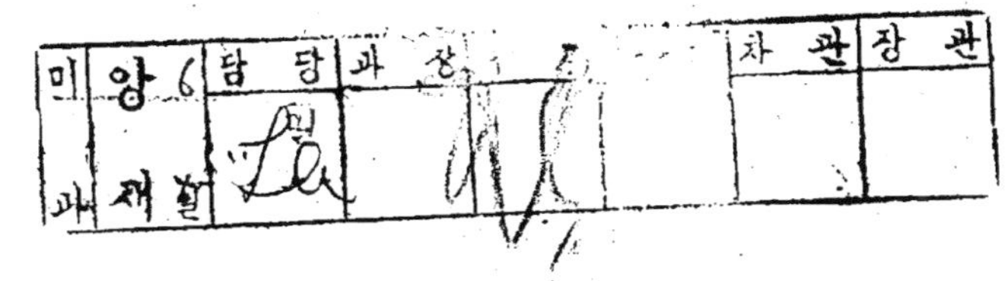

The Government of the Republic of Korea wishes to present to the Government of the United States for its consideration the Korean position regarding the Government's proposal to reopen the negotiations for the Status of Forces Agreement in order to revise some of the provisions of the major Articles dealing with Criminal Jurisdiction, Claims, and Labor. ~~upon which the negotiators of both countries have agreed through formal in informal meetings.~~

It may seem rather unusual to ~~bring up the problem~~ propose the reopening of negotiations ~~for~~ of an agrement, the text of which has been agreed upon through pains-taking negotiations. ~~and which has been ready for mere formalities to be effected into force.~~ However, there are a number of inevitable reasons and political considerations which have thus compelled the Government of the Republic of Korea to arrive at this conclusion. ~~and to take rather unusual steps in the orthodox doctrines of normal diplomatic relations.~~

Recently, the Korean Government has received a series of reports from the Korean Ambassador in Washington D.C., on initial responses of ~~those highly placed~~ officials of the U.S. State Department to the Korean proposal and, accordingly, fully understands that the U.S. Government has certain difficulties in accomodating the Korean proposal both in its intragovernmental and in Congressional relations. However, it could be said that the difficulties confronting the Korean Government would be even greater than those the U.S. Government faces.

Originally, the Government's plan was to conclude and sign the Status of Forces Agreement some time in last year, together with the Korea-Japan Treaty, both of which have been the two highly controversial issues. Nevertheless, partly because of very stiff defiance and persistent criticism of the opposition parties and of some aspect of the people ~~at the time of, and during the rest of the year ensuing from,~~ ratification of the Korea-Japan Treaty, and partly because of the heavy pressures from the leading members of the Government's own Democratic Republican Party, the Government has been unable to sign the agreement ~~as agreed upon~~.

Furthermore, during the period ~~stretching~~ from September of last year to March of this year, the Government of the Republic of Korea, after receiving the requests from the United States and the Republic of Vietnam, had to undergo once again another trying ordeals and had, notwithstanding considerable criticism from the opposition and from ~~the~~ people, deployed ~~two army divisions and one marine brigade~~ to the Republic of Vietnam, thus gladly responding to the calls from friendly nations in the time of emergencies.

In the meantime, as you are well aware, the Government, with a view to concluding the Status of Forces agreement based on the agreed texts, has had several opportunities to brief the contents of the agreement for, and has exchanged views with, leading members of the Korean Bar Associations, and eminent figures in academic and press circles, and, through them, has sounded out initial reactions thereon. It is needless to say that an important objective of the Government was to ~~create a favorable atmosphere for the occasions of conclusion and ratification of the prospective agreement~~. However, contrary to such expectations of the Government, the initial reactions and ensuing public opinions thereupon have been generally of negative nature. In particular, the response of the opposition parties have been far more serious than the Government has expected. Especially, severe criticism have been levelled at certain provisions of the major Articles dealing with Criminal Jurisdiction, Claims and Labor, which have been

0124

key issues for the past negotiations.

In additfon, it has been well known and oft-repeated facts that the initial goal of the Korean negotiators has been to attain the same objectives envisaged in the SOFA agreements with NATO countries and Japan. Nevertheless, the contents of agreement, upon which both negotiators of the Republic of Korean and the United States have agreed through numbers of formal and informal negotiations, are far below the standards of those agreements with other countries. In fact, the Korean Government has in the past stressed on numerous occasions to the visiting high officials of the State Department that the SOFA between Korea and the United States should exceed or at least, be equal to those agreements being negotiated between the United States and other Asian countries. Nevertheless, the Criminal Jurisdiction Article revised by the United States and the Philippines has indicated ~~has unfortunately proved~~ that the Government of the United States is reluctant to meet special emphasis of the Government and earnest desire of the people of the Republic of Korea. Thus, it is regretful to point out that the people and the Government of the Republic of Korea are, in fact, at a loss to understand the underlying reasons why Korea should be differentiated from the Philippines in SOFA negotiations.

On the other hands, the Korean Government, ~~taking into consideration foreseeable difficulties it would undoubtedly face in the~~ forthcoming Presidential and Congressional ~~elections which will held in the~~ early part ~~of the next year, may be able to delay~~ will be compelled to put off temporarily the conclusion of the agreement which neither the people nor the Government are satisfied with. However, the past experiences in Korea, not to mention those in other countries, teach us that to delaying the pending issues is not the rational approach to solving the points at issue, ~~but only to temporarily laying aside the sensitive and to some extent,~~ explosive issues, ~~which would in the coming elections~~ but only afford ample opportunities for the Opposition parties and the critics to make the most of the

0125

Furthermore

pending issues. Whereas, if the Government would sign the agreement as agreed upon, opposition parties would yet reap good harvests by blaming the Government forits failure to conclude an agreement based upon the principle of equality of sovereignty.

Accordingly, the Government believes that the contents of the agreement, rather, the principles upon which both sides have agreed nearly one year ago, would hardly be acceptable to the people and the National Assembly. Also, it should not be overlooked that the Government would certainly face a great deal of difficulties, which would place the Government in a very difficult position; and no one can rule out the possibility that the National Assembly may disapprove the agreement depending upon the political climate that may develop at the time of the Assembly's deliberation.

The Korean Government, therefore, emphasizes once again that, on this occasion the Government of the United States would sincerely give its special considerations to the Korean proposal to reopen the negotiations, and accept, will before the next year's election, the newly proposed revisions, thereby help strengthening the considerably weakened position of the Government in the forthcoming Presidential and Congressional elections, and thus further contributing towards the promotion of traditionally friendly relations existing between the Republic of Korea and the United States.

June 7, 1966.

Seoul.

0126

The Government of the Republic of Korea wishes to present to the Government of the United States for its consideration the Korean position regarding the Government's proposal to reopen the negotiations for the Status of Forces Agreement in order to revise some of the provisions of the major Articles dealing with Criminal Jurisdiction, Claims, and Labor.

It ~~may seem~~ rather unusual to propose the reopening of negotiations for an agreement, the text of which has ~~in the past~~ been agreed upon through pains-taking negotiations. However, there are numbers of ~~inevitable~~ reasons and political considerations which have thus ~~compelled~~ the Government of the Republic of Korea to ~~arrive at this conclusion.~~

Recently, the Korean Government has received a series of reports from the ~~Korean~~ Ambassador in Washington D.C., on initial responses of officials of the U.S. State Department to the Korean proposal and, accordingly, fully understands that the U.S. Government has certain difficulties in accomodating the Korean proposal both in its intra-governmental and in Congressional relations. However, it ~~could be said~~ that the difficulties confronting the Korean Government would be even greater than those the U.S. Government faces.

Originally, the Government's plan was to conclude ~~and sign~~ the Status of Forces Agreement some time in last year together with the Korea-Japan Treaty, both of which had been ~~the two~~ highly controversial issues. ~~Nevertheless,~~ ~~partly because of very stiff defiance and persistent criticisms from the opposition parties and some aspect of the~~

0127

people in the cause of the ratification of the Korea-Japan Treaty, and partly because of the strong objections from the leading members of the Government's own Democratic Republican Party to the signing of SOFA as agreed upon, the Government was unable to sign the two agreement at the same time.

Furthermore, during the period from September of last year to March of this year, the Government of the Republic of Korea, after receiving the requests from the United States and the Republic of Vietnam, had to undergo once again another trying ordeals and had, notwithstanding considerable criticism from the opposition and from some of the people, deployed its combat troops to the Republic of Vietnam, thus gladly responding to the calls from friendly nations in the time of emergencies.

In the meantime, As you are well aware, The Government, with a view to concluding the Status of Forces agreement based on the agreed texts, has had several opportunities to brief the contents of the agreement for, and has exchanged views with, leading members of the Korean Bar Association, and eminent figures in academic and press circles, and, through them, has sounded out initial reactions thereto. It is needless to say that an important objective of the Government has been to sign an agreement which would not become the subject of criticisms from the opposition parts and some segment of the public. However, contrary to such expectations of the Government, the initial reactions and ensuing public opinions thereupon have been generally of negative nature. In particular, the response

0128

of the opposition parties have been for more serious than the Government has expected. Especially, severe criticisms have been levelled at certain provisions of the major Articles dealing with Criminal Jurisdiction, Claims and Labor, which have been key issues for the past negotiations.

In addition, it has been well known and oft-repeated facts that the initial goal of the Korean negotiators has been to attain the same objectives envisaged in the SOFA agreements with NATO countries and Japan. Nevertheless, the contents of the agreement, upon which both negotiators of the Republic of Korean and the United States have agreed through numbers of formal and informal negotiations, are far below the standards of those agreements which the United States concluded with other countries. In fact, the Korean Government has in the past stressed on numerous occasions to the visiting high officials of the State Department that the SOFA between Korea and the United States should, in the light of specially close relations existing between the two countries, exceed or at least, be equal to those agreements being negotiated between the United States and other Asian countries. Nevertheless, the Criminal Jurisdiction Article revised last year by the United States and the Philippines indicated that the Government of the United States is reluctant to meet special emphasis of the Government and earnest desire of the people of the Republic of Korea. Thus, it is regretful to point out that the people and the Government of the Republic of Korea are, in fact, at a loss to understand the underlying reasons why Korea should be differentiated, in particular, from the Philippines, in SOFA negotiations.

0129

X. Further, in view of the fact that the ROK deployed its combat troops to the R.V.N. in order to share the common objective of the free countries notwithstanding considerable criticism from the opposition party, the ROK is unable to explain to the people that the R.O.K. came to an agreement with the United States on [illegible] terms, than other Asian countries. discriminatory basis.

0130

On the other hands, the Korean Government, will be compelled to put off temporarily the conclusion of the agreement with which neither the people nor the Government are satisfied. However, the past experiences in Korea, not to mention those in other countries, teach us that to delay the pending issues is not the rational approach to solving the points at issue, but would only afford ample opportunities for the opposition parties and the critics to make the most of the pending issues. Furthermore, if the Government would sign the agreement as agreed upon, opposition parties would yet reap good harvests by blaming the Government for its failure to conclude an agreement based upon the principle of equality of sovereignty.

Accordingly, the Government believes not only that the contents of the agreement, rather, the principles upon which both sides have agreed nearly one year ago, would hardly be acceptable to the people and the National Assembly, but also that the Government would certainly face a great deal of difficulties, should the Government try to sign the agreement as agreed upon. Besides, no one can, under the present circumstances, rule out the possibility that the National Assembly may disapprove the agreement depending upon the political climate that may develop at the time of the Assembly's deliberation. Naturally, such consequencies would be neither for the interests of the United States, nor for the interests of the Republic of Korea.

The Korean Government, therefore, emphasizes once again that the Governments of the United States would sincerely give its special considerations to the Korean proposal to reopen the negotiations, and accept the newly proposed revisions.

0131

due to the considerable objections from the Government's own Democratic Republican Party to the signing of SOFA as agreed upon, the Government was unable to sign the two agreement at the same time.

The Government, with a view to concluding the Status of Forces agreement based on the agreed texts, has had several opportunities to brief the contents of the agreement for, and has exchanged views with, leading members of the Korean Bar Association, and eminent figures in academic and press circles, and, through them, has sounded out initial reactions thereto. However, the Government realized that the initial reactions and ensuing public opinions thereupon have been generally of negative nature, and particularly, severe criticisms have been levelled at certain provisions of the major Articles dealing with Criminal Jurisdiction, Claims and Labor, which have been key issues for the past negotiations. Much criticisms are that the contents of the agreement are inferior to those of the agreements which the United States concluded with other countries, notably with Japan. In fact, the Korean Government has in the past stressed on numerous occasions to the visiting high officials of the State Department that the SOFA between Korean and the United States should, in the light of specially close relations existing between the two countries, at least be equal to those agreements. Nevertheless, the agreement between the United States and the Philippines, for example, indicated that the revised Criminal Jurisdiction Article thereof is much more favorable to the Philippines than the corresponding Article in the agreed text between Korea and the United States is to the Republic of Korea. Therefore, the people and the Government of the

0132

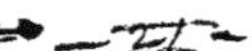

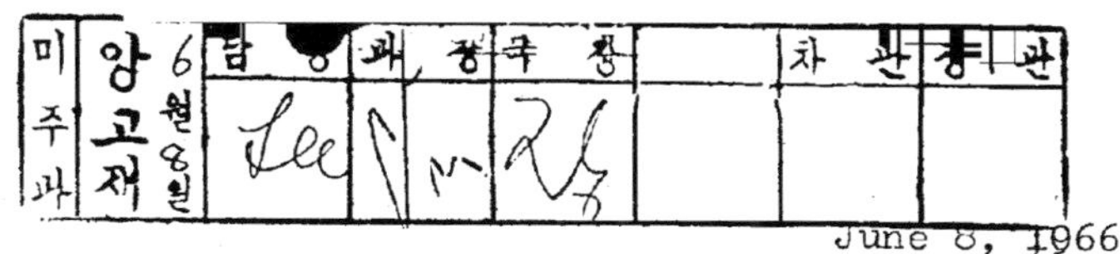

June 8, 1966

The Government of the Republic of Korea wishes to present to the Government of the United States for its consideration the Korean position regarding ~~the Government~~'s negotiation for ~~proposal to reopen~~ the negotiations for the Status of Forces Agreement in respect to ~~in order to revise some of~~ the provisions of the major Articles dealing with Criminal Jurisdiction, Claims, and Labor.

~~It is rather unusual and unprecedented, in certain respect, for the Government to propose the reopening of negotiations for an agreement, the text of which~~ Although the agreement has been informally agreed upon through ~~pains taking~~ working level negotiations, ~~However~~, there are numbers of compelling reasons and political considerations which have ~~been~~ led the Government of the Republic of Korea to propose ~~to continue~~ ~~reopening of~~ continuing the negotiations.

Recently, the Korean Government has received a series of reports from the Ambassador in Washington D.C., on initial responses of officials of the U.S. State Department to the Korean proposal and, accordingly, fully understands that the U.S. Government has certain difficulties in accomodating the Korean proposal both in its intra-governmental and in Congressional relations. However, it is to be noted that the difficulties confronting the Korean Government would be even greater than those the U.S. Government faces.

Originally, the Government's plan was to conclude negotiations for the Status of Forces Agreement some time in last year and submit to the National Assembly for its ratification, together with the Korea-Japan Treaty, both of which had been highly controversial issues. However,

0133

due to the ~~considerable objections from the~~ Government's own Democratic Republican ~~Party to~~ the signing of SOFA as agreed upon, the Government was unable to sign the two agreement at the same time.

The Government, with a view to concluding the Status of Forces agreement based on the agreed texts, has had several opportunities to brief the contents of the agreement for, and has exchanged views with, leading members of the Korean Bar Association, and eminent figures in academic and press circles, and, through them, has sounded out initial reactions thereto. However, the Government realized that the initial reactions and ensuing public opinions thereupon have been generally of negative nature, and particularly, severe criticisms have been levelled at certain provisions of the major Articles dealing with Criminal Jurisdiction, Claims and Labor, which have been key issues for the past negotiations. Much criticisms are that the contents of the agreement are inferior to those of the agreements which the United States concluded with other countries, notably with Japan.

In fact, the Korean Government has in the past stressed on numerous occasions to the visiting high officials of the State Department that the SOFA between Korean and the United States should, in the light of specially close relations existing between the two countries, at least be equal to those agreements. Nevertheless, the agreement between the United States and the Philippines, for example, indicated that the revised Criminal Jurisdiction Article thereof is much more favorable to the Philippines than the corresponding Article in the agreed text between

0134

77

Korea and the United States is to the Republic of Korea. Therefore, the people and the Government of the Republic of Korea are, in fact, at a loss to see the underlying reasons why Korea should be differentiated from other SOFA in the light of the fact that the Korean people highly value self-respect and equality of sovereignty.

Furthermore, in view of the fact that the Government of the Republic of Korea deployed its combat troops to the Republic of Vietnam in order to share the common objectives of the two countries notwithstanding considerable opposition ~~criticisms from the opposition parties,~~ the Government of the Republic of Korea is unable to explain to the people that the Government come to an agreement with the United States on a discriminatory basis. Therefore, it is the position of the Korean Government that ~~with the~~ the text ~~agreed~~ contents of the agreement, as negotiated, be in treatment of the world, the people and government of the R.O.K., the Government will be compelled to put off the conclusion of the agreement. ~~which neither the people nor the Government is satisfied.~~

Therefore, the Government of the Republic of Korea sincerely hopes that the Government of the United States would give its favorable consideration to the position of the Government of the Republic of Korea, and accept the proposal to continue ~~reopen~~ the negotiations along with the new~~ly~~ proposed ~~revisions~~.

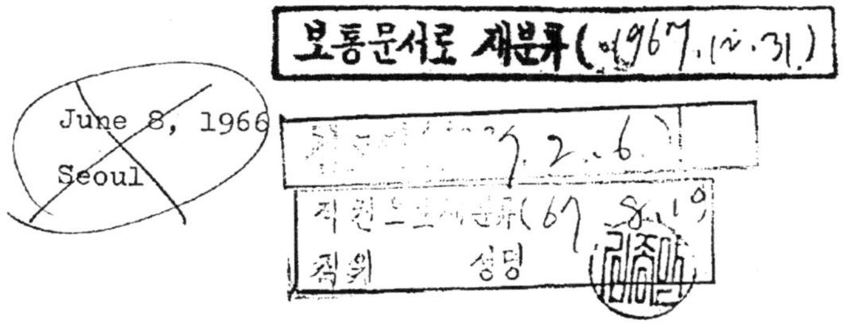

June 8, 1966
Seoul

0135

72

대한민국외무부

발신전보

번 호: WPH-0623
일 시: 091620

종 별

수신인 주비대사

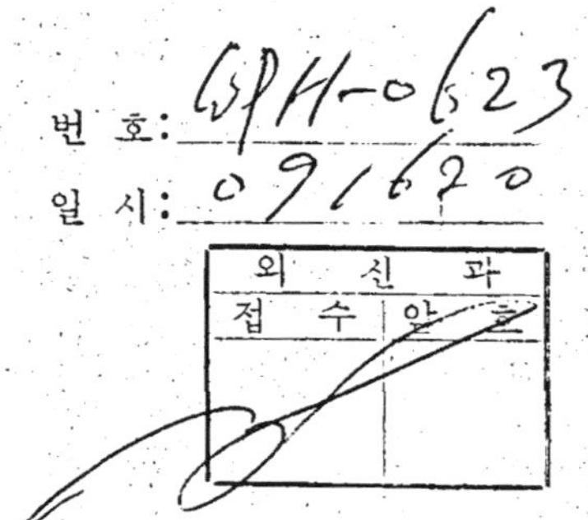

1. 미.비 기지협정(SOFA) 제13조 Criminal Jurisdiction Article 에 관한 Agreed Official Minutes 중 Paragraph 4 의 규정에 의하면, 비국은 비국이 재판권을 행사하는 것이 특히 중요하다고 결정하는 경우를 제외하고 기타 사건에 대한 제1차 재판권을 미군당국에 포기하게되어 있음.

2. 비국 관계당국과 공식 또는 비공식으로 접촉하여 비국이 재판하는 것이 특히 중요하다고 결정하여 미군당국에 재판권을 포기하지 않게 되어 있는 범죄의 종류에 관하여 미.비 양국간에 어떤 비밀 양해사항이 있는지 유무와 있다면 그 내용을 조사 지급보고 바람. (외구미)

장 관

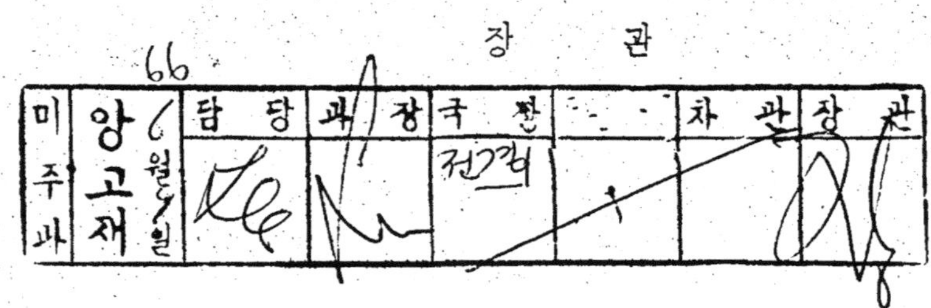

미주과	앙고재 6월 일	담 당	과 장	국 장		차 관	장 관

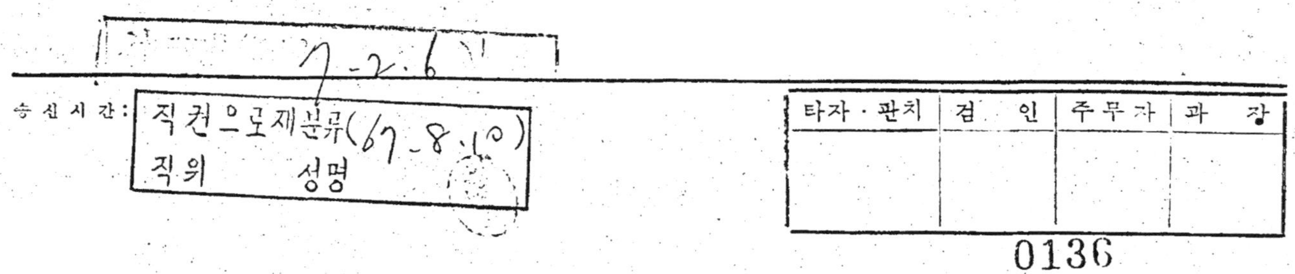

송신시간: 직권으로재분류(67.8.10) 직위 성명

타자 · 판치	검 인	주무자	과 장

0136

관리번호 1961

발신전보

대한민국외무부

지급

종 별

번 호: WUS-0646

일 시: 091805

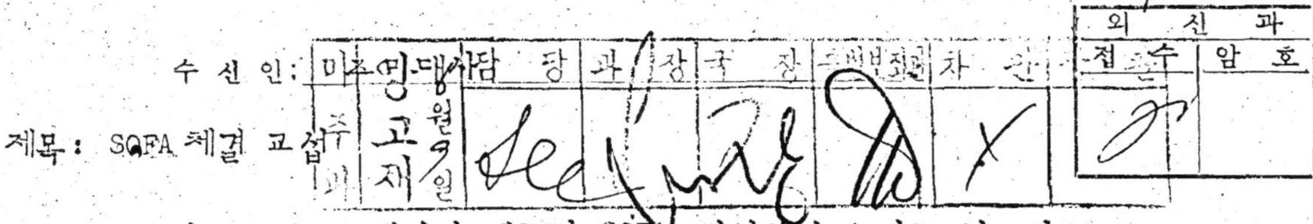

수 신 인: 주미대사

제목: SOFA 체결 교섭

담 당	과 장	국 장	차 관	외신과 접수	암 호

1. 정부는 6.7. 개최된 제81차 SOFA 회의에서 우리측 최종안을 미측에 수교하였는바, 그중 형사재판 관할권, 군계약자, 노무조달에 관하여 미측안에 대한 다음과 같은 중요 수정안을 제안하였음.

2. 귀관은 즉시 미국무성 당국과 접촉하여 우리측 수정안을 수락하여 줄것을 촉구하고 특히 정부가 국내 사정을 고려하여 한.일 회담의 타결과 동시에 SOFA 도 일괄 타결 조인코저 추진하고 있음을 강조하고 금주말 또는 늦어도 내주초 까지는 현지 대사관에 훈령 하도록 교섭하시고 그 결과를 지급 회전 바람.

가. 형사 재판 관할권

(1) Waiver of Primary Jurisdiction

미측의 포기 조항을 수락하고 실지 운영상의 오해나 분쟁을 해소하기 위하여 다음과 같은 규정을 포기조항 제4항 다에 합의 의사록으로 추가 할것을 제안하였음.:

"In case where the Government of the Republic of Korea, in resoliving disagreement in accordance with the fore-going provisions, determines that it is imperative that jurisdiction be exercised by the authorities

송신시간:

통제관		자체 통제		기안처	
결 재					

타자·판치	검 인	주무자	과 장

필 요 ☐ 보안불필요 ☐

0137

66-5-2

0138

대한민국외무부

발신전보

종 별

번 호;

일 시;

외 신 과	
접 수	암 호

수 신 인;

of the Republic of Korea, the recall of waiver shall be final and conclusive."

(2) 계엄령과 형사 재판 관할권 조항의 효력

미국은 "In the event that martial law is declared by the Republic of Korea, the provisions of this Article shall be immediately suspended in the part of the Republic of Korea under martial law, and the military authorities of the United States shall have the right to exercise exclusive jurisdiction over members of the United States armed forces or civilian component, and their dependents, in such part until martial law is ended. 를 주장하고 있으나 우리측은 다음과 같은 이유로 미측 주장을 철회 할것을 주장하였음.

(ㄱ) 우리측은 제1차 관할권의 포기는 물론, 전속적 관할권 까지도 미군당국이 포기를 요청하면 호의적 고려를 할것을 수락하였으며,

(ㄴ) 또한 "미군인, 군속, 가족은한국의 군법회의에 회부되지

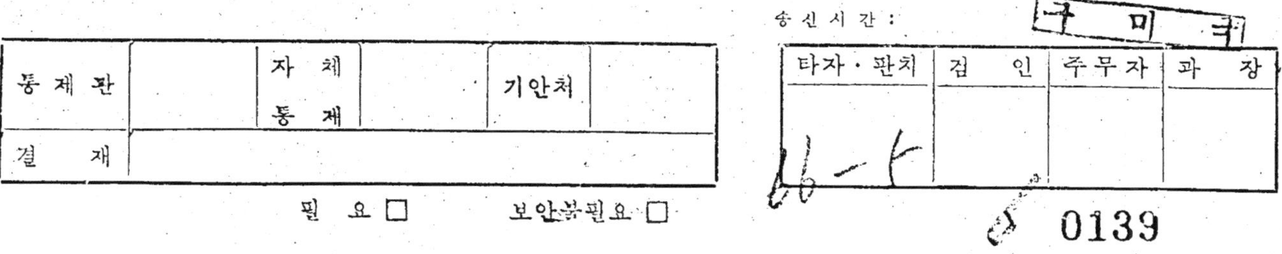

송신시간:

구미과

통 제 관		자 체 통 제		기안처	
결 재					

타자·판치	검 인	주무자	과 장
66-6			

필 요 ☐ 보안불필요 ☐

0139

0140

대 한 민 국 외 무 부

발신전보

종 별

번 호:

일 시:

외 신 과	
접 수	암 호

수 신 인:

- 3 -

아니한다" 는 미측제안을 수락하였음으로 개업명에 관한 미측 제안은 불필요한 것임.

(3) 공무의 정의, Definition of Official Duty

미측은 공무의 정의를 Understanding 으로 회의록에 기록할 것을 요구하고 있으나 우리측은 동 규정은 협정의 실지 운영상의 중요한 지침임으로 이를 Agreed Minute 로 협정문에 명백히 규정할 필요가 있음을 강조하였음.

(4) 기타 병의 복역 중인자의 신병인도, 정부대표의 참석권, 미군 시설내의 경찰권, 공무 집행 증명서 발행권자등 몇가지 문제에 관한 수정안도 동시에 제시하였는바, 이는 실지 운영상 상호 만족할 만한 결과를 얻기 위한 합리적인 것임.

나. Invited Contractors 및 그들의 가족에 대한 형사재판 관할권 조항의 적용

(1) 미측은 "The persons referred to in para. 1 shall be subject to those provisions of Article and the Agreed Minute thereto which pertain to members of the civilian

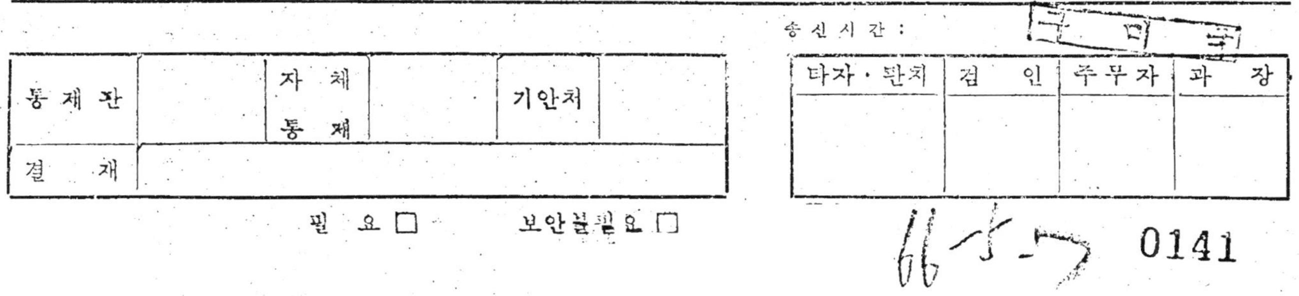

송신시간:

통 재 관		자 체 통 제		기안처	
결 재					

타자 · 판치	검 인	주무자	과 장

필 요 □ 보안불필요 □

66-5-7 0141

66-5-2

외문 708-5

0142

대한민국외무부

발신전보

번 호:
일 시:

외 신 과	
접 수	암 호

종 별

수 신 인:

- 4 -

component, and to dependents." 를 주장하고 있으나 우리측은 군계약자들이 미군관계 계약을 수행하는 일반 민간인이며 따라서 미국정부의 고용인으로 미군에 근무하는 미군속과는 구별하여야 하며, 또한미군당국이 적절히 처벌할수 있는 법이 없고, 다른 SOFA 에 선례를 볼수 없음을 지적하여 한국당국이 재판권을 행사 하여야 한다고 주장하였음.

다. 노무조항

(1) 미측은 고용 조건에 있어 한국법령을 준수치 못할 경우 가능한 한 사전에 합동위원회에 보고하여 심의한다는데 대하여 우리측은 가능한 한 사전에 Mutual agreement 를 위하여 합동위원회에 회부되어야 한다고 제의 하였음.

(2) 미측은 노동조합이 미국의 이익에 배반되는 경우에는 노동조합을 결성하지 못한다는 제안에 대하여 우리측은 노동조합은 그 목적이 미국과 한국의 " common interests " 에 상반되지 않는한

0143

송신시간:

통 재 관		자 체 통 제		기안처	
결 재					

타자·판치	검 인	주무자	과 장

필 요 ☐ 보안불필요 ☐

66-5-2

0144

발신전보

대한민국외무부

번 호;
일 시;

종 별

외 신 과	
접 수	암 호

수 신 인;

- 5 -

승인되어야 한다고 우리측 수정안을 제안하였음.

마. 협정 발효 조항

(1) 미측은 협정의 비준과 협정 발효에 필요한 입법 및 예산조치를 취하고 4개월후에 협정이 발효한다고 제의하였으나, 우리측은 협정의 비준과 발효에 필요한 조치는 별개 문제이며 이는 다른 SOFA 에도 없으므로 다만 비준 30일 이후에 발효하고 입법 및 예산조치는 별도로 규정 할것을 제안하였음.

(외구미)

장 관

송신시간 :

통 제 관		자 체 통 재		기안처	
결 재					

타자 · 판치	검 인	주무자	과 장

필 요 ☐ 보안불필요 ☐

0145

66-5-2 (6)

0146

발신전보

대한민국외무부

번 호: WGE-0632
일 시: 121250

종 별

외 신 과	
접 수	암 호

수 신 인: 주 독 대 사

SOFA 체결 교섭에 참고코저 하오니 다음 사항을 지급 조사 보고하시기 바람.

1. 4.22 일자 WGE-0456 호 제 1 항에서 지시한바와 같이 독일이 1959 년도에 서독보충협정을 체결할 당시의 독일정부의 입장 또는 국내 사정.(외무성관계관, 대학교수, 또는 언론인과의 접촉과 그 당시의 국회의 증언록, 신문등을 조사하면 알 수 있을 것이며 가능하면 국회증언록 사본, 또는 신문 크립핑등 자료를 입수 송부바람.)

2. 독일국에 주둔하고 있는 미군인, 군속, 및 그들의 가족의 대체적인 숫자. 끝.(외구미)

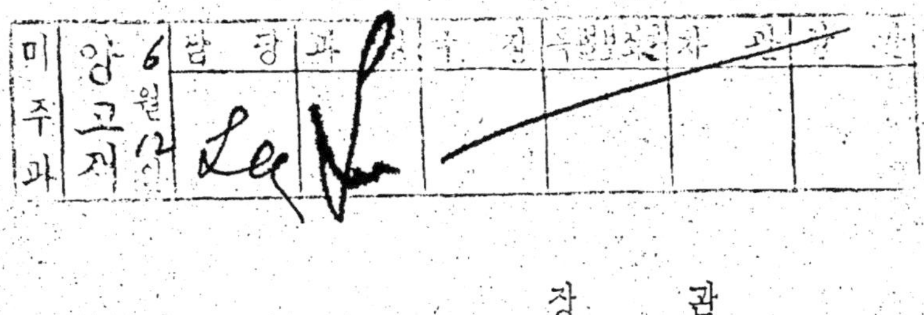

장 관

송신시간:

통 제 관		자 체 통 제		기안처	
결 재					

타자·판치	검 인	주무자	과 장

필 요 ☐ 보안불필요 ☐

0147

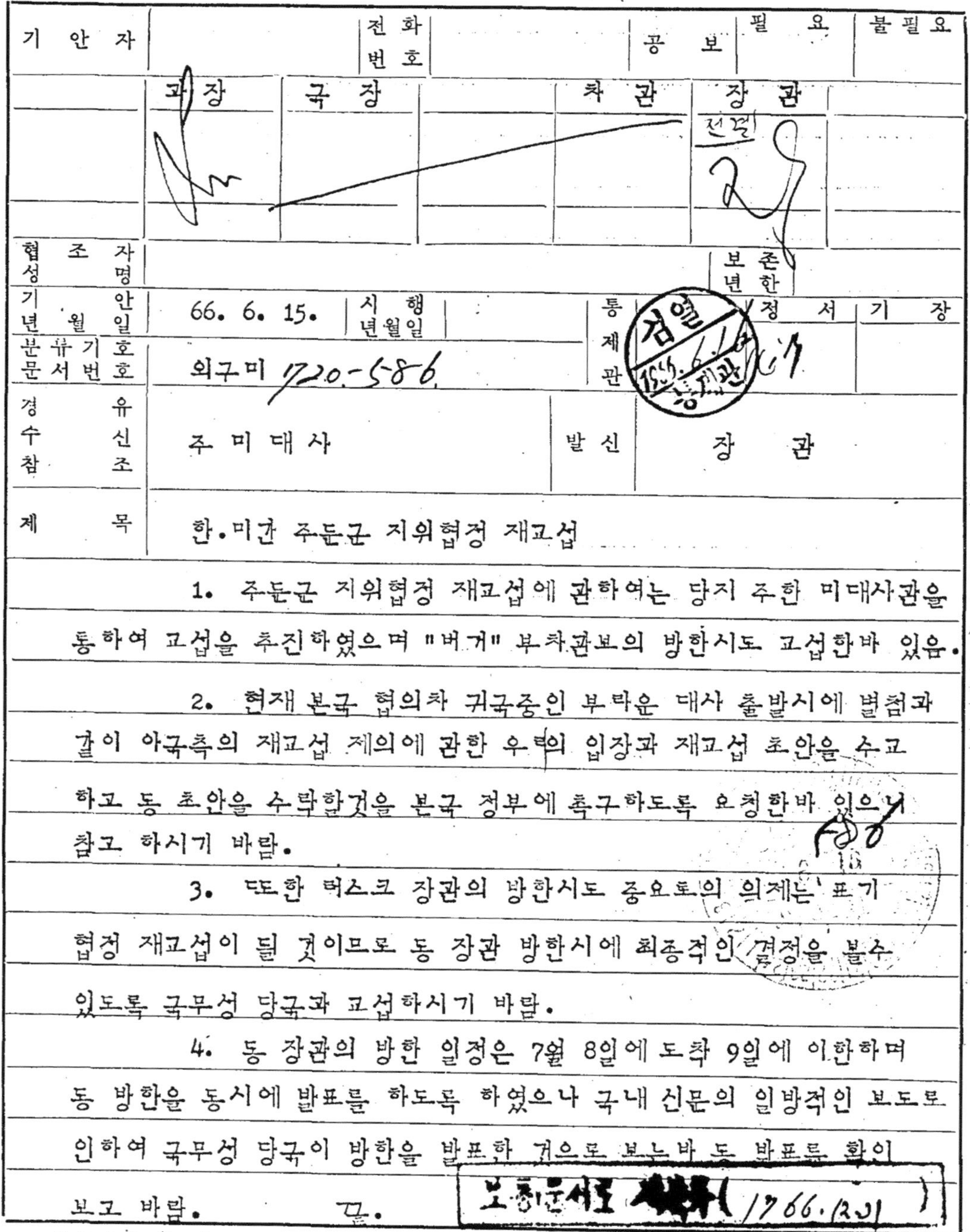

기 안 지

기 안 자		전화번호		공 보	필 요	불필요
	과 장	국 장		차 관	장 관	
					전결	
협조자 성명					보존 년한	
기안 년월일	66. 6. 15.	시행 년월일		통제관	정 서	기 장
분류기호 문서번호	외구미 720-586			검열 1966.6.1 통제관		
경유 수신 참조	주 미 대 사		발신	장 관		
제 목	한.미간 주둔군 지위협정 재교섭					

1. 주둔군 지위협정 재교섭에 관하여는 당지 주한 미대사관을 통하여 교섭을 추진하였으며 "버거" 부차관보의 방한시도 교섭한바 있음.

2. 현재 본국 협의차 귀국중인 부라운 대사 출발시에 별첨과 같이 아국측의 재교섭 제의에 관한 우리의 입장과 재교섭 초안을 수교하고 동 초안을 수락할것을 본국 정부에 촉구하도록 요청한바 있으니 참고 하시기 바람.

3. 또한 러스크 장관의 방한시도 중요토의 의제는 표기 협정 재교섭이 될 것이므로 동 장관 방한시에 최종적인 결정을 볼수 있도록 국무성 당국과 교섭하시기 바람.

4. 동 장관의 방한 일정은 7월 8일에 도착 9일에 이한하며 동 방한을 동시에 발표를 하도록 하였으나 국내 신문의 일방적인 보도로 인하여 국무성 당국이 방한을 발표한 것으로 보는바 동 발표를 확인 보고 바람. 끝.

보통문서로 재분류(1966.12.31)

공통서식 1—2 (갑)

(16절지)

별첨 1. 재교섭제의
2. 재교섭초안

0148

외 무 부

외구미 1966. 6. 16.

수 신 : 주 미 대 사

제 목 : 한.미간 주둔군 지위협정 재교섭

1. 주둔군 지위협정 재교섭에 관하여는 당지 주한 미대사관을 통하여 교섭을 추진하였으며 "버거" 부차관보의 방한시도 교섭한바 있음.

2. 현재 본국 협의차 귀국중인 부라운 대사 출발시에 별첨과 같이 아국측의 재교섭 제의에 관한 우리의 입장과 재교섭 초안을 수교하고 동 초안을 수락할 것을 본국 정부에 촉구하도록 요청한바 있으니 참고 하시기 바람.

3. 또한 러스크 장관의 방한시도 중요 토의 의제는 표기 협정 재교섭이 될 것이므로 동 장관 방한시에 최종적인 결정을 볼수 있도록 국무성 당국과 교섭 하시기 바람.

4. 동 장관의 방한 일정은 7월 8일에 도착 9일에 이한하며 동 방한은 동시에 발표를 하도록 하였으나 국내 신문의

0149

일방적인 보도로 인하여 국무성 당국이 방안을 발표한 것으로 보는바 동 발표를 확인 보고 바람.

유첨 : 1. 재교섭 제의
2. 재교섭 초안. 끝.

외무부장관 이 동 원

0150

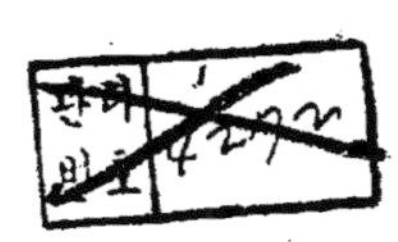

June 8, 1966

The Government of the Republic of Korea wishes to present to the Government of the United States for its consideration the Korean position regarding the negotiations for the Status of Forces Agreement in respect to the provisions of the major Articles dealing with Criminal Jurisdiction, Claims, and Labor.

7

Although the draft agreement has been informally agreed upon through working level negotiations, there are numbers of compelling reasons and political considerations which have led the Government of the Republic of Korea to propose the continued negotiations.

Recently, the Korean Government has received a series of reports from the Ambassador in Washington D.C., on initial responses of officials of the U.S. State Department to the Korean proposal and, accordingly, fully understands that the U.S. Government has certain difficulties in accomodating the Korean proposal both in its intra-governmental and in Congressional relations. However, it is to be noted that the difficulties confronting the Korean Government would be even greater than those the U.S. Government may face.

The Government, with a view to concluding the Status of Forces agreement based on the texts agreed on informally, has had several opportunities to brief the contents of the agreement for, and has exchanged views with, leading members of the Korean Bar Association, and eminent figures in academic and press circles, and, through them, has sounded out initial reactions thereto. However, the Government realized that the initial reactions and ensuing public opinions thereupon have been generally of negative nature, and particularly, severe criticisms have been levelled at certain provisions of the major Articles dealing with Criminal Jurisdiction Claims and Labor which have been

0151

key issues for the past negotiations. Much criticisms are that the contents of the agreement are inferior to those of the agreements which the United States concluded with other countries, notably with Japan.

In fact, the Korean Government ~~has~~ in the past stressed on numerous occasions to the visiting high officials of the State Department that the SOFA between Korea and the United States should, in the light of specially close relations existing between the two countries, be at least ~~be~~ equal to those agreements. Nevertheless, the agreement between the United States and the Philippines, for example, indicates that the revised Criminal Jurisdiction Article thereof is much more favorable (to the Philippines) than the corresponding Article in the above-mentioned ~~agreed text~~ between Korea and the United States (is to the Republic of Korea.) Therefore, the people and the Government of the Republic of Korea are, in fact, at a loss to see the underlying reasons why Korea should be differentiated from other SOFAs in the light of the fact that the Korean people highly value self-respect and equality of soveriegnty.

Furthermore, particularly when ~~in view of the fact that~~ the Government of the Republic of Korea has ~~deployed~~ its combat troops deployed in ~~to~~ the Republic of Vietnam in order to share the common objectives of the two countries notwithstanding considerable opposition, the Government of the Republic of Korea is unable to explain to the people that the Government come to an agreement with the United States on a discriminatory basis. Therefore, ~~it is the position of the Korean Government that if the text~~ Unless ~~of~~ the agreement cannot be negotiated to the satisfaction of ~~both the people and the Government of the Republic of Korea,~~ the Republic of Korea, the public opinion

0152

the Government will ~~be compelled to put off the conclusion of the agreement~~ be placed in a difficult position.

Therefore, the Government of the Republic of Korea sincerely hopes that the Government of the United States would give its favourable consideration to the position of the Government of the Republic of Korea, and accept the proposal to continue the negotiations along with the ~~new~~ present proposal.

0153

ARTICLE XXII CRIMINAL JURISDICTION

Present Draft	New Draft
1. Subject to the provisions of this Article.	1. Subject to the provisions of this Article.
(a) the military authorities of the United States shall have the right to exercise within the Republic of Korea all criminal and disciplinary jurisdiction conferred on them by the law of the United States over members of the United States armed forces or civilian component, and their dependents;	(a) the military authorities of the United States shall have the right to exercise within the Republic of Korea all criminal and disciplinary jurisdiction conferred on them by the law of the United States over all persons subject to the military law of the United States; (To be consistent with the above revision, the following relevant portions in this Article and these Agreed Minutes shall also be revised: 1. Article : Paragraphs 2(a), 3(a). 2. Agreed Minutes : Re Paragraph 1(b), Re Paragraph 3(a).
None	Re Paragraph 1(a) The term "all persons subject to the military law of the United States" as referred to in this Article and in these Agreed Minutes does not apply to members of the civilian component or dependents, with respect to whom there is no effective military jurisdiction at the time this agreement enters into force. If the scope of U.S. military jurisdiction changes as a result of subsequent legislation, constitutional amendment or decision by

It is nothing

0154

appropriate authorities of the United States, the Government of the United States shall inform the Government of the Republic of Korea through diplomatic channels.

Re Paragraph 2

The Republic of Korea, recognizing the effectiveness in appropriate cases of the administrative and disciplinary sanctions which may be imposed by the United States authorities over members of the United States armed forces or |vilian component, and their dependents, will give sympathetic consideration in such cases to requests in the Joint Committee for waivers of its right to —ercise jurisdiction under paragraph 2.

Delete

Re Paragraph 3(b)

1. The Government of the Republic of Korea waives in favor of the United States the primary right granted to the authorities of the Republic of Korea under subparagraph (b) of paragraph 3 of this Article in cases of concurrent jurisdiction, in accordance with paragraphs 2,3,4,5,6, and 7 of this Minute.

Re Paragraph 3(b)

1. The authorities of the Republic of Korea, recognizing that it is the primary responsibility of the United States military authorities to maintain good order and discipline where persons subject to the military law of the United States are concerned, will, upon the request of the military authorities of the United States pursuant to paragraph 3(c), waive their primary right to exercise jurisdiction under paragraph 3(b), except where they determine that it is of particular importance that jurisdiction

0155

be exercised by the authorities of the Republic of Korea.

(In accordance with the above proposal regarding waiver formula, changes shall be made in the Paragraphs 2,3,4, 6(a), and 7 of this Minute.)

0156

ARTICLE XVII LABOR

(Underlined parts are modifications.)

Present Draft

4. (b) The Joint Committee, taking into consideration the role of the employees of the United States armed forces in the defense of the Republic of Korea and pertinent provisions of legislation of the Republic of Korea, shall determine those categories of essential employees who shall not exercise the right of further collective action in the event a labor dispute is not resolved by the foregoing procedures. In the event an agreement cannot be reached on this question in the Joint Committee, it may be made the subject of review through discussions between appropriate officials of the Government of the Republic of Korea and the diplomatic mission of the United States of America.

New Draft

4. Employees or any employee organization shall have the right of further collective action in the event a labor dispute is not resolved by the foregoing procedures except in cases where the Joint Committee determines such action seriously hampers military operations of the United States armed forces for the joint defense of the Republic of Korea. In the event an agreement cannot be reached on this question in the Joint Committee, it may be made the subject of review through discussions between appropriate officials of the Government of the Republic of Korea and the diplomatic mission of the United States of America.

AGREED MINUTES

Present Draft

4. When employers cannot conform with provisions of labor legislation of the Republic of Korea applicable under this Article on account of the military requirements of the United States armed forces, the matter shall be referred, in advance whenever possible, to the Joint

New Draft

4. When employers cannot conform with provisions of labor legislation of the Republic of Korea applicable under this Article on account of the military requirements of the United States armed forces, the matter shall be referred, in advance, to the Joint Committee for

0157

Committee for consideration and appropriate action. In the event mutual agreement cannot be reached in the Joint Committee regarding appropriate action, the issue may be made the subject of review through discussions between appropriate officials of the Government of the Republic of Korea and the diplomatic mission of the United States of America.

mutual agreement. In the event mutual agreement cannot be reached in the Joint Committee regarding appropriate action, the issue may be made the subject of review through discussions between appropriate officials of the Government of the Republic of Korea and the diplomatic mission of the United States of America.

0158

-8-

ARTICLE XXIII CLAIMS

Agreed Minutes

1. Unless otherwise provided,	1. Delete
(a) The provisions of paragraphs 5,6,7 and 8 of this Article will become effective six months from the date of entry into force of this Agreement as to claims arising from incidents in the Seoul Special City Area.	(To be consistent with the above revision, the ensuing Agreed Minutes #2 and 3 shall also be deleted.)
(b) The provisions of paragraph 5, 6, 7 and 8 will be extended, at the earliest date practicable, to other areas of the Republic of Korea and determined by the Joint Committee.	

0159

대한민국 외무부

착신암호전보

번 호: PHW-0659

일 시: 150830

종 별

수 신 인: 장 관

발 신 인: 주비대사

대: WPH -0623

1. 당지외무성 법무국장에게 문의했든바 미군당국에 재판권을 포기하지않는 요건으로서의 특히 중요한 경우라는것은 예컨데 큰 데모의 발생등으로그것이 특히 필요한때를 말하며, 범죄의 종류나 상황에관하여 문서 또는 구두상으로 합의한바없다함.

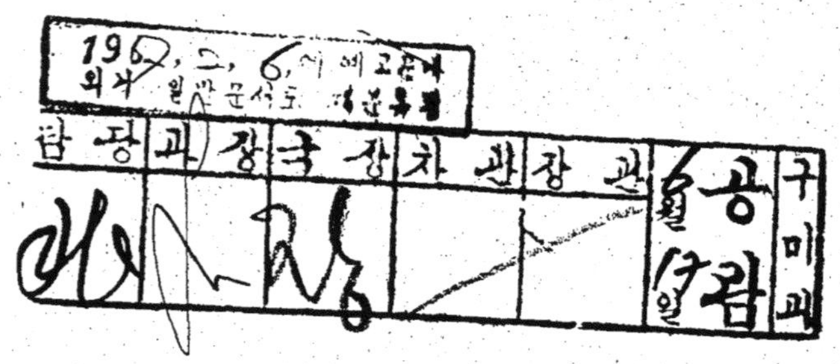

1966 JUN 15 수신시간: PM

비서		아주	√	통상		상공		청와대	
총무		구미	0	경기		농림		총리실	
의전		정문	√	정공		조달		수 산	
여권		방교		중정	√	외연		공보부	
육군		해군		공군		해병		합 참	

외 신 과

검 인 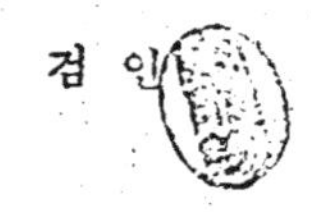

담 당	주 무 자	과 장

0160

착신전보

종 별

번 호: GEW-0647

일 시: 151500

수신인: 외무부장관 귀하

발신인: 주독대사

대호 WGE -0632

대호전문으로 지시하신 주둔군 법적지위에 관한 협정에 관하여는 이미 GEW -0503 호 GEW -0505 및 주독대 700--381 호로 보고한바 있으나 1959 년도에 보충협정을 체결하였을당시의 독일정부의 입장 또는 국내사정등에 관하여 조사한바를 아래와같이 보고함.

1. 당시 수상이던 "아데나워" 박사는 독일이 (국회 또는 언론기관) 미독행정협정 체결에 관하여 논쟁함을 꺼리고 조속 이를 체결할것에 특히 유의하였다고 하는데 그 이유로서는 이는 적은문제이기 때문에 이러한 문제를 가지고 양국간의 좋은 분위기를 어지럽게 할필요가 없다고 판단하였으며 NATO 에서의 독일의 입장을 확고히 함이 도리혀 중요한 문제라고 생각하였다는것임.

2. 따라서 본협정은 60 년 11 월 17 일 서명되고 61 년 5 월 5 일 국회의 비준동의를 얻었을때에도 단지 분과위원회에서의 약간의 질의가 있었을뿐 본회의에는 일체 이에 관한 토의가 없었다고하며 신문지상에서도 이문제를 별로 다루지않었다고 담당관은 말하였음.

3. 본문제를 분과위원회가 취급하였을때에는 대학교수 또는 언론기관등에서 증언한바 없다고하며 단지 외상의 증언과 의원의 토의내용에 관하여는 이를 발췌하여 명일 파우치편으로 송부하겠으나 본토의 내용도 형사 관할권문제에 관하여는 일체 언급이 없으며 다

비	✓	아주		통상		상공		청와대
총		구미	✓	경기		농림		총리실
의		정문	✓	국방		조달		재무부
여		방교		중정		공보관		공보부

검 인:

수신시간: JUN 16 PM 10 37

0161

지 일반적인데 끝쳤음.

4. 본문제는 그후 국회에서 개정의 필요성을 느끼고 약간의 토의가 되었는데 그 발취 문제는 역시 다음 파운치에 보고 위계이나 개정은 "66 년 7 월 1 일" 부터 가능하다고 함. (구미)

외 신 과

0162

발신전보 관리번호 1974

대한민국 외무부

번호: WUS-0682

일시: 181830

166 종별

수신인: 주미대사

연: WUS — 0646호 및 USW — 0687호

1. 정부는 조속한 시일내에 교섭을 타결하기 위하여 6.7. 일자 제 81 차 SOFA 회의 개최 후 미측과 최종적 절충을 계속하고 있음.

2. 이와 같은 절충의 결과 우리측은 대호 지시 내용 중 가. 형사재판관할권의 제 (2)항 계엄령에 관한 미측안을 수락할 것을 미측에 시사한바 있음.

3. 귀관은 미국무성관계당국과 재접촉하여 우리 정부가 미해결로 남아있던 여러 조항과 이번에 또 Martial Law 에 관한 미측 요구를 전적으로 수락한 것은 기타 문제점에 관한 우리측 제안을 미측이 수락할 것을 기대한 것임을 지적하고 남어지 문제에 관한 우리측 제안이 수락되도록 교섭하시기 바람.

4. 정부가 본 협정의 비준동의를 앞두고 국민이나 국회의 협조를 얻기 위하여서는 특히 형사재판관할권조항중 Waiver of Primary Jurisdiction 의 제 4 항 끝에 추가할 것을 제안한 Additional Sentence 및 Invited Contractors 와 그들의 가족에 대한 형사재판관할권 행사에 관한 우리측 입장이 관철되어야 함을 강조하시고 그 결과를 회보하시기 바람.

일반문서로 재분류 (1966.12.31)

장 관 (미주과)

통제관		자체 통제		기안처	
결 재					

타자·판치	검 인	주무자	과 장

필 요 ☐ 보안불필요 ☐

0163

66-

66-5-3 (1)

0164

발신전보

대 한 민 국 외 무 부

번 호: WUS-0678

일 시: 221515

종 별

수 신 인 주 미 대 사

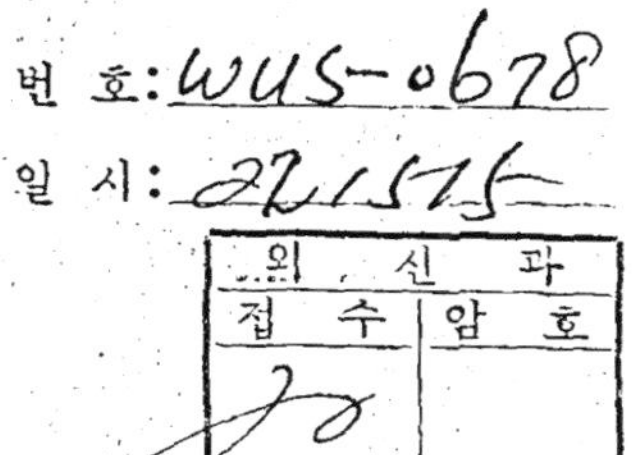

1. 연 : 1966. 6. 16. 외구미 720-586

2. 연호로 알려드린 SOFA 재교섭에 대하여 아래 사항을 보고 바람.

가. 현재 귀국중인 Brown 대사와 접촉 SOFA 재교섭에 관한 미국측 반응타진.

나. Bundy 차관보와 만나 SOFA 재교섭에 관한 그간의 미국 측의 반응 타진. (외구미)

장 관

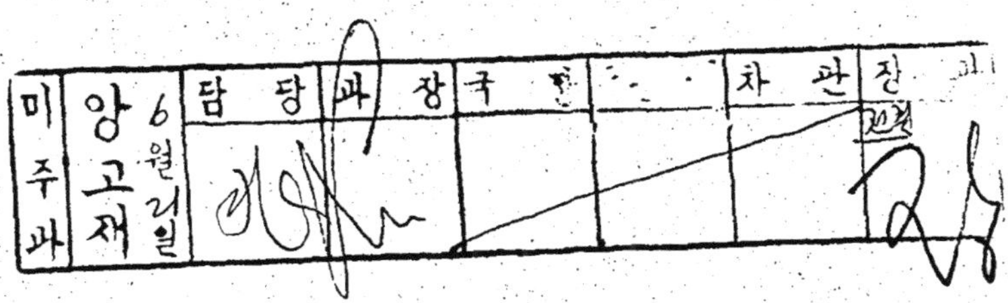

미주과	안고재	6월 21일	담당	과장	국장		차관	장관

수신시간:

타자·판치	검 인	주무자	과 장

0165

대한민국 외무부

착신암호전보

번 호: USW-06I29

일 시: 2II730

종 별

수 신 인: 장 관

발 신 인: 주미대사

대: 외구미720-586

대호공문 지시에 따라 본직은 금6월21일 하오 3시 국무성으로 극동담당차관보서리 바넷트씨(번디차관보는 부재중)를 방문하고 약30분간 요담하였는바 그요지를 아래와같이 보고함.

1. 먼저 본직은 러스크장관 방한시 군대지위협정문제를 최종적으로 해결할수 있도록 희망하고있으며 그동안 미국측에서 검토한결과에 대하여 문의하고 조속한 해결을 촉구하였던바 바넷스차관보서리는 한국측 제의를 예의검토 하였으며 그결과 러스크장관 방한시까지 이문제에대한 해결을 하기에는 시간적으로 비현실적이라고 말하였음.

2. 바넷트씨는 또한 주한미대사 부라운씨가 협의차 귀국하였을시 동대사는 미국정부의 지시를 휴대하였으며 부라운대사는 한국정부에 적절한 회답을 할수있는 입장에 있다고 부언하였음.

3. 본직은 계속 대호 공문에 지적된 제반사정 및 이유를 설명하고 미.비군대기지 협정. 일미협정에 비하여 한미군대지위협정은 많은 차별점이 있음을 지적하고 조속한재교섭을 재차강조하였던바 바넷트씨는 아국측제의를 매우 신중히검토 하였으며 이문제에 대하여 부라운씨가 장관께 회답을 전달할것이라고 말하고 이런차별점에 대한 우려를할 하등의 근거가 없는것으로 알고있으며 매우 좋은 협정이라고 생각한다고말하였음. 또한 수일내에 한국과장 후렉씨가 당관에 미국측 회답을 전달할예정이라고 부언하였음.

1966 JUN 22 AM 11 33

수신시간:

비서		아주		통상		상공		청와대
총무		구미	0	경기		농림		총리실
의전		정문		정공	√	조달		수 산
여권		방교	√	중정	√	외연		공보부
육군		해군		공군		해병		합 참

검인

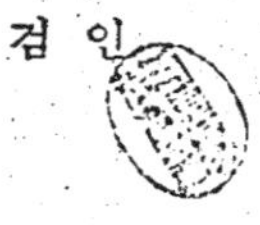

담 당	주무자	과 장

외 신 과

0166

66-5-4 (1)

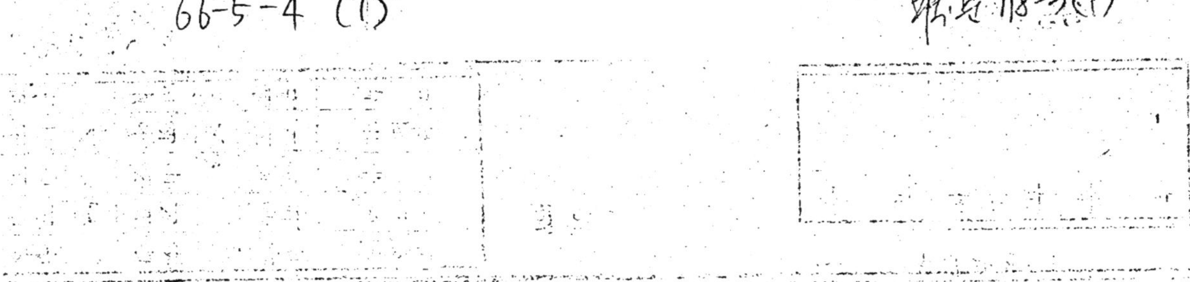

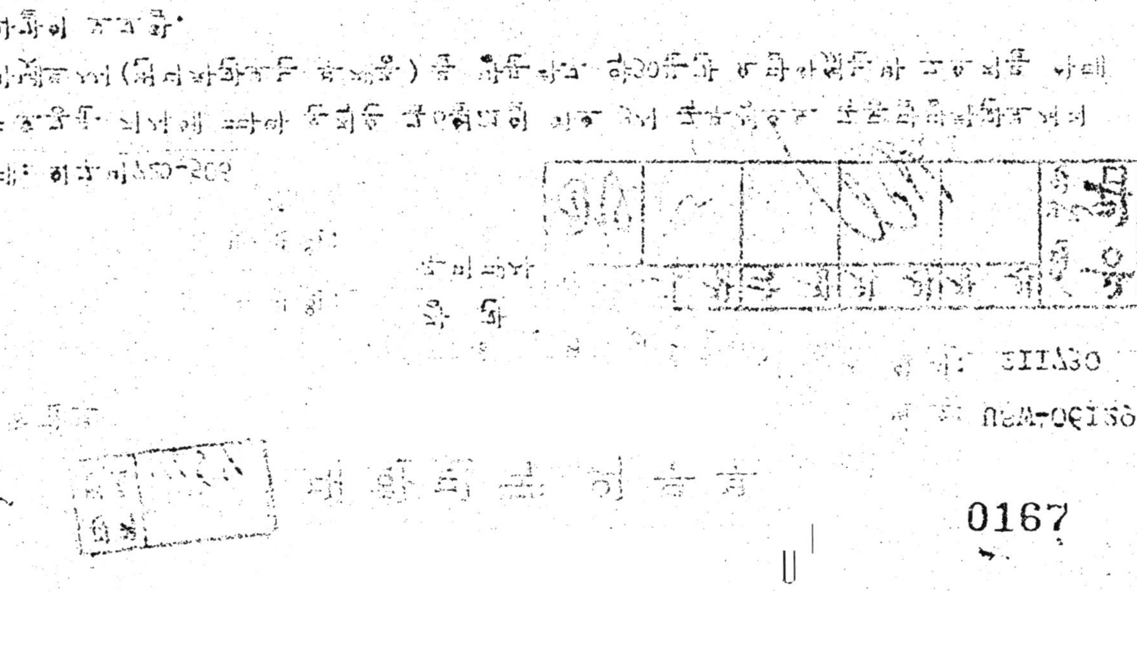

0167

지 급
URGENT

대한민국외무부

발신전보

번 호: COUS-0688

일 시: 231730

지 급
종 별

외 신 과	
접 수	암 호

수 신 인 주미대사

대외비

다음전문을 방미중인 국방장관에게 전달 바람.

1. 멕나마라 미 국방장관과 재차 면담하여 우리가 제의한 SOFA 수정안을 수락토록 교섭하시고 미국이 일본과 맺은 SOFA 와는 절대로 차별이 있어서는 안됨을 강조하시기 바람.

2. 멕 장관과의 면담이 불가능시는 국방성의 SOFA 관계 최고 책임자와 면담하시고 주미대사와 동행하시기 바람.

3. SOFA 재교섭 및 수정안에 관한 우리측 입장은 주미 대사관에 시달된바 있으니 참고 하시기 바람 (외구미)

장 관

미주과	앙고재 6월 23일	담 당	과 장	국 장		차 관	장 관

송신시간:

타자·판치	검 인	주무자	과 장

0168

WLA-0607

WHL-0607

대한민국외무부

발신전보

번 호:

일 시: 271720

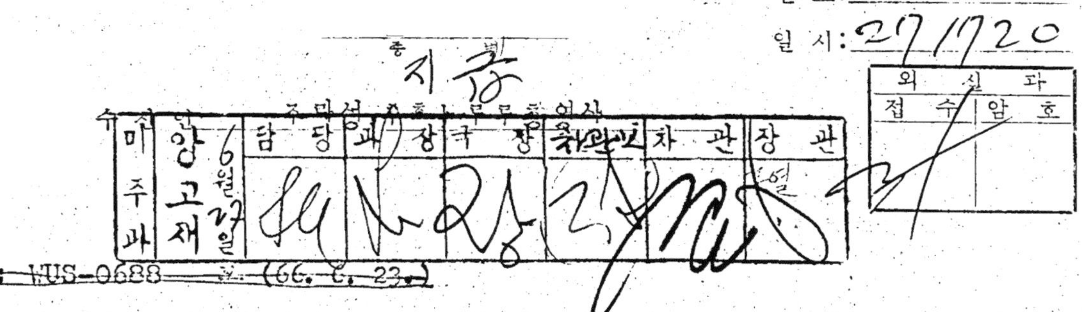

~~WUS-0688 호 (66. 6. 23.)~~

귀지를 방문예정인 김성은 국방부 장관에게 다음 내용을 전달 바람.

1. ~~오는부부~~에서 미국 태평양 지구 총사령관 Ulysses S. Sharp 제독을 방문시 WUS-0688호(66.6.23)에 언급 ~~하여~~ 대하여 동 제독에게 우리가 제의한 SOFA 수정안을 미측이 받아 수락도록 영향력을 발휘하여 줄 것을 요청 하시기 바라며, 특히 한.미간 협정이 미.일간 협정과 차이가 있어서는 아니되겠다는 우리 정부의 입장을 강조 하시기 바람.

2. 당지 미대사관측 정보에 의하면 SINCPAC 의 Sharp 제독은 SOFA 문제에 관하여 ~~미측 입장 내에서~~ 상당한 영향력이 있다함. (외구미)

장 관

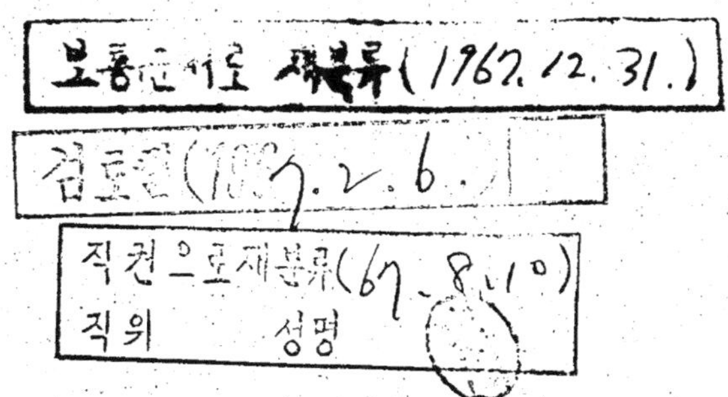

보통문서로 재분류(1967. 12. 31.)

검토필(1967. 2. 6.)

직권으로재분류(67. 8. 10)

직위 성명

(국방 장관 귀청 도착 6.27. — 출발 6.30 ...)

송신시간:

타자 · 판치	검 인	주무자	과 장

0169

발신전보

대한민국외무부

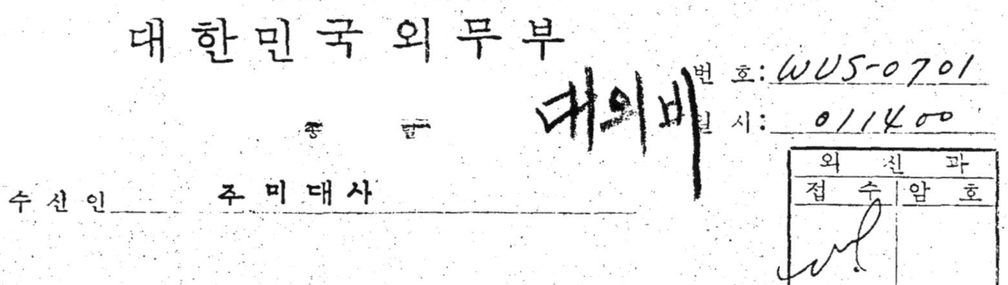

번 호: WUS-0701
일 시: 011400
대외비
외신과
접수
암호

수신인 주미대사

WUS-0688

SOFA 재교섭에 관한 연호 지시에 따라 김성은 국방부 장관이 "맥나마라" 국방장관과 면담한 내용을 지급 회전바람. (외구미)

장 관

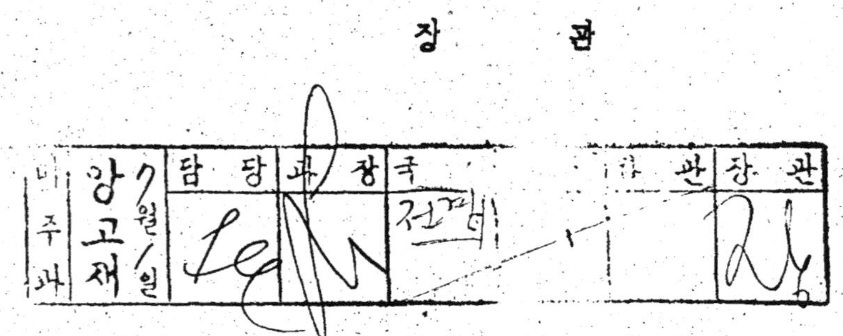

송신시간:

타자·판치	검 인	주무자	과 장

0170

기 안 지

기 안 자	미주과 이근팔	전화번호		공 보	필 요	불필요
	과 장	국 장	차관보	차 관	장 관	
협조자 성명				보존 년한		
기안 년월일	66. 7. 1.	시행 년월일		통제관	정 서	기 장
분류기호 문서번호	외구미					
경 유 수 신 참 조	대통령 : 비서실장 국무총리 : 비서실장 법무부장관 보건사회부장관 : 노동청장		발 신	장 관		
제 목	한.미간 주둔군 지위협정 체결교섭					

1. 1965. 6. 7. 일자 제 81차 교섭회의 개최 시 7가지도 합의를 보지 못하였던 형사 재판권, 노무, 청구권등 제조항에 관하여 그후 한.미 양국은 접촉을 계속하여 협정안 전반에 비공식 합의를 본바 있었읍니다.

2. 당부에서는 신중을 기하기 위하여 동 비공식 합의내용대로 협정을 체결하기 전에 1965년 말 경부터 1966년 초에 걸쳐 수차 법조계, 학계 및 언론계등 각계 저명인사를 초청하여 합의된 내용을 중심으로 의견을 교환한 결과 형사 재판권, 노무 및 청구권등 제조항의 일부 합의내용을 수정하는 것이 좋겠다는 요망이 있었으며, 그후 국내 여론 또한 대체적으로 이를 뒷받침한바 있읍니다.

3. 따라서 당부에서는 이와같은 사계의 권위자들의 요망과 국민의 여론을 존중하는 한편, 한.미간에 체결될 협정이 결코 미국이 나토 제국, 일본 또는 비율빈등 여러나라와 체결한 협정과 차이가 있어서는 아니되겠다는 결론에 도달, 비공식 합의안을 예의 재검토한

공통서식 1—2 (갑) (16절지)

0171

66-5-5 (11) 미이:우 113-3(13)

끝에 지난 4월 15일 협정안의 핵심인 형사재판권, 청구권, 노무 등 조항의 중요내용을 일부 수정하기 위한 재교섭을 미측에 제의하는 한편, 6월 9일에는 본국 정부와의 정무 연락차 귀국하는 "부라운" 주한 미국대사에게 수정안 수교와 더불어 우리측의 재교섭 제의에 대한 입장을 밝히고 미국정부의 성의를 촉구하여 계속 미측의 의향을 타진 중에 있었읍니다.

4. 우리측의 이와같은 제의에 대하여 미측은 우리측의 재교섭 제의에 응하여 6월 30일 대안을 제시하여 왔읍니다. 따라서 당부에서는 비공식 합의내용, 6월 9일자 우리측 수정안, 및 6월 30일자 미측대안에 관한 대비표를 별첨과 같이 작성하여 보고하오니 참고하시기 바랍니다.

각 관계조항에 관한 미측 대안을 검토하시와 귀부 의견을 조속 회보하여 주시기 바랍니다. 법무부 노사부

유 첨 : 한.미간 주둔군 지위협정안 대비표 1부. 끝.

보통문서로 재분류(1967.12.31.)

검토필(1967.2.6.)

직권으로재분류(67.8.10)
직위 성명

0172

장관 외 ~~廢~~ 폐기 1966. 7. 2

외 무 부

외구미 722.2- 1966. 7. 1.

수 신 : 대통령

참 조 : 비서실장

제 목 : 한.미간 주둔군 지위협정 체결교섭

1. 1965. 6. 7. 일자 제 81차 교섭회의 개최시 7가지도 합의를 보지 못하였던 형사 재판권, 노무, 청구권등 제 조항에 관하여 그후 한.미 양국은 접촉을 계속하여 협정안 전반에 비공식 합의를 본바 있었읍니다.

2. 당부에서는 신중을 기하기 위하여 동 비공식 합의내용대로 협정을 체결하기 전에 1965년 말 경부터 1966년 초에 걸쳐 수차 법조계, 학계 및 언론계등 각계 저명인사를 초청하여 합의된 내용을 중심으로 의견을 교환한 결과 형사 재판권, 노무 및 청구권등 제 조항의 일부 합의내용을 수정하는것이 좋겠다는 요망이 있었으며, 그후 국내 여론 또한 대체적으로 이를 뒷받침한바 있읍니다.

3. 따라서, 당부에서는 이와같은 사계의 권위자들의 요망과 국민의 여론을 존중하는 한편, 한.미간에 체결될 협정이 결코 미국이 나토 제국, 일본 또는 비율빈등 여러나라와 체결한 협정

0173

0174

과 차이가 있어서는 아니되겠다는 결론에 도달, 비공식 합의안을 예의 재검토한 끝에 지난 4월 15일 협정안의 핵심인 형사 재판권, 청구권, 노무등 조항의 중요내용을 일부 수정하기 위한 재교섭을 미측에 제의하는 한편, 6월 9일에는 본국 정부와의 정무 연락차 귀국하는 "부라운" 주한 미국대사에게 수정안 수교와 더불어 우리측의 재교섭 제의에 대한 입장을 밝히고 미국정부의 성의를 촉구하여 계속 미측의 의향을 타진중에 있었읍니다.

4. 우리측의 이와같은 제의에 대하여 미측은 우리측의 재교섭 제의에 응하여 6월 30일 대안을 제시하여 왔읍니다. 따라서, 당부에서는 비공식 합의내용, 6월 9일자 우리측 수정안 및 6월 30일자 미측대안에 관한 대비표를 별첨과 같이 작성하여 보고하오니 참고 하시기 바랍니다.

유첨 : 한.미간 주둔군 지위협정안 대비표 1부. 끝.

보통문서로 재분류(1967.12.31.)

직권으로 재분류(67.8.10)
외무부 장관 이 동 원

검토필(1967.2.6)

0175

~~0174~~

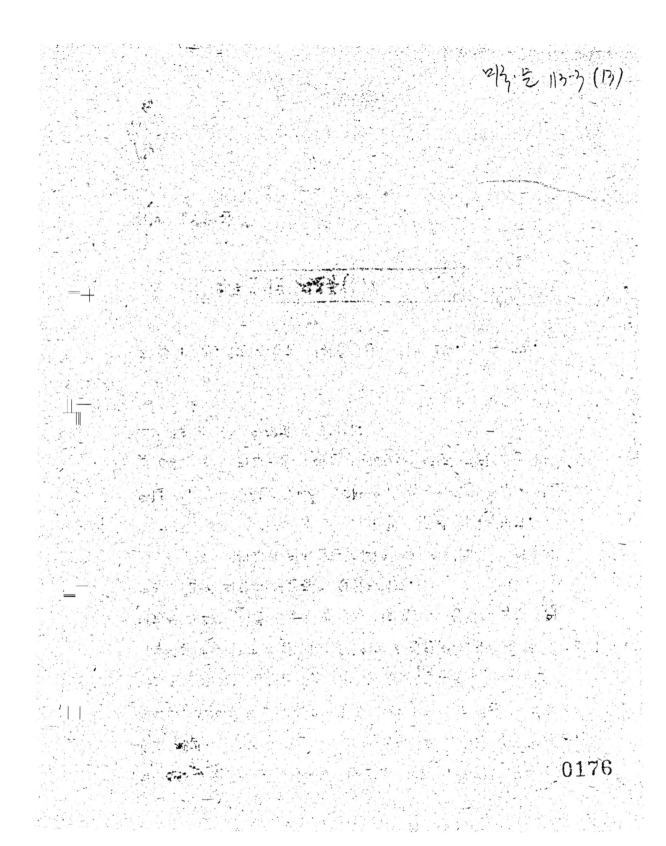

장관 [illegible] 폐

외 무 부

외구미 722.2- 1966. 7. 1.

수 신 : 국무총리

참 조 : 비서실장

제 목 : 한.미간 주둔군 지위협정 체결교섭

1. 1965. 6. 7. 일자 제 81차 교섭회의 개최시 까지도 합의를 보지 못하였던 형사 재판권, 노무, 청구권등 제 조항에 관하여 그후 한.미 양국은 접촉을 계속하여 협정안 전반에 비공식 합의를 본바 있었읍니다.

2. 당부에서는 신중을 기하기 위하여 동 비공식 합의내용대로 협정을 체결하기 전에 1965년 말 경부터 1966년 초에 걸쳐 수차 법조계, 학계 및 언론계등 각계 저명인사를 초청하여 합의된 내용을 중심으로 의견을 교환한 결과 형사 재판권, 노무 및 청구권 등 제 조항의 일부 합의내용을 수정하는것이 좋겠다는 요망이 있었으며, 그후 국내 여론 또한 대체적으로 이를 뒷받침한바 있읍니다.

3. 따라서, 당부에서는 이와같은 사계의 권위자들의 요망과 국민의 여론을 존중하는 한편, 한.미간에 체결된 협정이 결코 미국이 나토 제국, 일본 또는 비율빈등 여러나라와 체결한 협정

0177

~~0175~~

과 차이가 있어서는 아니되겠다는 결론에 도달, 비공식 합의안을 예의 재검토한 끝에 지난 4월 15일 협정안의 핵심인 형사 재판권, 청구권, 노무등 조항의 중요내용을 일부 수정하기 위한 재 교섭을 미측에 제의하는 한편, 6월 9일에는 본국 정부와의 정무 연락차 귀국하는 "부라운" 주한 미국대사에게 수정안 수교와 더불어 우리측의 재교섭 제의에 대한 입장을 밝히고 미국정부의 성의를 촉구하여 계속 미측의 의향을 타진중에 있었읍니다.

4. 우리측의 이와같은 제의에 대하여 미측은 우리측의 재 교섭 제의에 응하여 6월 30일 대안을 제시하여 왔읍니다. 따라서, 당부에서는 비공식 합의내용, 6월 9일자 우리측 수정안 및 6월 30일자 미측대안에 관한 대비표를 별첨과 같이 작성하여 보고하오니 참고 하시기 바랍니다.

유첨 : 한.미간 주둔군 지위협정안 대비표 1부. 끝.

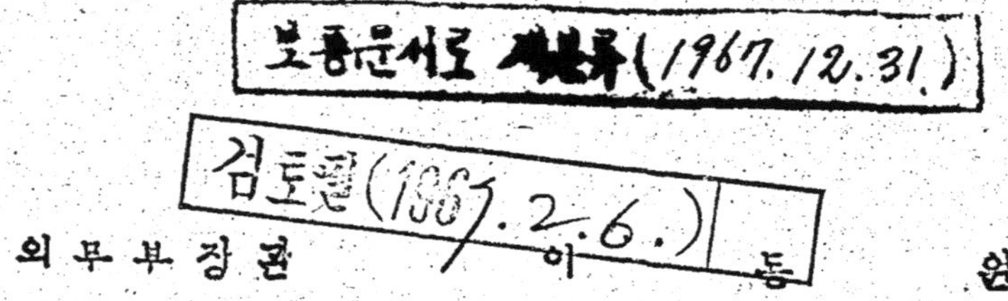

외무부장관 이 동 원

0178

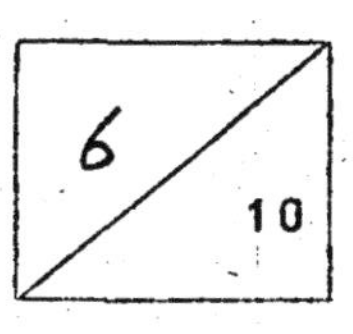

韓。美間駐屯軍地位協定案対比表

(労務，刑事裁判権，請求権 条項)

1966. 7. 1.

一般文書로 再分類 (1967.12.31)

外 務 部

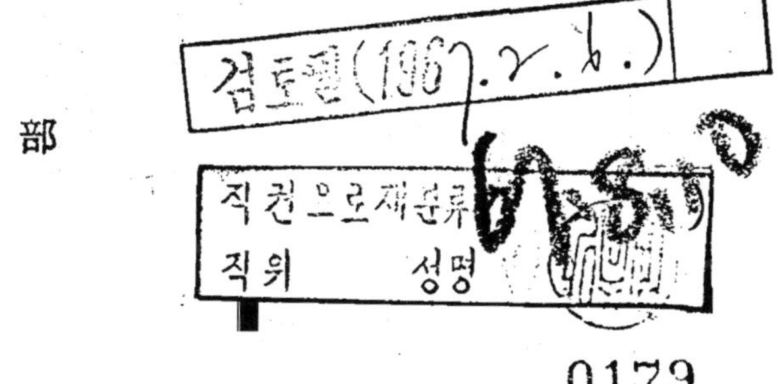

0179

66-5-5

미·문 113-3

0180

第17条 労務

非公式合意内容	韓国側再交渉修正案 (6月9日)	美側代案 (6月30日)
4. (나) 合同委員会는, 合衆国軍隊雇傭員의 大韓民国防衛에 있어서의 役割과 大韓民国 法令의 関係規定을 考慮하여, 労動争議가 前記節次에 依하여 解決되지 아니하는 境遇에는 더以上 団体行動権을 行使하여서는 아니될 緊要한 雇傭員의 諸範疇를 決定한다。合同委員会에서 이 問題에 関하여 合意에 到達할 수 없을 境遇에는 그 問題는 大韓民国政府의 関係官과 아메리카合衆国 外交使節間의 討議를 通한 再検討의 対象이 될 수 있다。	4. (나) 雇傭員 或은 雇傭員団体는, 労動争議가 前記節次에 依하여 解決되지 아니하는 境遇에는, 合同委員会가 大韓民国의 共同防衛를 為한 合衆国軍隊의 軍事作戰을 甚히 妨害한다고 決定한 境遇를 除外하고는, 더以上의 団体行動権을 가진다。(以下 左同…………………………)	4. (나) 左 同 (韓国案受諾)
合意議事録	合意議事録	合意議事録
4. 雇傭主가 合衆国軍隊의 軍事上 必要때문에 本条에 따라 適用되는 大韓民国 労動法令을 따를 수 없을 때에는, 그 問題는 可能한限 事前에 検討와 適当한 措置를 為하여 合同委員会에 回附되어야 한다。合同委員会에 適当한 措置에 ▓하여	4. 雇傭主가 合衆国軍隊의 軍事上 必要때문에 本条에 따라 適用되는 大韓民国労動法令을 따를 수 없을 때에는, 그 問題는 事前에 相互合意를 為하여 合同委員会에 回附되어야 한다。	4. 無

0181

—1—

66-5-5

기·문 113-3

0182

非公式合意內容	韓国側再交涉修正案(6月9日)	美側代案(6月30日)
相互合意가 이루어질 수 없는 境遇에는, 그問題는 大韓民国政府의 関係官과 아메리카合衆国의 外交使節間의 討議를 通한 再検討의 対象이 될 수 있다。	(以下 左同………)	

0183

-2-

66-5-5

미·로 113-3

0184

第22条 刑事裁判權

非公式合意内容	韓国側再交涉修正案 (6月9日)	美側代案 (6月30日)
1. 本条의 規定에따를것을 条件으로, (가) 合衆国軍当局은 合衆国軍隊의 構成員, 軍属및 그들의 家族에対하여 合衆国法令이 賦与한 모든 刑事裁判權및 懲戒權을 行使할 權利를 가진다.	1. 本条의規定에 따를것을 条件으로, (가) 合衆国軍当局은 合衆国軍法에 服하는 모든者에 対하여 合衆国法令이 賦与한 모든 刑事裁判權및 懲戒權을 行使할 權利를 가진다. 〔上記修正案과 一致시키기 為하여 本条및 本合意議事録의 다음条項의 関係部分도 修正되어야함. 1. 本条第2項(가),第3項(가) 2. 合意議事録：第1項(나),第3項(가)〕	1. (가) 無
	合意議事録 第1項(가)에 関하여, "合衆国軍法에服하는 모든者"라함은 本協定 発効時에 有効한 軍事裁判權이 없는 軍属또는 家族에는 適用되지아니한다. 追後의立法, 憲法改定, 또는 合衆国政府関係当局의 決定의 結果 合衆国 軍事裁判權의 範囲가 変更될境遇에는 合衆国政府는 外交経路를 通하여 大韓民国政府에 通告하여야한다.	無

0185

-3-

66-5-5

미·문113-3

0186

非公式合意案	韓国側再交涉修正案 (6月9日)	美側代案 (6月30日)
合意議事録 **第2項에関하여** 大韓民国은 合衆国当局이 適当한境遇에 合衆国軍隊의 構成員, 軍属및 그들의家族에対하여 課할수있는行政的및 懲戒的인 制裁의 有效性을 認定하여 合同委員会에서 第2項에따라 裁判権을 行使한 権利의 抛棄를 要請하는 境遇에는 이要請에 対하여 好意的 考慮를한다.	削　除	無
合意議事録 第3項(나)에関하여, 1. 大韓民国政府는 裁判権이 競合하는 境遇에는 本条第3項(나)에 依하여 大韓民国当局에 賦与된 第一次的権利를 本合意議事録 第2項, 第3項, 第4項, 第5項, 第6項및第7項에따라 合衆国을 為하여 抛棄한다. 2. 本 合意議事録 第7項에 依하여 締結될수있는 特別한 約定에 따를것을 条件으로, 合衆国 軍 当局은 本 合意	合意議事録 第3項(나)에関하여, 1. 大韓民国当局은, 合衆国軍法에 服하는者에 関하여 秩序와 規律을 維持함이 合衆国軍当局의 主된 責任임을 認定하여, 本条第3項 (다)의規定에따른 合衆国軍当局의 要請이 있으면 大韓民国이 裁判権을 行使함이 特히 重要하다고 決定하는 境遇를 除外하고, 第3項(나)의 規定下에서 裁判権을 行使하는 第一次的権利를 抛棄한다. (上記修正案과 一致[illegible]기 為하여	合意議事録 第3項(나)에 関하여, 1. 左同(韓国側案受諾) [illegible]民国当局이 前記規定에따라 내리는

-4-

0187

66-5-5

外·문 113-3

0103

非公式合意案	韓国側再交渉修正案 (6月9日)	美側代案 (6月30日)
議事録 第1項에 規定된 權利拋棄에 該当하는 個別的 事件을 大韓民国 関係当局에 通告하여야 한다. 3. 大韓民国 関係当局이 特定事件에있어서 特殊한 事情을 理由로하여 大韓民国의 司法上의 重大한 利益이 大韓民国의 裁判権의 行使를 不可避하게 한다는 意見을 가지는 境遇에는, 本合意議事録 第2項에 規定된 通告를 받은 날로부터 21日 以内에 또는 本合意議事録 第7項에 따라 締結되는 約定에서 規定될 수 있는 그 보다 短期間内에 合衆国의 関係当局에 通告함으로써 本合意議事録 第1項에서 賦与된 権利 拋棄를 撤回할 수 있다. 大韓民国 当局은 또한 이러한 通告를 받기에 앞서 通告書를 提出할수도 있다. (가) 個個의 特定事件의 慎重한 調査와 이러한 調査의 結果에 따를것을 条件으로, 特히 다음과같은 事件에 있어서 前記第3項의 趣旨 内에서 大韓民国의 司法上의 重大한 利益이 大韓民	本合意議事録 第2, 3, 4, 6 (가)및 7項도 修正되어야한다.)	決定에 関한 問題가, 関係当局間의 討議에서 解決될수없을 境遇에는, 合衆国 外交使節은 大韓民国의 適切한 当局과 協議할 수 있는 機会가 賦与된다. 2項 現非公式合意案 第5項과同一. 3項 現非公式合意案 第6項과同一. 4. 本条의 規定을 実施함에있어서 犯罪의 迅速한 処理를 促進하기 為하여 合衆国軍当局과 大韓民国関係当局은 約定을 締結할 수 있다. 諒解事項 1. "特히 重要"하다는 用語는 個々의 特定事件의 慎重한 調査後 大韓民国이 裁判権을 行使함이 不可避하다고 [illegible]되는 境遇를 指称하며 一般的으로

-5-

0189

66-5-5

미·문 113-3

0190

非公式合意案	韓国側再交涉修正案 (6月9日)	美側代案 (6月30日)
国의 裁判權行使를 不可避하게 할 수 있는 것으로 한다. (1) 大韓民国의 安全에 関한 犯罪, (2) 사람을 죽음에 이르게한 犯罪, 強盜罪 및 強姦罪, 다만, 그 犯罪가 合衆国 軍隊의 構成員, 軍属 또는 家族에 対하여 行하여진 境遇에는 그러하지 아니하다. 및 (3) 前記 各 犯罪의 未遂 또는 共犯, (나) 本項 (가) 에 規定된 犯罪에 関하여, 関係当局은 本条第6項에 規定된 相互間의 助力을 提供하기 為하여 豫備捜査의 着手時부터 特히 緊密한 協力을 継続 行하여야 한다. 4. 本合意議事録 第3項에 따라 大韓民国 関係当局이 特定事件에 対한 權利 拋棄를 撤回하고 이러한 境遇 関係当局間의 討議에서 諒解가 이루어지지 아니할 때에는, 合衆国政府는 外交 経路를 通하여 大韓民国 政府에 異議를 提起할 수 [illegible]다. 大韓民国 政府		다음과 같은 犯罪型態에 限定되는것으로 諒解한다. (1) 大韓民国의 安全에 関한 犯罪, (2) 사람을 죽음에 이르게한 犯罪, 強盜罪 및 強姦罪, 다만, 그 犯罪가 合衆国軍隊의 構成員, 또는 家族에 対하여 行하여진 境遇에만 그러하지 아니한다, 및 (3) 前記各犯罪의 未遂 또는 共犯, 2. 前項에 規定된 犯罪에 関하여, 関係当局은 第22条6項에 規定된 相互間의 助力을 提供하기 為하여 豫備捜査의 着手時부터 特히 緊密한 協力을 継続 行하여야 한다. <u>交換公文</u> 相互防衛目的을 為하여, 大韓民国에 配置된 合衆国軍隊의 駐屯으로 말미아마 発生하는 事件의 処理를 迅速히 하기 為하여 第3項 (나) 에 関한 合意議事録의 規定을 施行함에 있어서 合衆国은 個々의 特定事件에 있어서 拋

0191

66-5-99

미·문 113-3

0192

<table>
<tr><th>非公式合意案</th><th>韓国側再交渉修正案
(6月9日)</th><th>美側代案 (6月30日)</th></tr>
<tr><td>는 大韓民国의 司法 上의 利益과 合衆国의 利益을 充分히 考慮하여 外交分野에 있어서의 그의 権限을 行使하여 意見差異를 解決하여야 한다. 大韓民国 政府가 前記規定에 따라 意見差異를 解決함에 있어서 大韓民国 当局이 裁判権을 行使함이 不可避하다고 決定하는 境遇에는, 権利 抛棄의 撤回는 最終的이며 確定的이다.

5. 合衆国 軍 当局은, 大韓民国 関係当局의 同意를 얻어, 捜査審理및 裁判을 為하여 合衆国이 裁判権을 가지는 特定刑事事件을 大韓民国의 法院이나 当局에 移送할 수 있다.

大韓民国 関係当局은, 合衆国 軍当局의 同意를 얻어, 捜査, 審理및 裁判을 為하여 大韓民国이 裁判権을 가지는 特定 刑事事件을 合衆国 軍当局에 移送할 수 있다.

6. (가) 合衆国 軍隊의 構成員, 軍属 또는 家族이 大韓民国 안에서 大韓民</td><td></td><td>棄를 要請할 必要가 없으며 또한 大韓民国政府가 特定事件에 있어서 大韓民国当局이 그事件에 있어서 裁判権을 行使함이 特히 重要하다고 決定하는 境遇를 除外하고는 大韓民国이 그裁判権을 行使할 第一次的権利를 抛棄한것으로 認定한다.

司法行政을 迅速化 하기 為하여 大韓民国政府에 依한 그와같은 決定은 大韓民国이 그의 第一次的 裁判権에 属하는 犯罪의 発生을 通告받거나 또는 알게된後 15日内(또는 第3項(나)에 関한 合意議事録 第4項에 따라 相互 合意될수있는 그보다 短期間内)에 法務部長官이 書面으로 関係合衆国当局에 通告되어야한다. 合衆国当局은 15日 또는 달리 合意된 期間 満了以前에 裁判権을 行使하지 아니할수있다.</td></tr>
</table>

0193

66-5-5

기.운 113-3

0194

非 公 式 合 意 案	韓国側再交渉 修正案 (6月9日)	美 側 代 案 (6月30日)
国의 利益에 反하여 犯한 犯罪 때문에 合衆国 法院에 訴追되었을 境遇에는, 그 裁判은 大韓民国 안에서 行하여져야 한다. (1) 다만, 合衆国의 法律이 달리 要求하는 境遇, 또는 (2) 軍事上 緊急事態의 境遇 또는 司法上의 利益을 為한 境遇에 合衆国 軍当局이 大韓民国 領域밖에서 裁判을 行할 意図가 있는 境遇에는 除外된다. 이러한 境遇 合衆国 軍 当局은 大韓民国 当局에 이러한 意図에 対한 意見을 陳述할 수 있는 機会를 適時에 賦与하여야 하며 大韓民国 当局이 陳述하는 意見에 対하여 充分한 考慮를 하여야 한다. (나) 裁判이 大韓民国 領域 밖에서 行하여질 境遇에는, 合衆国 軍 当局은 大韓民国 当局에 裁判의 場所와 日字를 通告하여야 한다. 大韓民国 代表는 그 裁判에 立会할 権利를 가진다. 合衆国 当局은 判決과 訴訟의 最終 結果를 大韓民国 当局에 通告하여야 한다. 7. 本条 및 本合意議事録의 規定의 施行과 軽微한 犯罪의 迅速한 処理를 為하여, 大韓民国 関係 当局과 合衆国 軍 当局은 約定을 締結할수있다. 同 約定은 또한 通告없이 —는 処理와 本 [illegible]議事録 第3項에 規定된 権利 [illegible]를 撤回할수있 [illegible] 期間에도 미칠수있다.		

0195

-8-

66-5-5

미·문 113-3

0196

才23条 請求權

非公式合意內容	韓国側再交涉修正案（6月9日）	美側代案（6月30日）
合意議事錄 1. 달리 規定하는 境過를 除外하고는, (가) 本条의 才5項, 才6項, 才7項및才8項의 規定은, 서울特別市의 地域에서 일어난 事件으로부터 發生한 請求權에 關하여는, 本協定의 效力発生日後 6個月만에 效力이 発生하게 된다。 (나) 才5項, 才6項, 才7項및 才8項의 規定은 實行可能한 가장빠른 時日에, 合同委員会가 決定하는바에따라, 大韓民国의 其他地域에 그適用을 拡大한다。	1. 削除 (本修正에따라, 그다음의 合意議事錄 才2項과 才3項도 亦是 削除한다)	合意議事錄 1. 달리 規定하는 境過를 除外하고는, 本条의 才5項, 才6項, 才7項및才8項의規定은, 서울特別市의 地域에서 일어난 事件으로부터 発生한 請求權에 關하여는, 本協定의 效力発生日後 6個月만에, 그리고 大韓民国안 다른 곳에서 発生한 請求權에 關하여는, 그날로부터 1年만에, 效力이 発生하게 된다。 0197

66-5-5 (11)

미·일 113-3

0198

6/30 10:30 a.m. 1/3

AGREED MINUTE RE PARAGRAPH 3(b) OF ARTICLE XXII: CRIMINAL JURISDICTION

1. The authorities of the Republic of Korea, recognizing that it is the primary responsibility of the United States military authorities to maintain good order and discipline where persons subject to United States military laws are concerned, will, upon the request of the military authorities of the United States pursuant to paragraph 3(c), waive their primary right to exercise jurisdiction under paragraph 3(b) except when they determine that it is of particular importance that jurisdiction be exercised by the authorities of the Republic of Korea. In cases where any question concerning such determination as may be made by the authorities of the Republic of Korea in accordance with the foregoing provisions cannot be resolved in discussions between the authorities concerned, the United States diplomatic mission will be afforded an opportunity to confer with the proper authorities of the Republic of Korea.

2. With the consent of the competent authorities of the Republic of Korea, the military authorities of the United States may transfer to the courts or authorities of the Republic of Korea for investigation, trial and decision, particular criminal cases in which jurisdiction rests with the United States.

With the consent of the military authorities of the United States, the competent authorities of the Republic of Korea may transfer to the military authorities of the United States for investigation, trial and decision, particular criminal cases in which jurisdiction rests with the Republic of Korea.

3. (a) Where a member of the United States armed forces or civilian component, or a dependent, is arraigned before a court of the United States, for an offense committed in the Republic of Korea against Korean interests, the trial shall be held within the Republic of Korea

(i) except where the law of the United States requires otherwise, or

(ii) except where, in cases of military exigency or in the interests of justice, the military authorities of the United States intend to hold the trial outside the Republic of Korea. In this event they shall afford the authorities of the Republic of Korea timely opportunity to comment on such intention and shall give due consideration to any comments the latter may make.

(b) Where the trial is held outside of the Republic of Korea the military authorities of the United States shall inform the authorities of the Republic of Korea of the place and date of the trial. A representative of the Republic of Korea shall be entitled to be present at the trial. The

0200

of minor importance,

authorities of the United States shall inform the authorities of the Republic of Korea of the judgment and the final outcome of the proceedings.

4. In the implementation of the provisions of this Article, and to facilitate the expeditious disposal of offenses, arrangements may be made between the military authorities of the United States and the competent authorities of the Republic of Korea..

1. These arrangements may also extend to dispensing with notification ~~to~~ and to the period of time referred to in para 3 of this Article...

2. to dispense with necessity for a request for waiver of jurisdiction to be made ~~in~~ in each particular case.

AGREED UNDERSTANDING IN AGREED JOINT SUMMARY REGARDING AGREED MINUTE RE PARAGRAPH 3(b), OF ARTICLE XXII - CRIMINAL JURISDICTION

1. It is understood that the term "of particular importance" has reference to those cases in which, after a careful examination of each specific case, the exercise of jurisdiction by the Republic of Korea is deemed imperative, and, in particular, (is limited, in general,) to the following types of offenses:

(a) security offenses against the Republic of Korea;

(b) offenses causing the death of a human being, robbery, and rape, except where the offenses are directed against a member of the United States armed forces, the civilian component, or a dependent; and

(c) attempts to commit such offenses or participation therein.

2. In respect of the offenses referred to in the above paragraph, the authorities concerned shall proceed in particularly close cooperation from the beginning of the preliminary investigation in order to provide the mutual assistance envisaged in paragraph 6 of Article XXII.

0202

LETTER FROM THE AMERICAN AMBASSADOR TO THE FOREIGN MINISTER

Dear Mr. Minister:

Today the Governments of the United States of America and the Republic of Korea have formally signed the Agreement between the United States of America and the Republic of Korea regarding Facilities and Areas and the Status of United States Armed Forces in the Republic of Korea.

Article XXII of that Agreement and its Agreed Minutes provide for the exercise of jurisdiction over members of the United States armed forces, the civilian component, and their dependents in the Republic of Korea. In this regard, I would be grateful for your confirmation of the following understandings:

That, to facilitate the processing of cases resulting from the presence of United States armed forces deployed in Korea for mutual defense purposes, in implementation of the provisions of Agreed Minute Re Paragraph 3(b), it shall not be necessary for the United States to make a request for waiver in each particular case, and it shall be taken for granted that the Republic of Korea has waived its primary right to exercise jurisdiction thereunder except where the Government of the Republic of Korea determines in a specific case that it is of particular importance that jurisdiction be exercised therein by the authorities of the Republic of Korea;

That, in the interest of expediting the administration of justice, any such determination by the Government of the Republic of Korea shall be provided in writing by the Minister of Justice to the appropriate United States authorities within fifteen days (or such shorter period as may be mutually agreed upon pursuant to paragraph 4 of the Agreed Minute Re Paragraph 3(b)) after the Republic of Korea is notified or is otherwise apprised of the commission of an offense falling within its primary jurisdiction. The authorities of the United States may not exercise jurisdiction before the expiration of the fifteen day or other agreed period.

Sincerely yours,

/s/

0203

LETTER FROM THE FOREIGN MINISTER TO THE AMERICAN AMBASSADOR

Dear Mr. Ambassador:

As requested in your letter of __________, I am pleased to confirm our understandings:

That, to facilitate the processing of cases resulting from the presence of United States armed forces deployed in Korea for mutual defense purposes, in implementation of the provisions of Agreed Minute Re Paragraph 3(b), it shall not be necessary for the United States to make a request for waiver in each particular case, and it shall be taken for granted that the Republic of Korea has waived its primary right to exercise jurisdiction thereunder except where the Government of the Republic of Korea determines in a specific case that it is of particular importance that jurisdiction be exercised therein by the authorities of the Republic of Korea;

That, in the interest of expediting the administration of justice, any such determination by the Government of the Republic of Korea shall be provided in writing by the Minister of Justice to the appropriate United States authorities within fifteen days (or such shorter period as may be mutually agreed upon pursuant to paragraph 4 of the Agreed Minute Re Paragraph 3(b)) after the Republic of Korea is notified or is otherwise apprised of the commission of an offense falling within its primary jurisdiction. The authorities of the United States may not exercise jurisdiction before the expiration of the fifteen day or other agreed period.

Sincerely yours,

/s/

0204

PARAGRAPH 4. (b) OF ARTICLE XVII: LABOR

4. (b) Employees or any employee organization shall have the right of further collective action in the event a labor dispute is not resolved by the foregoing procedures except in cases where the Joint Committee determines such action seriously hampers military operations of the United States armed forces for the joint defense of the Republic of Korea. In the event an agreement cannot be reached on this question in the Joint Committee, it may be made the subject of review through discussions between appropriate officials of the Government of the Republic of Korea and the diplomatic mission of the United States of America.

0205

AGREED MINUTE 1 TO ARTICLE XXIII: CLAIMS

1. Unless otherwise provided, the provisions of paragraphs 5, 6, 7 and 8 of this Article will become effective six months from the date of entry into force of this Agreement with respect to claims arising from incidents in the Seoul Special City area, and one year from that date with respect to claims arising elsewhere in the Republic of Korea.

0206

대한민국 외무부

착신전보

대외비

종별

번호: USW-0703

일시: 011700

수신인: 장관

발신인: 주미대사

미주과	공람	담당	과장	국장			차관	장관
	월 일							

대: WUS-0701 및 WUS-0688

대호전문지시에 관하여 아래와같이 회보함.

1. 김성은 국방장관 방미중 제 1차 맥나마라 장관과의 회담은 6.22 오후 이루워 졌으며, 본부지시전문 WUS-0688 호는 6.23일 접수하였기때문에 군대지위 협정에 관하여 논의하지못하였음.

2. 6.23일본부지시전문을 접수한후 본직은 즉시 김국방장관에게 전달하고 맥나마라 장관 또는 기타 국방성 고위관리와의 접촉을 시도하였으나 일정 및 기타사유로 이루워지지못하였음.

3. 6.25 김장관께서 당지를 출발하기전에 맥나마라 국방장관과 단독 회견을 가졌는바 동 단독회견시 군대지위협정문제를 제기하였는지 여부는 확인할 도리가 없음. 그이유는 김장관은 국방성에서부터 직접 공군기지로 헬리콥타로 비행(태)한후 출발하였기때문에 김장관에게 확인하지못하였으며 현재 김장관은 호노루루를 방미 방문후 곧 귀국하게될것이므로 김장관 귀국후 직접 확인하여 주시기바람.

(구미)

Send cable to Tokyo and inquire about this question today!

비서		아주		통상		상공		청와대	
총무		구미	○	경기		농림		총리실	
의전		정문		정공		조달		수산	
여권		방교		중정		외연		공보부	
육군		해군		공군		해병		합참	✓

수신시간: 1966 7 2 11 09

0207

발신전보

대 한 민 국 외 무 부

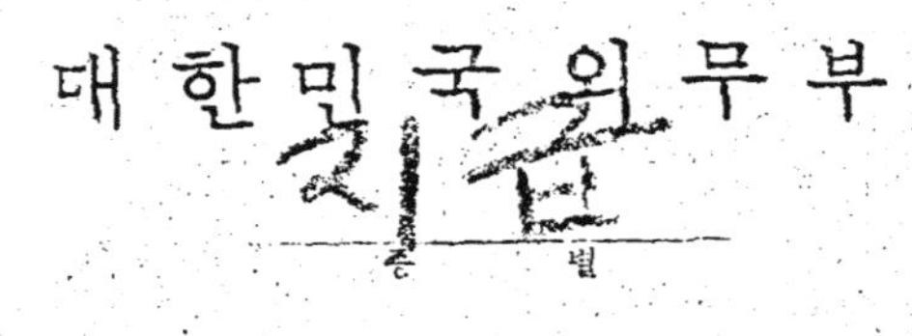

번 호: WJA-07079

일 시: 041900

외 신 과	
접 수	암 호

수 신 인 주 일 대 사

다음 전문내용을 귀지에 체재중인 김성은 국방부 장관에게 전달바람.

SOFA 재교섭에 관하여 연 WUS-0688 (6.23) 및 WUS-WLA-0607(6.27) 호에 따라, 방미중 미국방성 당국자 및 태평양 지구 사령관 Sharp 제독과 면담한 내용을 회전 바람. (외구미)

장 관

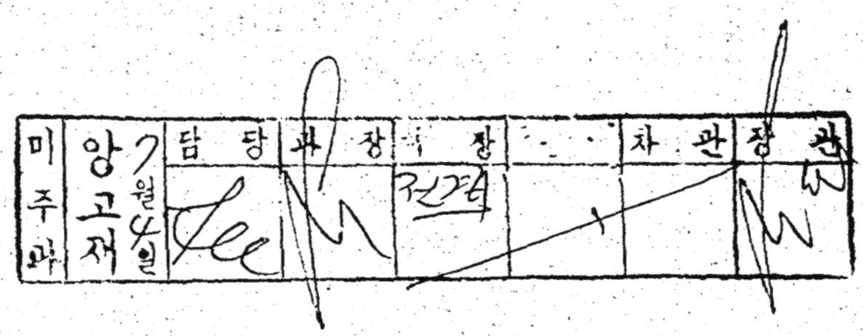

미주과	앙고재 7월 4일	담 당	과 장	국 장		차 관	장 관

송신시간:

타자 · 판치	검 인	주무자	과 장

0208

대한민국 외무부

착신암호전보

지급

종별

번 호: JAW-07111

일 시: 051050

수신인: 외무부장관

발신인: 주일대사

대: WJA-07079

대호를 김국방장관에게 금 5일 아침 전달하였음.

김장관으로부터 아래 사항의 타전요청이 있으므로 이를 전달함.

- 아래 -

1. 체미중 토의할 기회없었음.

2. SHARP 제독은 사시토회의관계로 부재중.

3. 머스크 장관과 토의할 가능성 있을것으로 사료됨. (머스크 장관 방한시)

(주일정, 외구미)

예고: 접수후 재분류

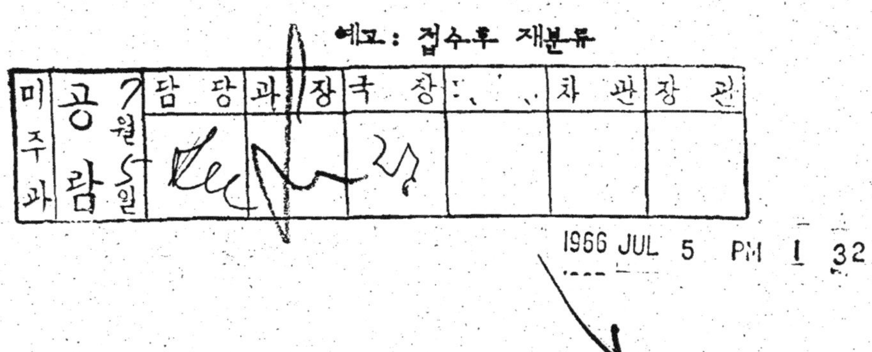

미주과	공람 7월 5일	담당	과장	국장		차관	장관

1966 JUL 5 PM 1 32

비서	√	아주		통상		상공		청와대
총무		구미	9 √	경기		농림		총리실
의전		정문		정공		조달		수산
여권		방교		중정	√	외연		공보부
육군		해군		공군		해병		합참

의신과

검인

수신시간:

담당	주무자	과장

0209

1966, 10, 7, 에 예고문에 의거 일반문서로 재분류됨

대 한 민 국 외 무 부

착신암호전보

번 호: USW-0722

일 시: 061700

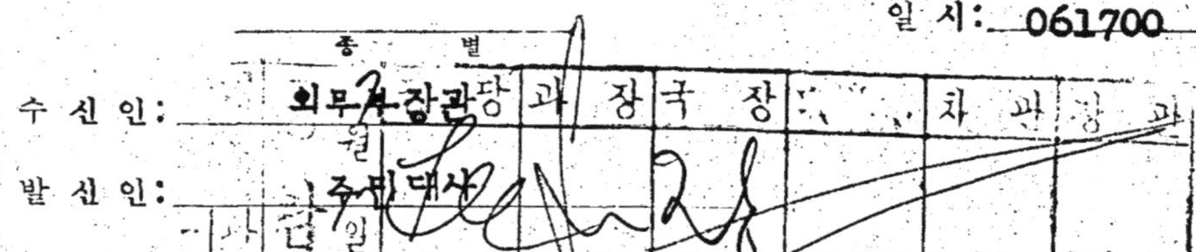

수 신 인: 외무부장관

발 신 인: 주미대사

1. 7.6 일자 DI 에의하면 그동안 현안중이든 한미 군대지위협정은 거이 합의에 도달하였다고하므로 동정보에의하여 국무성 한국과에 문의하였던바, 한미간에 완전합의에 도달하고 러스크 장관의 방한을 이용하여 7.9 일 서울에서 조인하게될것이라고함.

2. 국무성 한국과에 의하면 노동조항은 거이 한국측안을 수락하였으며 민사청구권문제는 서울에서는 6 개월후, 기타지역에서는 12 개월후에 발효하도록 합의에 도달하였고 재판관할권문제에 관하여는 ~~미국측안~~ 방식에의거 한미간에 합의되었다고하는바 당관 사무처리상 참고코저하오니 한미간에 합의된 내용을 회전하여주십시기바람. (구미)

66. 12. 31 일반문서로 재분류

1966 JUL 7 PM 4 22

비서	√	아주		통상		상공		청와대	
총무		구미	○	경기		농림		총리실	
의전		정문	√	정공		조달		수 산	
여권		방교	√	중정	√	외연		공보부	
육군		해군		공군		해병		합 참	

외 신 과

검 인

수신시간:

담 당	주무자	과 장

0210

대 한 민 국 외 무 부

발신전보

번 호: WUS-0718

일 시: 072100

종 별

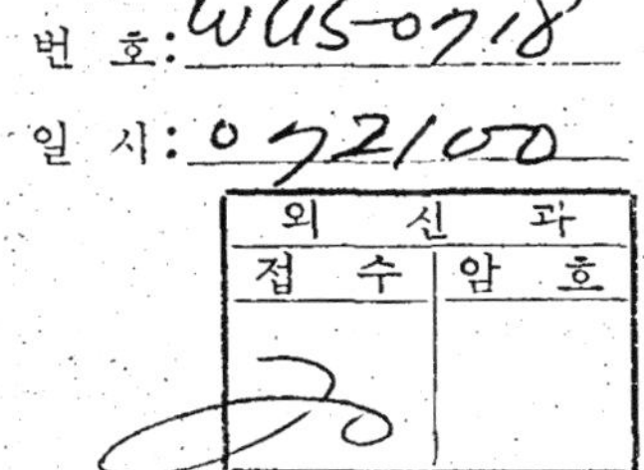

수 신 인 주 미 대 사

참 조 : 정무과장

대: USW-0722

1. 대호 전문 1항, 2항의 내용 확인함.
2. 2항 내용중 재판관할권문제에 관하여서는 화란, 희랍과 같은 표준형 Formular 에 의한 해결을 본 것이며 상세한 내용은 Pouch 편으로 알리겠음. (외구미)

장 관

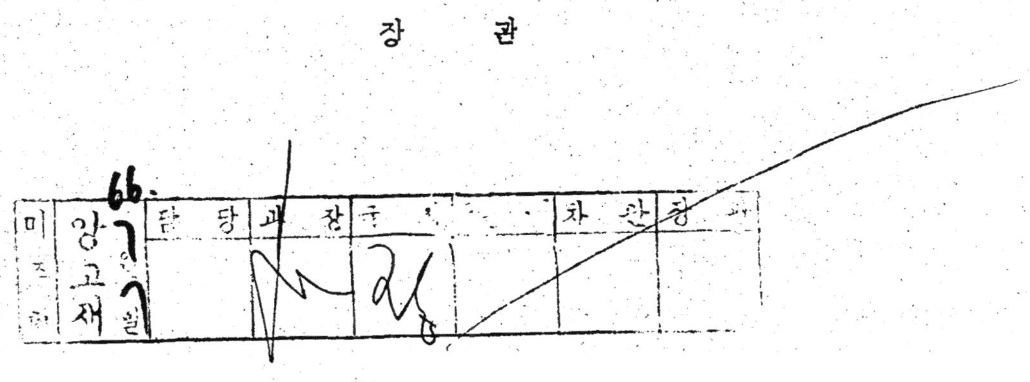

미주과	66. 7. 7. 기안	담 당	과 장	국 장		차 관	장 관

수신시간:

타자·판치	검 인	주무가	과 장

0211

대한민국 외무부

착신전보

종별

번 호: UNW-0706
일 시: 061700

수 신 인: 외무부장관 (중앙정보부장)
발 신 인: 주국련대사

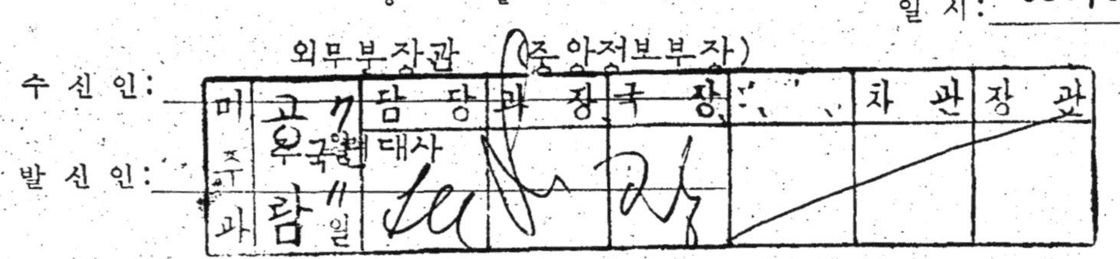

7.6 일자 뉴욕 타임스는 서울발신 기사로서 한미행정협정에 관한 이외무장관의 기자회견 내용을 아래와 같이 보도하였음.

SEOUL INSISTS ON TRYING G.I.'S FOR OFF DUTY CRIMES

SEOUL, KOREA, JULY 5- THE SOUTH KOREAN FOREIGN MINISTER, LEE TONG WON, DECCARED TODAY THAT UNLESS THE UNITED STATES RECOGNIZE SOUTH KOREA'S PRIMARY RIGHT TO TRY UNITED STATES SERVICEMEN FOR OFF-DUTY CRIMES, HE WOULD REFUSE TO SIGN ANY STATUS-OF-FORCES AGREEMENT. AFTER CONFERRING WITH THE UNITED STATES AMBASSADOR, WINTHROP G. BROWN, FOR AN HOUR ON THE MATTER MR. LEE SAID AT A NEWS CONFERENCE. HE WOULD SEEK A "POLITICAL SOLUTION" IN TALKS WITH SECRETARY OF STATE DEAN RUSK. MR. RUSK DUE HERE FRIDAY FOR AN OVERNIGHT VISIT ON HIS CURRENT ASIAN TOUR.

"IF THIS FAILS," MR. LEE SAID "WE WOULD HAVE TO SCRAP THE WHOLE NEGOTIATIONS AND WAIT 10 OR 20 YEARS UNTIL A SATISFACTORY STATUS-OF-FORCES AGREEMENT CAN BE SIGNED."

MR. LEE SAID SOUTH KOREA WANTED AN AGREEMENT SIMILAR TO THOSE

비서		아주	✓	통상		상공		청와대	
총무		구미		경기		농림		총리실	
의전		정문	✓	정공		조달		수산	
여권		방교	✓	중정		외연		공보부	
육군		해군		공군		해병		합참	

검 인:

수신시간: '66 7 7 17 05

0212

WHICH THE UNITED STATES HAS WITH COUNTRIES OF THE NORTH ATLANTIC TREATY ORGANIZATION. THE FOURYEAR-OLD NEGOTIATIONS WERE ALMOST COMPLETED A YEAR AGO AND THE SEOUL GOVERNMENT HAD AGREED TO WAIVE THE PRIMARY RIGHT TO TRY UNITED STATES SERVICEMEN FOR OFF-DUTY OFFENSES IN KOREAN COURTS EXCEPT FOR CRIMES AGAINST KOREA'S NATIONAL SECURITY.

BUT IN THE FACE OF CRITICISM FROM OPPOSITION POLITICIANS, LEGAL GROUPS AND THE KOREAN PRESS, THE GOVERNMENT PROPOSED A RENEGOTIATION DEMANDING RETENTION OF THE RIGHT TO TRY THE SERVICEMEN ON ALL OFF-DUTY CHARGES.

외 신 과

0213

발신전보

대 한 민 국 외 무 부

대 긴 급

번 호: WUS-0719
일 시: 080950

외 신 과	
접 수	암 호

수 신 인 주 미 대 사

Rusk 미국무장관의 방한을 마지하여 명 7월 9일 한국을 대표하여 이동원 외무부장관 및 민복기 법무부장관, 미측의 Rusk 국무장관 및 Brown 주한미국대사간에 현안이던 SOFA 를 체결함에 앞서 금 7월 8일 한.미 양측은 82차 회의를 개최한 후 다음과 같은 공동발표를 금일 오전 10시(한국시간)를 기하여 한.미 동시에 발표할 예정이오니 그 시간에 P.R. 에 자하시기 바랍니다.(외구미)

장 관

미주과	안고재 66.7월 8일	담 당	과 장	국 장		차 관	장 관

송신시간:

타자 · 판치	검 인	주무자	과 장

0214

한미공동발표

1966.7.8.

한미양국대표는 1966 년 7월 8 일에 개최된 제 82차회의에서 한미간 미주둔군 지위에 관한 협정 조인에 완전한 합의에 도달하였다.

제 82차 회의에서 중요조항인 형사재판권, 노동, 및 청구권조항과 기타 모든 미결 조항의 자구에 관하여 최종합의를 보았다.

동협정문은 대한민국을 대표하여 이동원 외무부장관 과 민복기 법무부장관, 미합중국을 대표하여 "러스크" 국무장관 과 "부라운" 주한미대사에의하여 서명될것이다. 동조인식은 1966년 7월 9일 토요일 오전 10시에 대한민국 서울의 중앙청 중앙 홀에서 거행될 예정이다.

동협정은 대한민국정부와 주한미군간의 모든관계를 다루고 있으며 전문과 31개조문으로 되어있다.

동협정은 대한민국정부가 그의 법적절차에 따라 동협정을 승인하였음을 미국정부에 통고한날로 부터 3개월후에 발효한다. 이군대 지위에관한 협정은 1950년 7월 12일자의 대전협정과 대한민국에 주둔하는 미군대에 관련하여 대한민국과 통합사령부간의 1952년 5월 24일자의 경제조정에관한 협정을 폐기하고 대치하게된다.

0215

66-8-H

66-5-8 (2)　　　　대국민 118-32(2)

0216

ROK-US Joint Press Release, to be Issued at the
Conclusion of the 82nd SOFA Negotiating Meeting

July 8, 1966

The Korean and United States negotiators reached full agreement on the text of the Republic of Korea-United States of Forces Agreement at the 82nd negotiating session on July 8, 1966.

At the 82nd meeting, final agreement was reached on the wording of three key Articles, Criminal Jurisdiction, labor, and Claims, as well as on all other previously unresolved Articles.

The document will be signed for the Republic of Korea by Minister of Foreign Affairs Tong Won Lee and Minister of Justice Bok Ki Min, and for the United States of America by Secretary of State Dean Rusk and Ambassador Winthrop G. Brown. It is anticipated that the signing ceremony will take place at 10:00 a.m. on Saturday, July 9, 1966, in the Main Hall of the Capitol Building in Seoul, Korea.

The Agreement includes a Preamble and 31 Articles covering all aspects of relations between the Government of the Republic of Korea and the United States military forces in the Republic of Korea.

The Agreement will enter into force three months after the date on which the Government of the Republic of Korea notifies the Government of the United States that it has approved the Agreement in accordance with its legal procedures. The Status of Forces Agreement will supersede and replace the Taejon Agreement of July 12, 1950 and the Agreement on Economic Coordination of May 24, 1952, between the Republic of Korea and the Unified Command, as related to United States armed forces in the Republic of Korea.

0217 66-1-60

66-5-8 (2)

마이크로 78-2(2)

0218

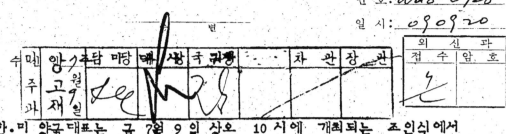

지급

대 한 민 국 외 무 부

발신전보

번 호: WUS-0728

일 시: 090920

수신	주미대사
발신	장관

1. 한·미 양국대표는 금 7월 9일 상오 10 시에 개최되는 조인식에서 SOFA 에 서명할 것임.

2. 동 서명식에서 양측 대표가 서명후 행할 외무부장관 및 Rusk 국무장관의 연설문 및 조인식후 발표할 공동발표문(영문)을 다음과 같이 알리오니 금 7월 9일 상오 11 시(한국시간)를 기하여 발표하시기 바람.

3. 최종적으로 합의된 협정문은 다음 파우치 편으로 송부할 것임.(외구미)

(1) Text of Remarks by Foreign Minister Tong Won Lee:

" 별첨 (1) "

(2) Text of Secretary Rusk's Remark:

" 별첨 (2) "

(3) Press Release on Formal Signing of SOFA, July 9, 1966:

" 별첨 (3) "

장관

송신시간:

타자·관치	검 인	주무자	과 장

0219

TEXT OF REMARKS BY FOREIGN MINISTER TONG WON LEE AT THE SIGNING CEREMONY OF THE STATUS OF FORCES AGREEMENT

(Not to be released prior to 11:00 a.m.Saturday, July 9, 1966)

July 9, 1966

His Excellency Secretary of State and Members of his Party,
His Excellency Prime Minister and Fellow Cabinet Members,
and Distinguished Guests:

It is my great honor and personal privilege to be present here at this signing ceremony together with His Excellency Secretary Rusk whose timely visit to this country has made this occasion significant. This ceremony, we believe, is a memorable event in the close relations which have existed between the Republic of Korea and the United States since the establishment of relations between our two countries.

As the Distinguished Guests have just witnessed, I have signed with Secretary Rusk and Agreement covering the facilities and areas and the status of the United States forces in the Republic of Korea, the conclusion of which, as you are well aware, has keenly been desired by the people and the Government of the Republic of Korea since the early 1950s.

It is also to be noted that, at the time of the Korean War, the United States armed forces came to the aid of this country, responding to the call of a nation facing Communist aggression, and have been deployed since then in the Republic

0221

of Korea under the Mutual Defense Treaty to play their vital role with the Korean armed forces in the common defense of this nation. Today, more than a decade later, our troops are fighting in Vietnam shoulder to shoulder with the troops of the United States to repel the Communist aggression supported and directed by Communist regimes. I firmly believe that the materialization of this Agreement, putting, once and for all, an end to the pending negotiations of many past years, is a reflection of the strong ties which bind our two countries and which have been strengthened by our comradeship in Vietnam, and will further contribute to the fraternity and understanding between our two peoples.

Furthermore, I am very proud of the fact that this Agreement is a product of, and is based upon, the mutual respect and friendship which exists between the two countries. It is my belief, therefore, that if our two countries observe and implement the Agreement faithfully it will serve to improve our already excellent relations.

Finally, I would like to take this opportunity to extend my most sincere and warmest appreciation to those who have participated directly or indirectly in the negotiations for their tireless efforts and their dedication in working toward this day, which marks another high point in the annals of the relations between our two countries.

Thank you,

0223

PRESS RELEASE ON FORMAL SIGNING OF SOFA-9 JULY 1966

(Note: The following is not for release by any media prior to 11 a.m. Saturday, July 9, 1966.)

The Foreign Minister of the Republic of Korea, Mr. Tong Won Lee and the United States Secretary of State, Dean Rusk, on 9 July 1966, signed at the Capitol Building in Seoul the Status of Forces Agreement between the United States of America and the Republic of Korea. The document was also signed by US Ambassador, Winthrop G. Brown, and the ROK Minister of Justice, Bok Ki Min.

This new US-ROK Agreement, which will supersede and replace the Taejon Agreement of July 12, 1950 and the May 24, 1952 Agreement on Economic Coordination between the Unified Command and Republic of Korea, as related to United States armed forces in the Republic of Korea, will enter into force three months after the Government of the Republic of Korea notifies the Government of the United States that it has approved the Agreement in accordance with its legal procedures.

The new US-ROK agreement provides that a US-ROK Joint Committee will be established to supervise implementation of the Agreement. The Joint Committee will be composed of a senior Representative from each of the two Governments, and each representative shall have several deputies and a staff.

Under the Taejon Agreement, the United States exercised exclusive jurisdiction over members of the US armed forces, civilian component and dependents. This will be altered under the Criminal Jurisdiction Article of the SOFA. This article, patterned after

0224

- 1 -

0225

the NATO SOFA's, provides that the United States has the primary right of jurisdiction where the offense arose out of the performance of official duty or where it solely concerns US personnel or property. The ROK has the primary right of jurisdiction in all other cases. However, the ROK agrees to waive this right except when it determines that it is of particular importance that jurisdiction be exercised by the authorities of the Republic of Korea.

The Criminal Jurisdiction Article also provides for rights of US personnel tried in a court of the Republic of Korea under this Agreement. These include trial safeguards similar to those provided under the U.S. Constitution, the right to have a representative of the United States Government present at all interrogations, pre-trial hearings and the trial itself, and pre-trial custody of the accused in US facilities except in cases of offenses against the security of the Republic of Korea.

The Labor Article of the new Agreement provides that the US armed forces will continue the system of direct-hire of its Korean personnel, with the recruitment services of the Government of the Republic of Korea being utilized insofar as is practicable. The Agreement also provides for continued conformance with the provisions of labor legislation of the Republic of Korea, regarding conditions of employment and compensation. The US armed forces will withhold from wages and pay to the Korean Government the withholdings required by Korean income tax legislation.

0226

마문 178-1

0227

New procedures are established for resolution of labor disputes which cannot be settled through the established grievance and labor relations procedures of the US armed forces. The disputes procedure includes three stages, as follows: (1) First, conciliation by the Office of Labor Affairs; (2) Second, in the event the dispute is not settled by the above conciliation effort, it shall be referred to the Joint Committee, which may establish a Special Committee for further conciliation efforts; and (3) finally, the Joint Committee shall resolve the dispute and its decisions shall be binding. Neither employee organizations nor employee shall engage in any practices disruptive of normal work requirements unless a period of at least 70 days has elapsed after the dispute has been referred to the Joint Committee, the second stage of mediation procedures.

Decisions of the Joint Committee shall be binding. However, employees and labor unions have the right of further collective action in the event a labor dispute is not resolved by the foregoing procedures, except in cases where the Joint Committee determines such action seriously hampers military operations of the United States armed forces for the joint defense of the Republic of Korea.

The two Governments agree that a union or other employee groups will be recognized by the employers unless its objectives are inimical to the common interests of the United States and the Republic of Korea. Membership or non-membership in such groups

0228

0229

shall not be a factor in employment or other actions affecting employees.

V. Heretofore, all claims for death, injury or property damage caused by members of the United States armed forces in Korea have been handled solely by U.S. authorities. The Claims Article of the Agreement provides for a progressive transfer of claims settlement authority and responsibility to the Government of the Republic of Korea. The Republic of Korea Government will assume the responsibility for settling claims in the Seoul special city area six months after entry into force of the SOFA, and in the rest of the ROK six months thereafter. These claims will be settled or adjudicated in accordance with the laws and regulations of the Republic of Korea. The United States will pay 75% of the cost of such claims and the Republic of Korea will pay 25%, in accordance with standard practice in the NATO SOFA's. Henceforth the Claims Services of both the United States and the Republic of Korea will work together in mutual cooperation to insure the speedy and equitable settlement of all claims arising as a result of action by members of the U.S. armed forces.

VI. The 31 Articles of the US-ROK SOFA cover almost all aspects of relations between the Government of the Republic of Korea and the US military forces in Korea. Four of the Articles pertain to the question of facilities and areas, the use of which is granted to the US by Article IV of the US-ROK Mutual Defense Treaty. The SOFA

0230

- 4 -

0231

Agreement provides that the records of US facilities and areas in the Republic of Korea shall be maintained through the Joint Committee after the SOFA enters into force. Other Articles in the Agreement cover subjects such as: Utilities and Services, Respect for Local Laws, Entry and Exit, Customs and Duties, Access of Vessels and Aircraft, Meteorological Services, Air Traffic Control and Navigational Aids, Non-appropriated Fund Organizations, Taxation, Invited Contractors, Local Procurement, Foreign Exchange Controls, Military Payment Certificates, Military Post Offices, Accounting Procedures, Vehicle and Driver's Licenses, Security Measures, Health and Sanitation, Enrollment and Training of Reservists.

VII This new Agreement is to remain in force as long as the US-ROK Mutual Defense Treaty remains in force unless the two Governments agree to terminate it earlier. Either Government may, at any time, request revision of any Article in the Agreement, in which case the two Governments shall enter into negotiations through appropriate channels.

0232

- 5 -

0233

대 한 민 국 외 무 부

발신전보

번 호: WUS-07140

일 시: 091450

수 신: 주미대사

미주과	암고재	담당과장	국장	차관	장관	외신과 수암호

대 :USW-0748 호 및 동 741호

연 :WUS-0735 호

1. 국무성과 계속 접촉함에 있어서 다음 사항을 참고 하시기 바람.

   가. 미국 대사관측에 의하면 국무성에서는 윤공사가 우리측 입장을 제시한후 미국 대사관에 의견을 문의하여 왔다 하며,

   나. 미국 대사관 측에서는 연 WUS-0735 호에서 언급한 우리측 입장을 검토후 금 7월 9일 오전중에 본국 정부에 현지 의견을 상신하였다함.

2. 내주중에 있을 최종회의 후 협정문 작성이 완료되는 대로 다음 파우치 편에 협정문을 송부할 예정이며 최종회의 후 다음과 같은 Press Release 를 발표할 예정이오니 참고 하시기 바람. (발표 시기는 차후 지시하겠음).

Press Release on US-ROK Agreement on SOFA

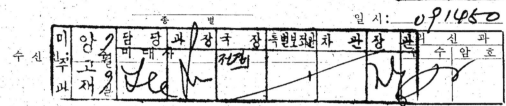

" "The Korean and American negotiators reached full agreement on the US-ROK Status of Forces Agreement at the 82nd negotiating session on July____, 1965. Final Agreement was reached on the wording of three key articles, Criminal Jurisdiction, Labor, and Claims, as well as on all other previously unresolved articles.

0234

송신시간:

타자 • 판치	검 인	주무자	과 장

The ROK Foreign Minister, Mr. Lee Tong-won, and the American Ambassador, Mr. Winthrop G. Brown, will sign the document in Seoul as soon as the formal texts have been prepared. The Agreement includes a Preamble and 31 articles covering all aspects of relations between the Government of the Republic of Korea and the United States military forces in Korea.

The new agreement will enter into force three months after the date the Korean Government notifies the U. S. Government that it has approved the Agreement in accordance with its legal procedures. The Status of Forces Agreement will supercede and replace Taejon Agreement of July 12, 1950 and Agreement on Economic Coordination of May 24, 1952 between Unfied Command and the Republic of Korea, as related to U.S. armed forces in Korea."

3. 한.미간 정식조인은 국무회의 의 의결이 끝나는대로 있을 것인바 내주말 경이 될 것이며 그후 국회에 동의를 요청할 계획임. (외구미)

장 관

보통문서로 재분류 (1966.12.31)

0235

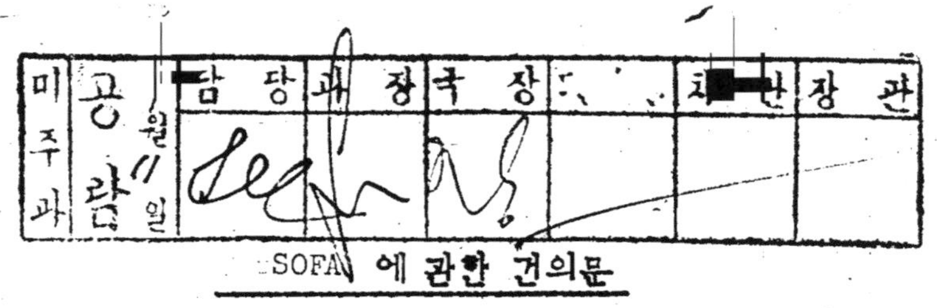

SOFA에 관한 건의문

1966. 7. 11.

가. 대한 변호사 협회에서는 SOFA 비공식 합의내용에 대한 다음과 같은 보완 건의문을 존슨 미대통령에게 발송하였다함.

1. 형사 재판권

가) 한국은 제1차 재판권을 일괄적으로 포기하여서는 아니되며 미국당국으로 부터 요청을 받을 때에는 호의적인 고려를 할수 있도록 보완하여야 함.

나) 공무집행중 범죄 여부의 판정은 미군 지휘관에게 부여하여서는 아니되며, 한.미 양국 법무관으로 구성된 합동위원회가 결정하여야 함.

다) 미군이 사용중인 시설과 구역에서의 체포권이 인정되어야 함.

2. 청구권

가) 공무집행중 여부에 불구하고, 손해배상액은 한.미 양국이 25%-75% 비율로 부담할 것이 아니라 미국이 전적으로 부담하여야 하며,

나) 청구권의 적용시기를 서울 지역과 기타지역으로 구분함이 없이 일률적으로 6개월 이내로 하여야 함.

0236

3. 노 무

가) 미군당국의 노무자의 모집은 간접 고용제도로 하여야 하며,

나) 한국 노무자에 대하여서는 한국의 노동법령을 적용하여야 하며,

다) 노동쟁의의 냉각 기간을 70일 대신 30일로 보완하고,

라) 군사상의 필요는 한·미 합동위원회에서 결정하도록 하여야 함.

나. 금번 체결된 SOFA 에서 건의안중 형사 재판권의 (가) 및 (나) 청구권의 (나), 노무의 (나) 및 (라) 항의 건의는 이를 대체적으로 충족하였으며, 기타 부분에서도 한국측 의견이 반영될수 있도록 강구 하였음.

0237

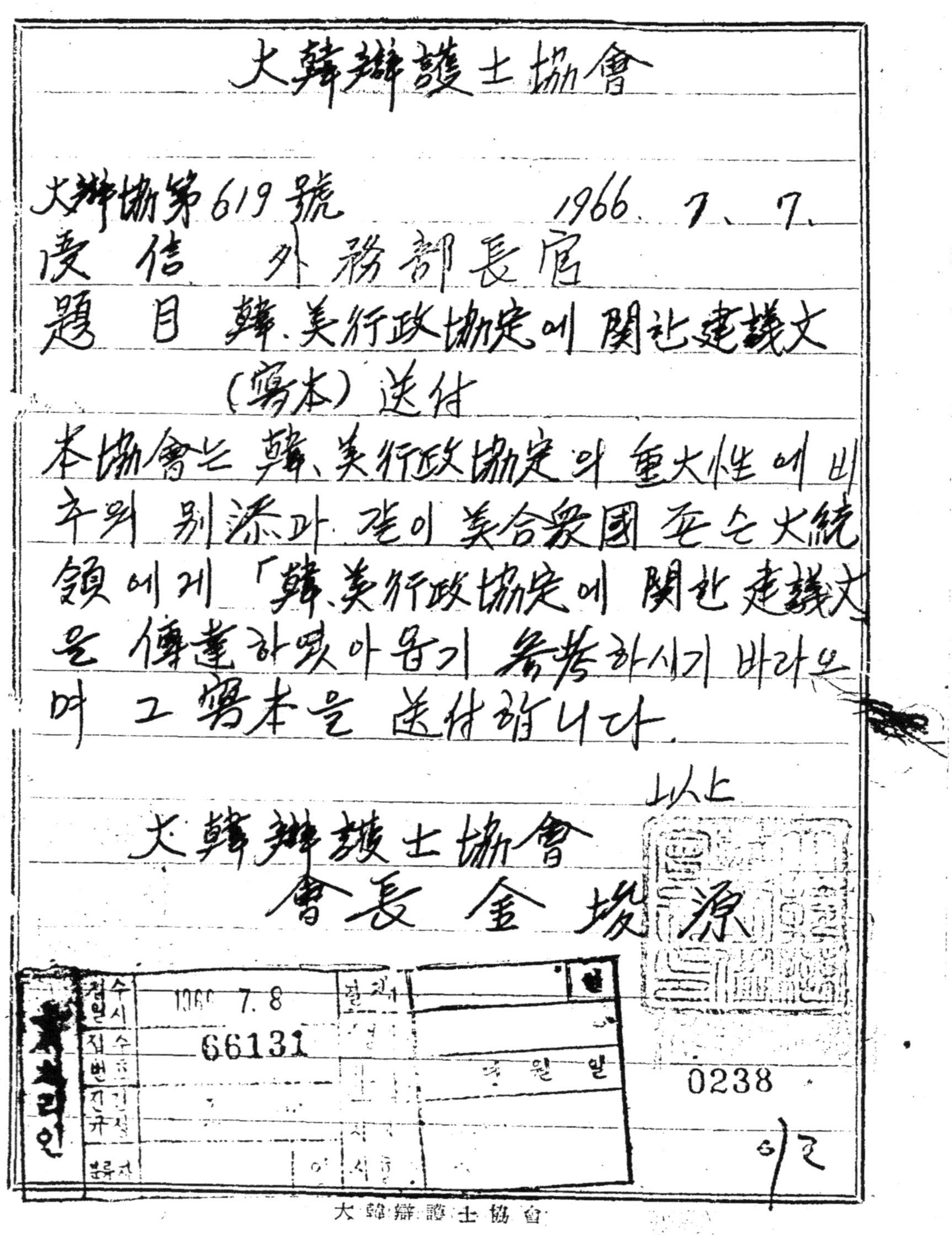
大韓辯護士協會

大辯協第619號 1966. 7. 7.
受信 外務部長官
題目 韓.美行政協定에 関한 建議文 (寫本) 送付

本協會는 韓.美行政協定의 重大性에 비추워 別添과 같이 美合衆國 존슨大統領에게 「韓.美行政協定에 関한 建議文」을 傳達하였아옵기 參考하시기 바라오며 그 寫本을 送付합니다.

以上

大韓辯護士協會
會長 金埈源

접수일시	1966. 7. 8	결재
접수번호	66131	
처리기간		
분류기호		

처리인

0238

大韓辯護士協會

美合衆國大統領 존슨閣下에게 보내는

韓·美行政協定에 關한 建議文

大韓辯護士協會

0239

134

尊敬하는

美國존슨大統領閣下

本協會는 韓美行政協定의 締結을 앞두고 全國辯護士会의 聯合団体인 大韓辯護士協会의 議決을 거쳐 閣下께 이 建議文을 드리게 된것을 無限히 기쁘게 생각합니다.

本協会는 閣下가 韓國의 自由와 安全을 保障하기 為하여 美合衆國軍隊를 韓國에 駐屯시키고 있는 事実에 対하여 衷心으로 敬意를 表하는 바입니다.

本協会는 集団的安全保障下에 오늘의 國際社会에 있어서 韓國을 防禦하는것이 곧 自由世界를 防禦하는 길이라고 確信합니다. 그러므로 共産侵略의 危險性이 아직 가시지않는 韓國에 있어서는 美合衆國軍隊의 駐屯이 継續必要한 것입니다.

이에 있어서 힘의 支配를 排斥하고 法의 支配를 이룩하고저하는 自由世界의 理念에 立脚하여 韓國에 駐屯하고 있는 美合衆國軍隊의 地位에 関한 協定이 [illegible] 그

-1-

0240

무엇보다 時急한에도 不拘하고 長久한 時日을 거친 오늘에 이르기까지 아직 締結되지 않고 있다는 事实은 法治主義를 追求하고 있는 韓國民에게 커다란 失望을 던저주고 있읍니다.

그뿐만 아니라 國際社会에 있어서의 모든 外交協定은 國家의 領土나 人口의 多小 國力의 强弱等으로 因하여 何等 差别을 받음이 없이 언제나 主權平等의 原則下에 이루어져야 한다고 本協会는 믿는 바입니다.

그러나 國内新聞에 報道된 韓美行政協定의 草案内容中에는 主權國家인 大韓民國의 國威宣揚에 未洽한 條項이 包含되어 있어 이를 反対하는 韓國民의 輿論을 惹起시키고 있다는 事実을 閣下께 말씀드리지 않을 수 없는 것입니다.

0241

本協会는 大韓民國의 憲法에 保障된 國民의 基本的人權을 侵害하거나 또는 主權國家인 韓國의 司法權에 重大한 制限을 加하는 如何한 協定內容에 対하여도 이를 斷乎히 反対합니다.

本協会는 韓美行政協定의 具体的內容에 対하여 여기서 仔細히 言及하려고는 하지 않읍니다.

다만 위 協定의 草案內容中 大韓民國의 主權行使에 重大한 制限을 加하고 있는 다음 몇가지 條項에 対하여 閣下께서 是正하여 주시기를 建議하오니 閣下의 誠意있는 配慮를 促求하는 바입니다.

本協会는 韓美行政協定의 草案內容에 対한 補完與否가 法의 支配를 이룩하고

0242

-4-

저하는 韓國에 있어서 하나의 試金石이 되고 있다는 事実을 여기에 다시금 強調하면서 閣下의 職務에 榮光이 있기를 바라마지 않읍니다.

記

(一) 刑事裁判管轄權

(1) 草案內容에 依하면

韓國은 美軍所属員의 非公務中에 犯한 事件에 対하여 第一次的裁判権을 가지되 위 裁判権을 美國当局에 一括的으로 抛棄한後 必要에 따라서 그 撤回를 美國当局에 要請할 수 있다는 趣旨의 規定을 두고 있읍니다.

0243

그러나

이와 같은 規定은

主權優先의 原則에 어긋날 뿐만아니라 美軍所屬員에게 治外法權과 類似한 特權을 賦與하게 되므로 主權國家인 韓國으로서는 絶對的으로 容納될 수 없는 屈辱的인 規定이라고 보지 않을 수 없읍니다.

國際慣例上 美國은 敗戰國家가 아닌 韓國政府에게 屈辱的인 裁判權拋棄를 强要할수 없는것입니다.

따라서

韓國은 第一次的裁判權을 一括的으로 拋棄할것이 아니라 美國当局으로부터

裁判權抛棄의 要請을 받을때에는 國際禮讓上 그 要請에 好意的인 考慮를 할 수 있도록 補完하여야 합니다.

(2) 또한 草案內容에 依하면 公務, 非公務의 判定은 美軍准將級以上의 指揮官이 発給한 公務証明書에 依하여 이를 決定한다는 趣旨의 規定을 두고 있읍니다.

그러나 韓國에 賦與된 第一次的裁判權行使에 重大한 影響을 미치고 있는 公務, 非公務의 判定權限을 美軍指揮官에게 一任하는 境遇에는 美軍指揮官이 그 權限을 濫用할 憂慮가 있는 것입니다.

萬一 美軍指揮官이 非公務中의 犯罪行爲를 公務中에 発生한 犯罪라고 独断解釋하는 境遇에는 韓國은 第一次的裁判權을 行使할 수 없게 되는 것입니다.

따라서

實재로 公務, 非公務의 判定權限을 美軍指揮官에게 賦與할것이 아니라 韓美合同委員會에서 決定하도록 補充하여야하며 둘째로 韓美合同委員會는 韓美軍 法務官과 韓國法官으로써 構成하도록 補充하여야 합니다.

(3) 또한 草案內容에 依하면 美軍地域과 그 附近에서 發生한 犯罪事件에 對하여는 韓國搜査官憲이 被疑者인 美軍所屬員을 逮捕할수 없다는 趣旨의 規定을 두고 있읍니다.

그러나 美軍地域內에서 發生한 犯罪事件에 對하여는 一理가 있으나 「그 附近에서」 發生한 犯罪事件에 對해서까지 이를 逮捕할수 없다는 規定은 韓國의 領土主權을 侵害하는 規定이라고 보지않을수 없읍니다.

따라서

0246

첫째로 위 草案內容中 「그附近에서」 라는 部分은 削除되어야 하며

둘째로 韓國이 裁判權을 行事할수있는 犯罪事件에 對하여는 韓國捜査當局에게 逮捕權을 賦與하도록 補完되어야 합니다.

(二) 民事請求權

(1) 草案內容에 依하면 美軍이 公務執行中 韓國民間人에게 입힌 損害補償은 그 補償額이 一, 四〇〇弗以上일 境遇에는 美國이 75% 韓國이 25%의 比率로 分割補償한다는 趣旨의 規定을 두고 있읍니다.

그러나

美國의 經濟的援助에 依存하고있는 韓國實情으로서는 法理上 美國이 負担하여야할 補償金까지 이를 分割補償할수 없는 것입니다.

따라서

美軍이 公務執行中에 韓國民間人에게 입힌 損害는 勿論이요 非公務中에 입힌 損害에 對하여도 美國이 全的으로 이를 負担하도록 補完하여야 합니다.

라) 또한 草案內容에 依하면 民事請求權의 適用時期를 「서울地域」은 六個月以內에 「其他地域」은 韓美合同委員會에서 合意를 보는 時期에 適用한다는 趣旨의 規定을 두고 있읍니다.

그러나 韓國에 있어서의 美軍人 犯罪의 75%는 서울以外의 地域에서 發生하고 있는 것입니다. 그러므로 韓·美 合同委員會가 서울以外의 地域에 對한 適用時期에 對하여 合意를 보지못할 境遇에는 韓國民間人은 事實上 民事請求權을 行使할수 없는것입니다.

이와같은 規定은 韓國憲法에 保障된 「裁判을 받을 權利」를 侵害하는 規定

~9~

0248

이라고 보지않을수 없는것입니다

따라서

民事請求權의 適用時期를 「서울地域」과 「其他地域」으로 區分함이 없이 一律的으로 六個月以内로 補完하여야 합니다.

(三) 勞動條項

(1) 草案内容에 依하면 美軍當局은 韓國政府를 거치지않고 勞務者를 募集하는 直接雇傭制度를 採擇하는 趣旨의 規定을 두고 있읍니다

그러나

첫째로 이와같은 規定은 國際的 先例에 어긋남으로 韓國政府가 勞務者를 募集하여 美軍에게 보내는 間接雇傭制度를 採擇하도록 補完하여야하며

둘째로 韓國勞動者에 對하여는 主權優先의 原則에 依하여 韓國의 勞動法令을

0249

適用하도록 補完하여야 합니다

(2) 또한 草案內容에 依하면 勞動爭議가 發生한 境遇에는 七○日間의 仲裁冷却期間을 둔後에 罷業할수 있도록 規定하였으며 軍事上 必要한 때에는 罷業을 中止시킬수 있다는 趣旨의 規定을 두고있읍니다.

그러나

첫재로 七○日間의 冷却期間은 罷業權行使에 相當한 時日을 要하게 되므로 그期限을 三○日로 短縮하도록 補完하여야 하며

둘재로

「軍事上 必要」의 有無에 對한 決定權限을 美軍當局에 一任하는 境遇에는 美軍當局이 그權限을 濫用할 憂慮가 있읍니다. 따라서 韓美合同委員會에서

이를 決定하도록 補完하여야 합니다.

以上

一九六六年 七月 六日

大韓辯護士協會

會長 金 埈 源

0251

노　　　　동　　　　청

노정노　722.2 - 27　　22 - 4295　　1966. 7. 14.

수신　외무부장관

제목　한미간 주둔군 지위협정 체결 교섭.

1. 66. 7. 1 외무미 722.2 - 606 에 대한 응신 입니다.

2. 제17조 제4항에 있어 66. 6. 9한국측 재교섭 수정안과 같이 고용주가 합중국군대의 군사상 필요 때문에 본조에 따라 적용되는 대한민국 노동법령을 따를수 없을때에는 그 문제는 사전에 상호 합의를 위하여 합동 위원회에 회부 하여야 하는 것이며 비공식 합의내용과 같이 가능한 사전에 검토와 적당한 조처를 위하여 합동위원회에 회부한다.면 사전에 합동 위원회에 회부안할수 있고 또 이로 인하여 필요이상의 분규나 알륵이 생길 우려가 있음으로 한국측 재교섭 수정안과 같이 사전에 상호 합의를 위하여 합동 위원회에 회부함이 타당 할것임. 끝.

노　동　청　장

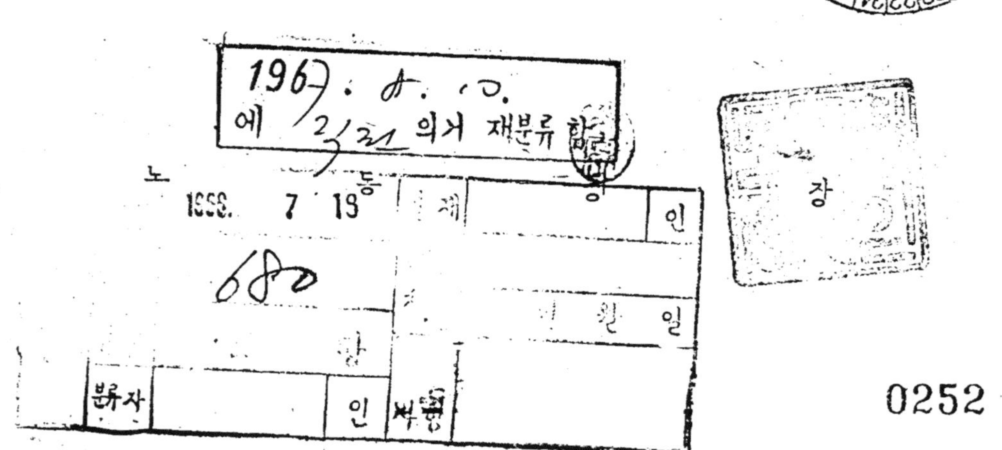
1967. 12. 31. 에 예고문에 의거 재분류 함

0252

군사상 필요와 쟁의행위

1. 제17조 제3항은 "본조의 규정과 합중국 군대의 필요에 배치되지 아니하는 한도내에서,.... 노사관계는 대한민국의 노동법령의 제규정에 따라야 한다"고 규정하여 고용주인 합중국 군 당국은 원칙적으로 우리나라 노동관계법령을 존중하게 되어 있다.

2. 그러나 그들이 군사상 필요로 인하여 대한민국의 노동법령을 지킬수 없을때에는 합의의사록 제4항에 따라 사전에 검토와 적당한 조치를 위하여 합동위원회에 회부하여야 하며 여기서도 합의가 이루어질수 없을때에는 우리나라 정부 관계당국과 합중국 외교사절간의 토의를 통한 재 검토의 대상이 되어야 한다.

3. 따라서, 합의의사록 제2항 후단에서 "합중국 정부는 고용을 계속 하는것이 합중국 군대의 군사상 필요에 배치되는 경우에는 어느 때든지 어떠한 고용을 종료시킬수 있다"고 규정하고 있지만 이때에도 군사상 필요 여부는 합동위원회에서 한.미 양국 대표에 의하여 사전에 검토 합의되어야 하며 합중국 군당국이 이러한 재결권을 가지지 않고 일방적으로 해고하는 경우에는 고용원이나 노조는 쟁의행위를 할수 있음은 물론이다.

0253

7. 노 무

1. 노무조항은 미국군이나 그 초청계약자가 한국민간인을 고용함에 있어서의 방법, 조건, 보상 및 노사관계를 규정하는 조항이다. 이 조항은 먼저 고용주를 미군기관과 초청계약자로 하고 그들은 한국인 고용원을 직접 고용하는 종래의 제도를 지속하되 가능한 한 한국정부의 모집기관을 통하여 모집하기로 하였다. 이 조항은 고용조건, 보상 및 노사관계에 있어서 한국 노동관계법령을 준수할것을 원칙으로 하였으며 미군의 군사상 필요로 한국 법령을 준수치 못할 경우에는 사전에 합동위원회에 회부하여 해결방안을 강구하기로 하였다. 그리고 고용주와 고용원간의 노동쟁의는 우선 불평처리와 노동관계절차 (노사협의 절차)에 의하여 해결하되, (1) 노동청에 회부하여 조정하고, (2) 합동위원회에 회부하고 그는 특별분과위원회에 조정을 의뢰하며, (3) 합동위원회가 직접 해결하기로 하였다. 이 합동위원회의 결정은 구속력을 가지되 제2단계인 합동위원회에 회부된후 70일이 경과하여도 해결이 되지 않을 경우 모든 고용원과 고용원단체는 그 후에 계속하여 단체행동권을 가진다. 다만 그러한 행동이 한국의 공동방위에 있어서 미군의 군사작전을 격심하게 방해한다고 합동위원회가 결정하는 경우는 제외된다. 노동조합은 한.미 공동이익에 배반되지 않는한 당연히 승인되기로 되어 있다.

2. 이상과 같은 규정에 따라 이점을 보면 아래와 같다.

가. 미군과 초청계약자는 종래와 같이 직접 고용과 관리를 할수 있으나

가능한 한 한국정부의 모집기관을 통하여 모집하며, 그 모집에 소요된 경비는 판상하기로 되어있으며 고용주가 직접 모집하였을 시는 그 정보를 한국 노동청에 통보하게 함으로서 종래 소홀하였던 미군에 의한 한국인 고용상태를 한국정부가 파악할수 있게되었다.

나. 고용주는 고용의 조건, 보상 (임금 및 기타 급부등) 및 노사관계에 있어서 한국 노동법령을 준수하기로 하였으며, 미군의 군사적 사태때문에 한국 법령을 따를수 없을때에는 사전에 합동위원회에 회부하여 적절한 조치를 취하기로 하였으며, 합동위원회에서 그러한 조치에 관하여 상호 합의가 되지 않을 경우에는 외교경로를 통하여 재 검토하여 해결하게 된다.

다. 그리고 노동쟁의 조정에 있어서 미군은 국제법상 면제권을 갖기 때문에 우리 노동위원회의 재정에 복하게 할수는 없으며, 70일의 냉각기간을 설정한 것은 한국 노동쟁의의 조정법에 비추어 보아 장기간이라 할수 없다. (동 법에는 70일내지 80일이됨)

그리고 고용원의 단체 행동권이 조정기간 70일 경과후 한국방위에 있어서 미군의 군사작전을 방해 한다고 합동위원회가 결정하는 경우 그 행동권을 제한할수 있도록 결정하고 있으나 한국이 합의한 경우에 한하는 것이며, 이 규정은 한국 헌법 제29조 제1항과 제32조 제2항의 취지에 입각하여 설정한 것이다. 따라서 전체 고용원은 원칙상 모두 단체 행동권을 가지며 특별한 경우 즉, 군사 작전상 절대로 불가피할 경우에만 한국측의 합의하에 단체 행동권의 행사를 일시적으로 제한할 필요가 있을 것이라는 가상하에 설정한 것으로 그러한 경우는 대체로 비상사태가 발생하였을 때일 것이다.

라. 끝으로 이 규정으로 고용주는 고용원에게 급료를 지불하게 함에 있어서 한국 소득세 법에 따라 고용원의 급료중에서 소득에 대한 원천과세액을 공제하여 동 액을 한국 정부에 납부하게 되었다.

0256

7. 労　　務

1. 労務条項는 美軍이나 그 招請契約者가 韓国民間人을 雇傭함에 있어서의 方法, 条件, 補償, 및 労使関係를 規定하는 条項이다. 이 条項은 먼저 雇傭主를 美軍機関과 招請契約者로 하고 그들은 韓国人雇傭員을 直接雇傭하는 従来의 制度를 持続하되 可能한限 韓国政府의 募集機関을 通하여 募集하기로 하였다. 이 条項은 雇傭条件, 補償 및 労使関係에 있어서 韓国労動関係法令을 遵守할 것을 原則으로 하였으며 美軍의 軍事上 必要로 韓国法令을 遵守치 못할 境遇에는 可能한限 事前에 合同委員会에 回附하여 解決方案을 講究하기로 하였다. 그리고 雇傭主와 雇傭員間의 労動争議는 우선 不平処理와 労動関係節次 (労使協議節次)에 依하여 解決되지 않을 境遇 (1) 労動庁에 回附하여 調整하고, (2) 合同委員会에 回附하고 그는 特別分科委員会에 調整을 依頼하며 (3) 合同委員会가 直接解決하기로 하였다. 이 合同委員会의 決定은 拘束力을 가지되 第2段階인 合同委員会에 回附된後 70日이 経過하여도 解決이 되지 않을 境遇 雇傭員은 合同委員会가 定한 特別한 者를 除外하고는 団体行動権을 行使할 수 있게 된다. 労動組合은 韓美共同利益에 背反되지 않는限 当然히 承認되기로 되어 있다.

2. 以上과 같은 規定에 따라 利点을 보면 아래와 같다.

가. 美軍과 招請契約者는 従来와 같이 直接雇傭과 管理를 할 수 있으나 可能한限 韓国政府의 募集機関을 通하여 募集하며 그 募集에 所要된 経費는 弁償하기로 되었으며 雇傭主가 直接募集하였을 時는 그 情報를 韓国労動庁에 通報하게 함으로서 従来

-21-

(手書き: 解決되며, 모든 可能한 方法을 ... 계속하여 가진다 ; 다만 그러한 行動이 韓国의 共同防衛에 있어서 美軍의 軍事作戦을 [illegible]하게 妨害한다고 合同委員会가 決定하는 境遇는 [illegible]되어야 한다.)

0257

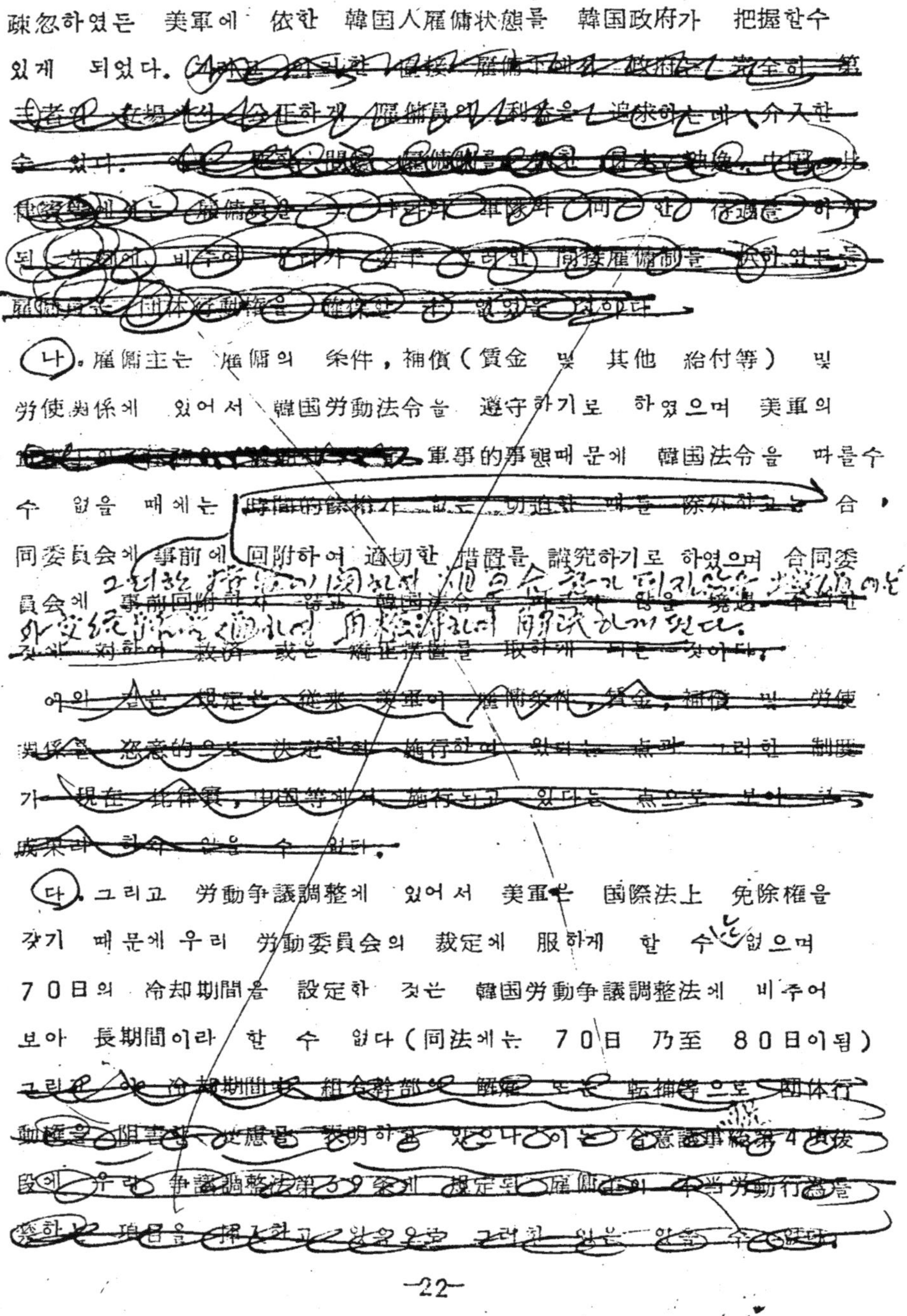
疎忽하였든 美軍에 依한 韓国人雇傭状態를 韓国政府가 把握할수 있게 되었다.

나. 雇傭主는 雇傭의 条件, 補償(賃金 및 其他 給付等) 및 労使関係에 있어서 韓国労動法令을 遵守하기로 하였으며 美軍의 軍事的事態때문에 韓国法令을 따를수 수 없을 때에는 合同委員会에 事前에 回附하여 適切한 措置를 講究하기로 하였으며 合同委員会에 그러한 措置에 関하여 合意가 되지 않을 때에는 外交經路를 通하여 再検討하여 解決하게 되었다.

다. 그리고 労動争議調整에 있어서 美軍은 国際法上 免除権을 갖기 때문에 우리 労動委員会의 裁定에 服하게 할 수는 없으며 70日의 冷却期間을 設定한 것은 韓国労動争議調整法에 비추어 보아 長期間이라 할 수 없다(同法에는 70日 乃至 80日이됨)

-22-

0258

그리고 雇傭員中 一部 緊要한 雇傭員에 対하여 合同委員会의 決定에 따라 团体行動權의 行使를 制限하기로 되여 있으나 이는 韓国側이 合意한 雇傭員에 限하는 것이며 团体行動權의 行使가 雇傭員全体의 權益을 向上시키는데 있음에 鑑하여 반드시 全体雇傭員이 行動에 加担할 必要는 없으며 多大數雇傭員의 行動으로 目的을 貫撤하고 制限받았든 雇傭員도 그 結果에 따라 自動的으로 恩択을 받으면 目的을 達하는 것으로 본다.

라) 끝으로 이 規定으로 雇傭主는 雇傭員에게 給料를 支払함에 있어서 韓国所得税法에 따라 雇傭員의 給料中에서 所得에 対한 源泉課税額을 控除하여 同額을 韓国政府에 納付하게 되있다.

이로서 從來 疎忽하였든 美軍関係雇傭員에 対한 合法的課税制度가 確立될 것이며 雇傭員들은 国民의 納税義務를 다하는 同時에 政府는 数億원의 達하는 国庫收入을 바로 잡게 된다.

이 規定은 韓國憲法 [illegible] 特別한 境遇 即 軍事作戰上 絶對로 不可避할 경우에만 韓國側의 合意下에 团体行動權의 行使를 一時的으로 制限할 경우도 있을 것이라는 假想下에 設定한 것으로 必要가 그러한 境遇는 大体로 緊急事態가 発生하였을 때일 것이다.

8. 外換管理

1. 合衆国軍隊関係者들에 対한 韓国의 外換管理法遵守義務를 規定하는 한편 例外的으로 이들의 韓国駐屯目的에 비추어 正当하고 公的이며 非営利的인 美貨移転行為의 自由를 保障해 주었다.

2. 그代身 合衆国当局은 前記 特権이 濫用되지 않도록 必要한 措置를 取하여야 한다고 規定하므로써 一部 合衆国軍関係者들에 依한 特権濫用이나 外換管理法의 違反行為에 対한 防止規定을 두었다.

3. 合衆国軍 및 軍機関의 韓国人雇傭員에 対한 報酬支払은 韓国의 外換管理法 및 関係規定에 따라야 한다고 規定하였다.

4. 上記한 去来에 適用될 換率은 換銭当時 違法이 아닌 最高換로 規定하였는바 이와 同一한 用語는 이미 1961年 2月 8日 韓国과 美国政府間에 締結된 "韓美経済協力에 関한 協定"에서도 採択된바 있는 것이다.

現在 韓国에 駐屯하고 있는 合衆国軍 및 軍機関이 雇傭하고 있는 韓国人従業員에 対한 報酬支払等을 為한 韓貨需要量이 莫大한 것임에 비추어 韓国으로서는 이들에게 "不法的이 아닌 最高換率"로 換銭해 주겠다는 保障을 주므로서 이들의 換銭意慾을 도구어 줄수 있다는 利点도 있을수 있으며 "違法이 아닌"이라는 条件을 붙이므로써 如何한 境遇에도 闇市場率과 같은 違法한 換率適用可能性을 完全히 排除하였다.

Handed to U.S. side 7/9/66

제 17 조 노 무

4. (나) 고용원 또는 고용원 단체는 노동 쟁의가 전기 절차에 의하여 해결되지 아니하는 경우에는 계속 단체 행동권을 가진다. 다만, 합동위원회가 이러한 행동이 대한민국의 공동 방위를 위한 합중국 군대의 군사 작전을 심히 방해한다고 결정하는 경우에는 제외한다. 합동위원회에서 이 문제에 관하여 합의에 도달할 수 없을 경우에는 그 문제는 대한민국 정부의 관계관과 아메리카 합중국 외교 사절 간의 토의를 통한 재 검토의 대상이 될수 있다.

합의의사록

4. 고용주가 합중국 군대의 군사상 필요 때문에 본 조에 따라 적용되는 대한민국 노동 법령을 따를 수 없을 때에는, 그 문제는 사전에 검토와 적당한 조치를 위하여 합동위원회에 회부되어야 한다. 합동위원회에서 적당한 조치에 관하여 상호 합의가 이루어질 수 없을 경우에는, 그 문제는 대한민국 정부의 관계관과 아메리카 합중국의 외교 사절 간의 토의를 통한 재 검토의 대상이 될 수 있다.

0261

OK

US-ROK SOFA LABOR ARTICLE - PARAGRAPH 4 (b)

"Employees or any employee organization shall have the right of further collective action in the event a labor dispute is not resolved by the foregoing procedures except in cases where the Joint Committee determines such action seriously hampers military operations of the United States armed forces for the joint defense of the Republic of Korea. In the event an agreement cannot be reached on this question in the Joint Committee, it may be made the subject of review through discussions between appropriate officials of the Government of the Republic of Korea and the diplomatic mission of the United States of America."

0262

ARTICLE XVII LABOR

AGREED UNDERSTANDING TO AGREED MINUTE NO. 4

Reference: 82nd Meeting, July 8, 1966

"It is understood that the deviation from Korean labor legislation need not be referred to the Joint Committee in cases when such referral would seriously hamper military operations in an emergency."

韓國 勞動法令으로부터의 離脫은 合同委員會에의 回附가 緊急時에 軍事作戰을 甚히 妨害할 境遇에는 回附할 必要가 없는 것으로 諒解한다.

0263

AGREED MINUTE OF ARTICLE 17

"4. When employers cannot conform with provisions of labor legislation of the Republic of Korea applicable under this Article on account of the military requirement of the United States armed forces, the matter shall be referred, in advance, to the Joint Committee for consideration and appropriate action. In the event mutual agreement cannot be reached in the Joint Committee regarding appropriate action, the issue may be made the subject of review through discussions between appropriate officials of the Government of the Republic of Korea and the diplomatic mission of the United States of America."

0264

ARTICLE XVII LABOR

4. Employees or any employee organization shall have the right of further collective action in the event a labor dispute is not resolved by the foregoing procedures except in cases where the Joint Committee determines such action seriously hampers military operations of the United States armed forces for the joint defense of the Republic of Korea. In the event an agreement cannot be reached on this question in the Joint Committee, it may be made the subject of review through discussions between appropriate officials of the Government of the Republic of Korea and the diplomatic mission of the United States of America.

AGREED MINUTES

4. When employers cannot conform with provisions of labor legislation of the Republic of Korea applicable under this Article on account of the military requirements of the United States armed forces, the matter shall be referred, in advance, to the Joint Committee for consideration and appropriate action. In the event mutual agreement cannot be reached in the Joint Committee regarding appropriate action, the issue may be made the subject of review through discussions between appropriate officials of the Government of the Republic of Korea and the diplomatic mission of the United States of America.

0265

第17條 勞務

4. (나) 雇傭員 또는 雇傭員 團体는, 勞動爭議가 前記 節次에 依하여 解決되지 아니하는 境遇에는 繼續 團体行動權을 가진다. 다만, 合同委員会가 이러한 行動이 大韓民國의 共同防衛를 爲한 合衆國 軍隊의 軍事作戰을 甚히 妨害한다고 決定하는 境遇에는 除外한다. 合同委員会에서 이 問題에 関하여 合意에 到達할 수 없을 境遇에는 그 問題는 大韓民國政府의 関係官과 아메리카合衆國 外交使節團의 討議를 通한 再檢討의 対象이 될 수 있다.

0266

US-ROK SOFA LABOR ARTICLE - PARAGRAPH 4 (b)

"Employees or any employee organization shall have the right of further collective action in the event a labor dispute is not resolved by the foregoing procedures except in cases where the Joint Committee determines such action seriously hampers military operations of the United States armed forces for the joint defense of the Republic of Korea. In the event an agreement cannot be reached on this question in the Joint Committee, it may be made the subject of review through discussions between appropriate officials of the Government of the Republic of Korea and the diplomatic mission of the United States of America."

OK

0267

韓美間 駐屯軍地位協定案 対比表

第17條 勞務

非公式合意案	韓國改正案	美國側代案
4. (나) 勞動爭議調整을 위한 70日間의 冷却期間經過後 団体行動权을 行使하여서는 아니될 緊要한 雇傭員의 範疇는 合同委員会에서 決定한다.	4. (나) 勞動爭議調整을 위한 70日間의 冷却期間經過後 모든 雇傭員은 団体行動权을 갖되, 다만 軍事作戰을 甚히 阻害하는 境遇에는 除外된다.	4. (나) 左 韓國案受諾.
合意議事錄 4. 美軍이 軍事上 必要로 韓國勞動法令을 지키지 못할 때에는 그 問題를 可能한 限 事前에 合同委員会에 回附하여 檢討하고 適当한 措置를 講究한다.	4. 美軍이 軍事上 必要로 韓國勞動法令을 지키지 못할 때에는 그 問題를 事前에 合同委員会에 回附하여 検討하고 適当한 措置를 講究한다.	4. (非公式合意案主張)
諒解事項 韓國勞動法으로부터의 離脫中 軍事作戰을 甚히 阻害하는 것은 合同委員会에 回附할 必要없다.	韓國勞動法으로부터 離脫中 緊急事態下에 軍事作戰을 甚히 阻害하는 것은 合同委員会에 回附할 必要없다.	(非公式合意案主張)

0268

DEPARTMENT OF STATE
WASHINGTON

July 19, 1966

Mr. Sang Mun Chang
Director, Europe and America Bureau
Ministry of Foreign Affairs
Seoul, Korea

Dear Mr. Chang:

Please accept my hearty congratulations on the signing of the SOFA! I have just finished reading the minutes of the 82nd negotiating meeting and I wish to associate myself with the remarks of the U.S. negotiators concerning the patience and friendly cooperation displayed by the Korean negotiators throughout the negotiations. I know that Phil Habib would join me in doing so, if he were here.

I trust that the successful outcome of these negotiations will provide a basis for cementing even more firmly the very close and friendly relations which exist between our two governments. And I hope that the experience gained during these negotiations will assist both sides in swiftly reaching full agreement on the provisions of the KSC Agreement.

I know that you personally must feel a great sense of relief that the long drawn-out SOFA negotiation has been finally brought to a successful conclusion. I am sure that your contributions, as chief Korean negotiator, to the success of the negotiations will receive the recognition they deserve.

Please extend my personal greetings and congratulations to the other members of the Korean negotiating team. Mr. Lee has indicated that he will be visiting Washington with the Foreign Minister and I look forward to welcoming him to Washington. Nothing would please me more than to be able to welcome you as well. I might even be able to produce a cup of ginseng tea for the occasion!

With best regards from Mrs. Fleck and me to you and Mrs. Chang,

Sincerely yours,

Ben Fleck

Benjamin A. Fleck
Country Director for Korea
Bureau of Far Eastern Affairs

0269

정/리/보/존/문/서/목/록					
기록물종류	문서-일반공문서철	등록번호	935 9608	등록일자	2006-07-27
분류번호	741.12	국가코드	US	주제	
문서철명	한.미국 간의 상호방위조약 제4조에 의한 시설과 구역 및 한국에서의 미국군대의 지위에 관한 협정 (SOFA) 전59권. 1966.7.9 서울에서 서명 : 1967.2.9 발효 (조약 232호) *원본				
생산과	미주과/조약과	생산년도	1952 - 1967	보존기간	영구
담당과(그룹)	조약	조약	서가번호	--	
참조분류					
권차명	V.37 실무교섭회의, 제82차, 1966.7.8 (I)				
내용목차	* 일지 : 1953.8.7 이승만 대통령-Dulles 미국 국무장관 공동성명 - 상호방위조약 발효 후 군대지위협정 교섭 약속 1954.12.2 정부, 주한 UN군의 관세업무협정 체결 제의 1955.1월, 5월 미국, 제의 거절 1955.4.28 정부, 군대지위협정 제의 (한국측 초안 제시) 1957.9.10 Hurter 미국 국무차관 방한 시 각서 수교 (한국측 제의 수락 요구) 1957.11.13, 26 정부, 개별 협정의 단계적 체결 제의 1958.9.18 Dawling 주한미국대사, 형사재판관할권 협정 제외 조건으로 행정협정 체결 의사 전달 1960.3.10 정부, 토지, 시설협정의 우선적 체결 강력 요구 1961.4.10 장면 국무총리-McConaughy 주한미국대사 공동성명으로 교섭 개시 합의 1961.4.15, 4.25 제1, 2차 한.미국 교섭회의 (서울) 1962.3.12 정부, 교섭 재개 촉구 공한 송부 1962.5.14 Burger 주한미국대사, 최규하 장관 면담 시 형사재판관할권 문제 제기 않는 조건으로 교섭 재개 통고 1962.9.6 한.미국 간 공동성명 발표 (9월 중 교섭 재개 합의) 1962.9.20~ 1965.6.7 제1-81차 실무 교섭회의 (서울) 1966.7.8 제82차 실무 교섭회의 (서울) 1966.7.9 서명 1967.2.9 발효 (조약 232호)				

마/이/크/로/필/름/사/항

촬영연도	*롤 번호	화일 번호	후레임 번호	보관함 번호
2006-11-23	I-06-0070	05	1-227	

0001

제23조 청 구 권

합의의사록

1. 달리 규정하는 경우를 제외하고는, 본조의 제5항, 제6항, 제7항 및 제8항의 규정은, 서울특별시의 지역에서 일어난 사건으로부터 발생한 청구권에 관하여는, 본 협정의 효력 발생일 후 6개월만에, 그리고 대한민국 안 다른 곳에서 발생한 청구권에 관하여는, 본 협정의 효력 발생일 후 1년만에, 효력이 발생하게 된다.

0002

AGREED MINUTE 1 TO ARTICLE XXIII: CLAIMS

Article XXIII

1. Unless otherwise provided, the provisions of paragraphs 5, 6, 7 and 8 of this Article will become effective six months from the date of entry into force of this Agreement with respect to claims arising from incidents in the Seoul Special City area, and one year from that date with respect to claims arising elsewhere in the Republic of Korea.

0003

④ Re Paragraph 1(a)

~~AGREED MINUTE RE PARA 1(A) of Article 22~~

~~Re Paragraph 1(a)~~

It is understood that under the present state of United States law, the military authorities of the United States have no effective criminal jurisdiction in peacetime over members of the civilian component or dependents. If the scope of United States military jurisdiction changes as a result of subsequent legislation, constitutional amendment, or decision by appropriate authorities of the United States, the Government of the United States shall inform the Government of the Republic of Korea through diplomatic channels.

合衆國 法律의 現狀態 下에서 合衆國 軍當局은 平和時에는 軍屬 및 家族에 對하여 有效한 刑事裁判權을 가지지 아니한다. 追後의 立法, 憲法改正, 또는 合衆國 關係當局에 依한 決定의 結果로서 合衆國 軍事裁判權의 範圍가 變更된다면, 合衆國 政府는 外交經路를 通하여 大韓民國 政府에 通告하여야 한다.

0004

US-ROK SOFA AGREED MINUTE RE PARAGRAPH 2 OF CRIMINAL JURISDICTION ARTICLE

Re Paragraph 2

The Republic of Korea, recognizing the effectiveness in appropriate cases of the administrative and disciplinary sanctions which may be imposed by the ~~United States authorities~~ military over members of the United States armed forces or civilian component, and their dependents, may, at the request of the military authorities of the United States, waive its right to jurisdiction under Paragraph 2.

exercise

small

그대로 살린것,
(United States authorities

大韓民國은, 合衆國 當局이 適當한 境遇에 合衆國 軍隊의 構成員, 軍屬 및 그들의 家族에 對하여 課할 수 있는 行政的 및 懲戒的 制裁의 有效性을 認定하여, 合衆國 軍 當局의 要請에 依하여 第2項에 따라 裁判權을 行使할 權利를 抛棄할 수 있다.

0005

page 263 ~ 266

(6)

US-ROK SOFA CJ ARTICLE - AGREED MINUTE RE PARAGRAPH 3(b):

Re paragraph 3 (b)

1. The authorities of the Republic of Korea, recognizing that it is the primary responsibility of the United States military authorities to maintain good order and discipline where persons subject to United States military laws are concerned, will, upon the request of the military authorities of the United States pursuant to Paragraph 3(c), waive their primary right to exercise jurisdiction under Paragraph 3(b) except when they determine that it is of particular importance that jurisdiction be exercised by the authorities of the Republic of Korea.

2. With the consent of the competent authorities of the Republic of Korea, the military authorities of the United States may transfer to the courts or authorities of the Republic of Korea for investigation, trial and decision, particular criminal cases in which jurisdiction rests with the United States.

With the consent of the military authorities of the United States, the competent authorities of the Republic of Korea may transfer to the military authorities of the United States for investigation, trial and decision, particular criminal cases in which jurisdiction rests with the Republic of Korea.

3. (a) Where a member of the United States armed forces or civilian component, or a dependent, is arraigned before a court of the United States, for an offense committed in the Republic of Korea against Korean interests, the trial shall be held within the Republic of Korea

0006

(i) except where the law of the United States requires otherwise, or

(ii) except where, in cases of military exigence or in the interests of justice, the military authorities of the United States intend to hold the trial outside the Republicof Korea. In this event they shall afford the authorities of the Republic of Korea timely opportunity to comment on such intention and shall give due consideration to any comments the latter may make.

(b) Where the trial is held outside of the Republic of Korea the military authorities of the United States shall inform the authorities of the Republic of Korea of the place and date of the trial. A representative of the Republic of Korea shall be entitled to be present at the trial. The authorities of the United States shall inform the authorities of the Republic of Korea of the judgment and the final outcome of the proceedings.

"4. In the implementation of the provisions of this Article, and to facilitate the expeditious disposal of offenses, arrangements may be made between ~~the United States military authorities and the competent authorities of the Republic of Korea~~."

the competent authorities of the Republic of Korea and the military authorities of the United States.

0007

(合意議事錄)

第32項 (나)에 關하여

1. 大韓民國 당국은, 合衆國 軍法에 服하는 者에 關하여 秩序와 規律을 維持함이 合衆國 軍 당국의 主된 責任임을 認定하여, 第32項 (다)에 依한 合衆國 軍 당국의 要請이 있으면 大韓民國 당국이 裁判權을 行使함이 特히 重要하다고 決定하는 境遇를 除外하고, 第32項 (나)에 依한 裁判權을 行使할 1次의 第一次的 權利를 抛棄한다.

2. 合衆國 軍 當局은, 大韓民國 關係 當局의 同意를 얻어, 捜査 審理 및 裁判을 爲하여 合衆國이 裁判權을 가지는 特定 刑事 事件을 大韓民國의 法院이나 當局에 移送할 수 있다. 大韓民國 關係 當局은, 合衆國 軍 當局의 同意를 얻어, 捜査, 審理 및 裁判을 爲하여 大韓民國이 裁判權을 가지는 特定 刑事 事件을 合衆國 軍 當局에 移送할 수 있다.

3. (가) 合衆國 軍隊의 構成員, 軍屬 또는 家族이 大韓民國 안에서 大韓民國의 利益에 反하여 犯한 犯罪 때문에 合衆國 法院에 訴追되었을 境遇에는, 그 裁判은 大韓民國 안에서 行하여져야 한다.

(1) 다만, 合衆國의 法律이 달리 要求하는 境遇, 또는

(2) 軍事上 緊急 事態의 境遇 또는 司法 上의 利益을 爲한 境遇에 合衆國 軍 當局이 大韓民國 領域 밖에서 裁判을 行할 意圖가 있는 境遇에는 除外된다. 이러한 境遇 合衆國 軍 當局은 大韓民國 當局에 이러한 意圖에 對한 意見을 陳述할 수 있는 機會를 適時에 賦與하여야 하며 大韓民國 當局이 陳述하는 意見에 對하여 充分한 考慮를 하여야 한다.

(나) 裁判이 大韓民國 領域 밖에서 行하여질 境遇에는, 合衆國 軍 當局은 大韓民國 當局에 裁判의 場所와 日字를 通告하여야 한다. 大韓民國 代表는 그 裁判에 立會할 權利를 가진다. 合衆國 當局은 判決과 訴訟의 最終 結果를 大韓民國 當局에 通告하여야 한다.

4. 本條의 規定의 施行과 犯罪의 迅速한 處理를 爲하여, 大韓民國 關係당국과 合衆國 軍 당국은 約定을 締結할 수 있다.

0008

AGREED UNDERSTANDINGS TO THE
AGREEMENT UNDER ARTICLE IV
OF THE MUTUAL DEFENSE TREATY
BETWEEN THE REPUBLIC OF KOREA
AND THE UNITED STATES OF AMERICA,
REGARDING FACILITIES AND AREAS AND
THE STATUS OF UNITED STATES ARMED
FORCES IN THE REPUBLIC OF KOREA
AND RELATED AGREED MINUTES

0009

ARTICLE IX

PARAGRAPH 5

1. Examination of parcels in the MPO mails in the ROK by ROK customs inspectors will be conducted so as not to damage the contents of the parcels inspected or delay delivery of the mail;

2. Such examinations will be conducted in U.S. IMPO installations in the presence of U.S. officials;

3. No parcel in the MPO mails will be removed from U.S. postal channels except as mutually agreed;

4. It is understood that the right of inspection will be exercised on a "sample check" basis so as not to unduly delay delivery or increase the administrative burden of the postal authorities.

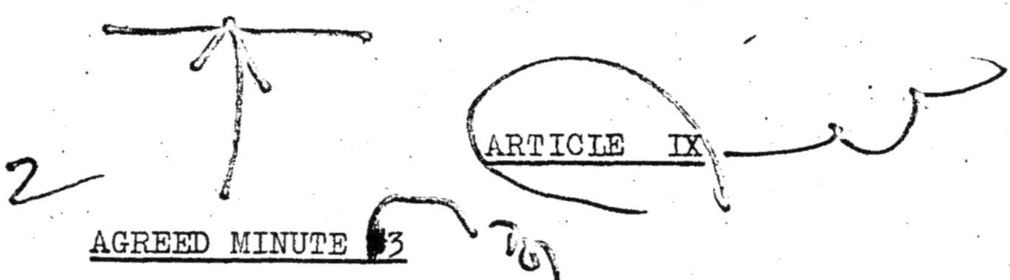

ARTICLE IX

AGREED MINUTE #3

1. Pertinent information shall include cargo

mainfests and shipping documents;

2. In addition to information provided on a routine basis, other pertinent information will be provided on request through the Joint Committee.

ARTICLE XIII

3 AGREED MINUTE

It is understood that the present use of Non-Appropriated Fund organizations by organizations and persons other than those referred to in items (a), (b), (c), (d), and (e) shall immediately be suspended at the time of the entry into force of this Agreement. The extent of organizations and persons to be granted the use of such organizations under item (f) of this minute shall be left to further negotiations between the appropriate authorities of the two Governments.

ARTICLE XV

4 PARAGRAPH 1

If the U.S. authorities determine that there

would be significant advantage for U.S. - ROK mutual defense to utilize one or more third-country corporations as USFK-invited contractors, the authorities of the Government of the Republic of Korea shall give sympathetic consideration to a U.S. request to extend the benefits of this agreement to such non-U.S. corporations.

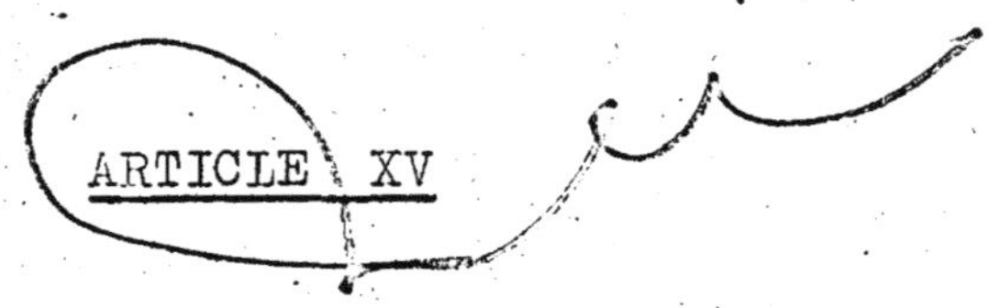

ARTICLE XV

5 PARAGRAPH 8

Unless otherwise agreed in Joint Committee, the privileges provided for in the second sentence of paragraph 8 of this Article shall be extended only to United States Nationals.

ARTICLE XVII

6 PARAGRAPH 1(b)

1. Local residents, who are third-country nationals and are also local-hire USFK employees and local-hire contractor employees paid in won, on the effective date of the agreement, shall be excluded

from the application of this provision.

2. The provisions of Paragraph 1(b) do not preclude the United States armed forces from bringing into Korea, without privileges, third-country contractor employees possessing special skills not available from the Korean labor force.

ARTICLE XVII

PARAGRAPH 3 AND AGREED MINUTE #4

It is understood that the deviation from Korean labor legislation need not be referred to the Joint Committee in cases when such referral would seriously hamper military operations in an emergency.

ARTICLE XIX

The ROK and U.S. negotiators agree that nothing in the Status of Forces Agreement in any way prevents the appropriate authorities of either the Republic of Korea or the United States from raising any appropriate matter at any time with each other. The U.S. negotiators recognize the desire of the ROK authorities to discuss the disposal of Military Payment Certificates under custody of the ROK Government. However, both the ROK and U.S. negotiators have agreed to remove from the SOFA text any reference to the question of compensation for Military Payment Certificates held by unauthorized persons. This agreement does not prejudice the position of either party in connection with discussion of this question through other channels.

ARTICLE XXII

PARAGRAPH 1(b)

The civil authorities of the Republic of Korea will retain full control over the arrest, investigation and trial of a member of the United States armed forces or civilian component or a dependent.

ARTICLE XXII

PARAGRAPH 5

With regard to the custody of the accused in

0014

the hands of the Korean authorities in connection with security offenses:

1. There must be mutual ROK - US agreement as to the circumstances in which such custody is appropriate;

2. Korean confinement facilities must be adequate by US standards.

ARTICLE XXII

AGREED MINUTE RE PARAGRAPH I(a)

The Government of the Republic of Korea agrees that upon notification under the second sentence of the Agreed Minute Re Paragraph 1 (a), the military authorities of the United States may exercise jurisdiction over such persons in accordance with the terms of the Criminal Jurisdiction Article.

ARTICLE XXII

AGREED MINUTE RE PARAGRAPH 2

It is understood that the United States authorities

shall exercise utmost restraint in requesting waivers of exclusive jurisdiction as provided for in the Agreed Minute Re Paragraph 2 of this Article.

ARTICLE XXII

AGREED MINUTE #1 RE PARAGRAPH 3(a)

With regard to the Agreed Minute Re Paragraph 3(a), a substantial departure from the acts a person is required to perform in a particular duty usually will indicate an act outside of his "official duty."

ARTICLE XXII

AGREED MINUTE RE PARAGRAPH 3(a)

A duty certificate shall be issued only upon the advice of a Staff Judge Advocate, and the competent authority issuing the duty certificate shall be a General Grade officer.

- 210 -

0016

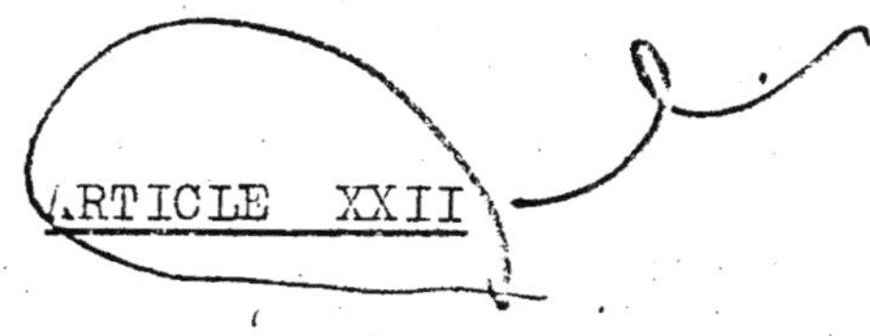

ARTICLE XXII

AGREED MINUTE RE PARAGRAPH 3(a)

13

1. The certificate will be conclusive unless modification is agreed upon. The United States authorities shall give due consideration to any objection which may be raised by the Chief Prosecutor for the Republic of Korea.

2. The accused should not be deprived of his entitlement to a prompt and speedy trial as a result of protracted reconsideration of the duty certificate.

ARTICLE XXII

16

AGREED MINUTE RE PARAGRAPH 3(b)

1. It is understood that the term "of particular importance" has reference to those cases in which, after a careful examination of each specific case, the exercise of jurisdiction by the Republic of Korea is deemed essential, and the term has reference, in general but not exclusively, to the following types of offenses:

(a) security offenses against the Republic of Korea;

(b) offenses causing the death of a human being, robbery, and rape, except where the offenses are directed against a member of the United States armed forces, or the civilian component, or a dependent; and

(c) attempts to commit such offenses or participation therein.

2. In respect of the offenses referred to in the above paragraph, the authorities concerned shall proceed in particularly close cooperation from the beginning of the preliminary investigation in order to provide the the mutual assistance envisaged in paragraph 6 of Article XXII.

ARTICLE XXII

AGREED MINUTE RE PARAGRAPH 3(b)

In cases where, in the view of the United States authorities, any question arises concerning the determination that a case is one "of particular importance", the U.S. diploamtic mission reserves the right a

United States

-212-

0018

and expects to be afforded an opportunity to confer with the proper authorities of the Republic of Korea.

ARTICLE XXII

AGREED MINUTE RE PARAGRAPH 9, SUB-PARAGRAPH (a) OF SECOND UNNUMBERED PARAGRAPH

Under the appellate procedure of the Courts of the Republic of Korea, the accused may request a re-examination of the evidence, including new evidence and witnesses, as a basis for new findings of fact by the appellate court.

ARTICLE XXIII

PARAGRAPH 12

The liability for claims generated by KSC personnel will be determined by other negotiations between the Republic of Korea and the United States.

ARTICLE XXV

20 PARAGRAPH 5

In cooperating with each other under this Article, the two Governments agree that each will take such measures as may be necessary to ensure the security and protection of the U.S. aremd forces, the members thereof, the civilian component, the persons who are present in the Republic of Korea pursuant to the Article dealing with Invited Contractors, their dependents and their property.

- 214 -

0020

대한민국과 아메리카 합중국 간의
상호 방위조약 제4조에 의한 시설과 구역 및
대한민국에서의 합중국 군대의 지위에 관한 협정의
합의 양해사항

0021

2304-
2374
Kenney

AGREED UNDERSTANDINGS TO THE AGREEMENT AND ~~ITS~~ Related AGREED MINUTES」

「협정 및 관계 합의의사록에 대한 합의 양해 사항」

1. 국문안
2. 영문안

0022

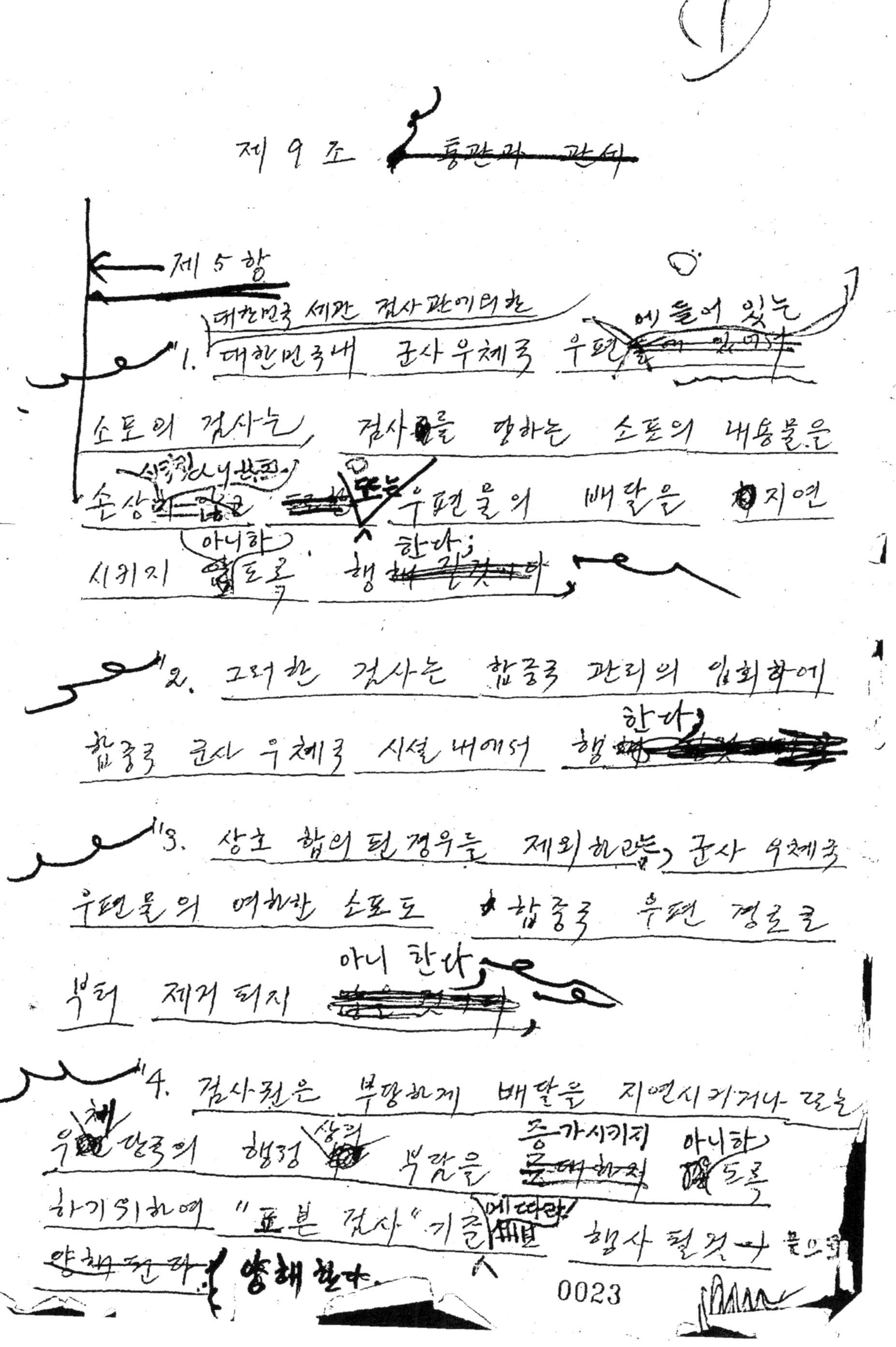

①

제 9 조

제 5 항

1. 대한민국 세관 검사관에 의한 대한민국내 군사우체국 우편에 들어 있는 소포의 검사는, 검사를 행하는 소포의 내용물을 손상시키거나 또는 우편물의 배달을 지연시키지 아니하도록 행한다;

2. 그러한 검사는 합중국 관리의 입회하에 합중국 군사 우체국 시설 내에서 행한다.

3. 상호 합의된 경우를 제외하고는 군사 우체국 우편물의 여하한 소포도 합중국 우편 경로로부터 제거되지 아니한다.

4. 검사관은 부당하게 배달을 지연시키거나 또는 우체당국의 행정상의 부담을 증가시키지 아니하도록 하기위하여 "표본 검사" 기준에 따라 행사될 것을 양해한다.

0023

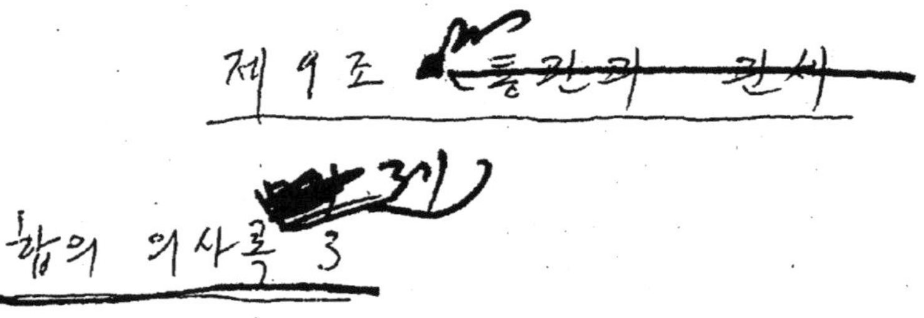

제 9 조 ~~통관과 관세~~

합의 의사록 3

1. 관계정보는 화물 ~~[illegible]~~ 적하목록 및 ~~[illegible]~~ 선적서류를 포함한다.

2. ~~[illegible]~~ ~~통상적인 주문에서~~ 정규적으로 제공되는 ~~[illegible]~~ 정보에 추가하여, 기타 관계정보는 합동위원회를 ~~통하여~~ 통한 요구에 따라 제시 ~~된다~~ 된 제공된다.

0024

제13조 비세출자금기관

합의 의사록

(가), (나), (다), (라) 및 (마) 항목에서 언급된 것 이외의 기관 및 인원에 의한 비세출자금기관의 현재의 사용은 본협정의 효력 발생시에 즉각 정지되는 것으로 양해한다. 본의사록 (바) 항목에 따라 그러한 기관의 사용이 허용된 기관과 인원의 범위는 양국정부의 관계 당국간의 계속적 협의에 의한다.

0025

제15조 ~~초청 계약자~~

제1항

합중국 당국이 하나 또는 둘 이상의 제3국 법인을 주한 합중국 군대의 초청 계약자로서 사용함이 대한민국과 합중국간의 상호 방위를 위하여 중대한 이익이 될것이라고 결정할 경우에는, 대한민국 정부 당국은 그러한 비합중국 법인에게 본협정의 혜택을 부여하도록 하는 합중국의 요청에 호의적 고려를 하여야 한다.

0026

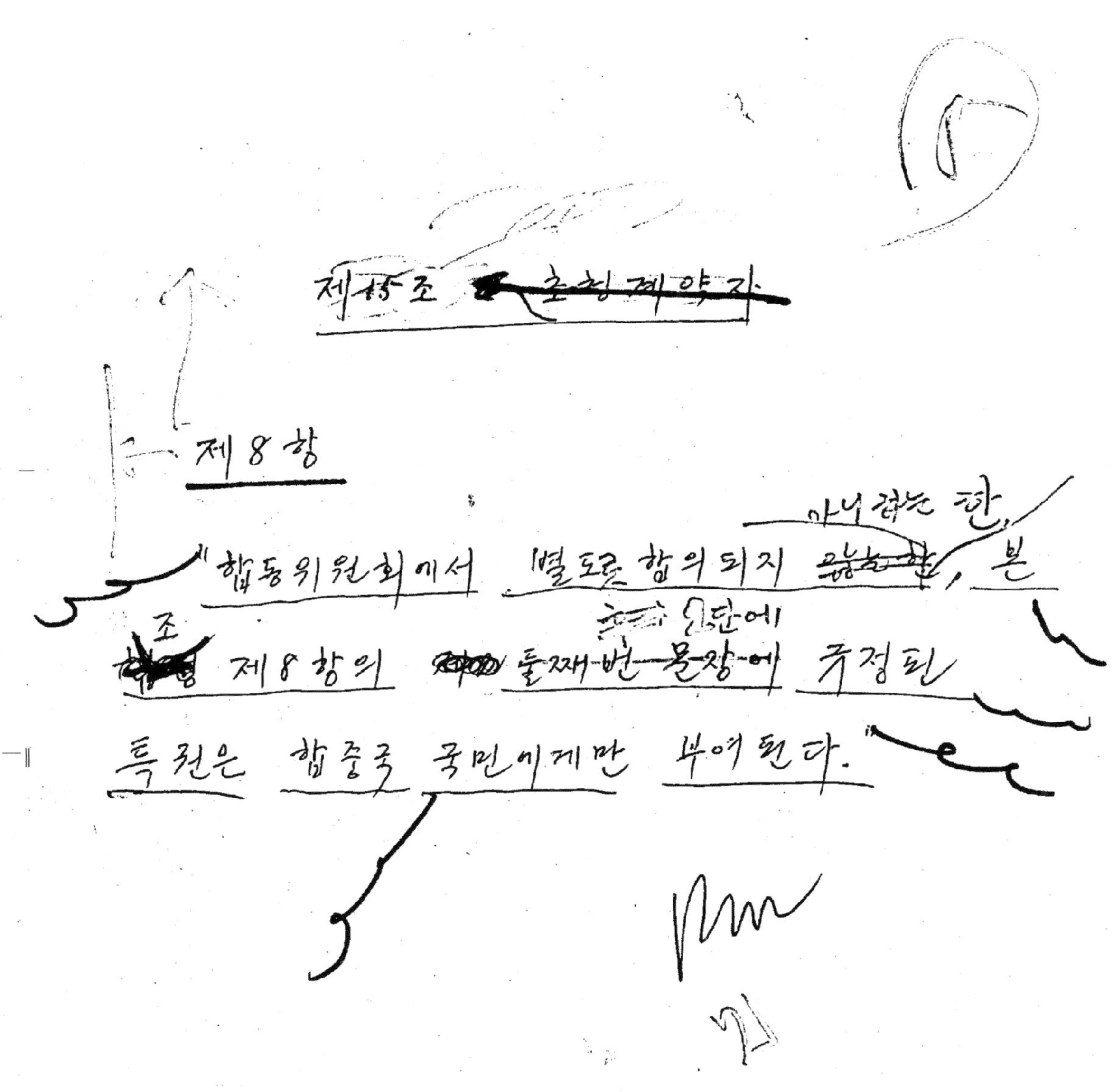

제15조 초청계약자

제8항

"합동위원회에서 별도로 합의되지 아니하는 한, 본조 제8항의 단서에 규정된 특권은 합중국 국민에게만 부여된다."

0027

제17조 ~~노무~~

제1항(나)

"1. 본협정 효력발생일자에 제3국 국민이며 또한 원화로서 지급되는 현지채용 주한 합중국 군대 고용원과 현지 채용 계약자 고용원인 현지 거주자는 본 규정의 적용으로 부터 제외된다."

"2. 제1(나)항의 규정은 합중국 군대가 한국 노동력으로 부터 획득할수 없는 특수기술을 가지고 있는 제삼국 계약자 고용원을 특권없이 한국으로 데리고 오는것을 배제하지 않는다."

0028

제17조 노무

제3항과 합의의사록 제4

"한국 노동 법령으로부터의 이탈은, 합동위원회에의 회부가 비상시에 있어서 군사작전을 심히 방해할 경우에는, 동위원회에 회부할 필요가 없는 것으로 양해한다."

0029

제19조 ~~군표~~

"대한민국과 합중국 교섭대표는 주둔군지위 협정의 어느것도 대한민국과 합중국의 ~~적절한~~ 관계당국이 상호간에 언제든지 여하한 적절한 사항을 제기하는 것을 전혀 방지하지 않는데 합의한다. 합중국 교섭대표는 대한민국 정부가 보관하고 있는 군표 처리문제를 토의하려는 대한민국 정부의 요망을 인정한다. 그러나 대한민국 및 합중국 양 교섭대표는 개인가 [illegible] 자에 의하여 보유되고 있는 군표에 대한 보상 문제에 관한 여하한 언급도 주둔군지위 협정 조문으로부터 제거하는데 합의하였다. 본 협정은 기타 경로를 통하여 본 문제의 토의와 관련하여 어느 일방 당사국의 입장을 침해하지 아니한다."

0030

제 22조 ~~형사재판관할~~

제 1항(나) ~~종~~

"대한민국 민간당국은 합중국 군대 구성원, 군속 또는 가족의 체포, 수사 및 재판에 대한 완전한 통할을 지속한다."

~~통할권을~~

통할권을 가진다.

0031

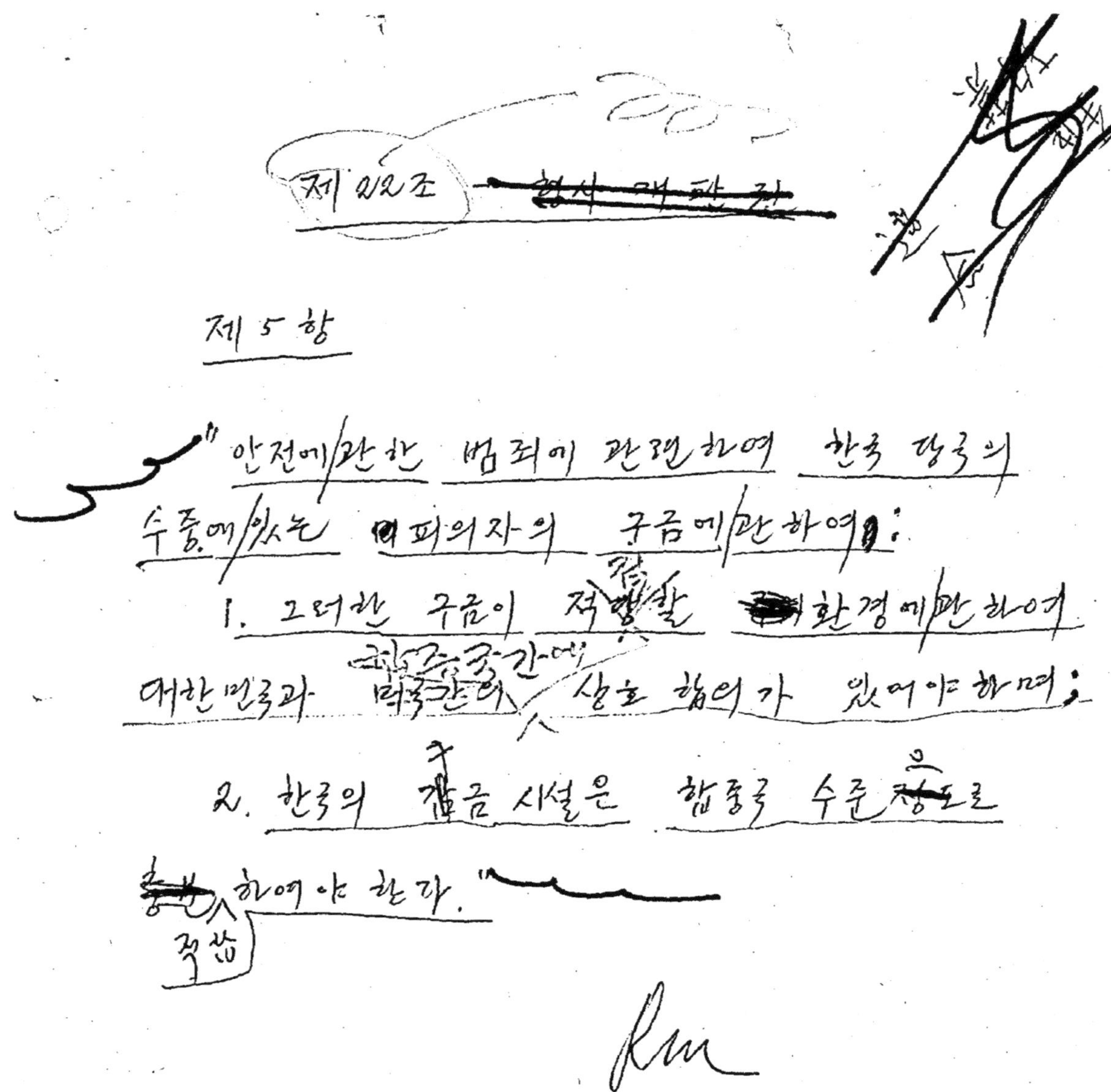

제 22조 ~~형사 재판권~~

제 5 항

"안전에 관한 범죄에 관련하여 한국 당국의 수중에 있는 피의자의 구금에 관하여:

1. 그러한 구금이 적합할 환경에 관하여 대한민국과 미국간에 상호 합의가 있어야 하며;

2. 한국의 구금 시설은 합중국 수준으로 적합하여야 한다."

Rm

0032

第22条 刑事裁判權

非公式合意案	最終合意案
第一項 (가) 1. 本条의 規定에따를것을 条件으로, (가) 合衆国軍当局은 合衆国軍隊의 構成員, 軍屬및 그들의 家族에 対하여 合衆国法令이 賦与한 모든 刑事裁判權및 懲戒權을 行使할 權利를 가진다.	第一項 (가) 左同 合意議事錄第 1 項 (가) 合衆国法律의 現状態下에서 合衆国軍当局은 平和時에는 軍屬및 家族에 対하여 有効한 刑事裁判權을 가지지 아니한다. 追後의 立法, 憲法改正, 또는 合衆国関係当局에 依한 決定의 結果로서 合衆国 軍事裁判權의 範囲가 変更된다면, 合衆国政府는 外交経路를 通하여 大韓民国政府에 通告하여야 한다. 第22條에 関한 合意議事錄 第1項 (가) 大韓民国政府는 第一項 (가)에 関한 合意議事錄의 後段에 依한 通告가 있으면 合衆国軍当局은 刑事裁判權条項의 規定에 依拠하여 그러한 者에 対하여 裁判權을 行使할수 있다는 것에 合意한다.

제22조 - 형사재판권

제2항에 관한 합의 의사록

"합중국 당국은 본조 제2항에 관한 합의 의사록에 규정된 전속적 재판권의 포기를 요청함에 있어서 최대한으로 자제할 것~~이 양해된다~~을 양해한다."

~~0033~~

0034

제3(a)항에 관한 합의 의사록 1

"제3(a)항에 관한 합의 의사록에 관하여, 어떤자가 특정 공무에 있어서 행할것이 요구되는 행위로부터의 실질적 이탈은, 통상 그의 "공무" 밖의 행위를 뜻한다.

0035

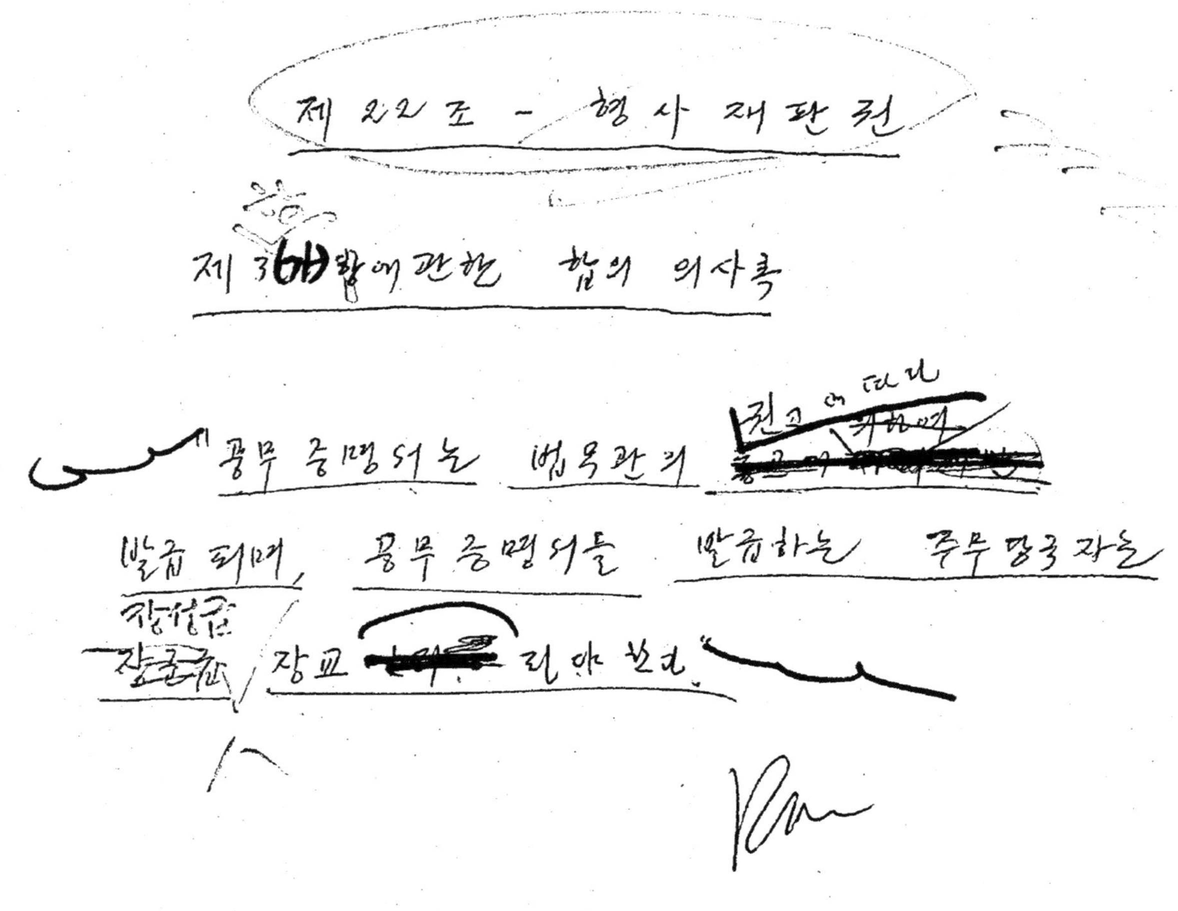

제22조 - 형사재판권

제3(바)항에 관한 합의 의사록

"공무 증명서는 법무관의 권고에 따라 발급되며, 공무 증명서를 발급하는 주무 당국자는 장성급 장교라야 한다."

0036

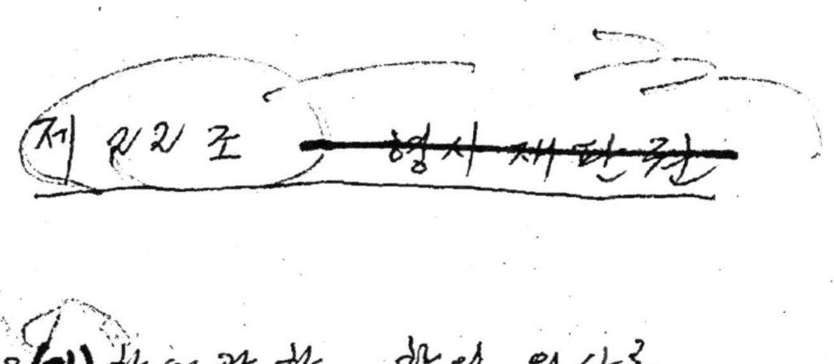

제22조 ~~형사재판권~~

제3(가)항에 관한 합의의사록

1. 수정이 합의되지 아니하는 한, 증명서는 결정적이다. 합중국 당국은 대한민국을 대신하여 검찰총장이 제기하는 대한민국의 이의에 정당한 고려를 ~~한다.~~" 해야 한다.

2. 피의자는 공무증명서의 지연된 재고 결과 즉각적이고도 신속한 재판에 대한 그의 권리가 박탈되어서는 아니된다."

0037

제 3항 (나)에 관한 합의 의사록

1. "특히 중요"하다는 용어는 개개의 특정 사건을 신중히 조사한 후 대한민국이 재판권을 행사함이 긴요하다고 생각되는 사건에 관련되며 또한 이 용어는 일반적으로 다음과 같은 종류의 범죄에 관련되나 그와같은 종류의 범죄에만 한정되는 것이 아니라고 양해한다.

(가) 대한민국의 안전에 관한 범죄

(나) 사람을 죽음에 이르게 한 범죄, 강도죄 및 강간죄. 다만, 그 범죄가 합중국 군대의 구성원, 군속 또는 가족에 대하여 행하여진 경우에는 그러하지 아니하다. 그리고

(다) 전기 각 범죄의 미수 또는 공범.

2. 전항에 규정된 범죄에 관하여, 관계 당국은 제 22조 제 6항에 규정된 상호 간 조력을 제공하기 위하여 예비 조사를 할 때부터 특히 긴밀하게 협력하면서 절차를 취하여야 한다.

0038

非公式合意案

4. 本合意議事錄 第3項에 따라 大韓民國 關係當局이 特定事件에 對한 權利 抛棄를 撤回하고 이러한 境遇 關係當局間의 討議에서 諒解가 이루어지지 아니할 때에는, 合衆國政府는 外交經路를 通하여 大韓民國 政府에 異議를 提起할 수 있다. 大韓民國 政府는 大韓民國의 司法上의 利益과 合衆國의 利益을 充分히 考慮하여 外交分野에 있어서의 그의 權限을 行使하여 意見差異를 解決하여야 한다. 大韓民國 政府가 前記規定에 따라 意見差異를 解決함에 있어서 大韓民國 當局이 裁判權을 行使함이 不可避하다고 決定하는 境遇에는, 權利 抛棄의 撤回는 最終的이며 確定的이다.

5. 合衆國 軍 當局은, 大韓民國 關係當局의 同意를 얻어, 捜査拘束 및 裁判을 為하여 合衆國이 裁判權을 가지는 特定刑事事件을 大韓民國의 法院이나 當局에 移送할 수 있다.

大韓民國 關係當局은, 合衆國 軍 當局의 同意를 얻어, 捜査, 審理 및 裁判을 為하여 大韓民國이 裁判權을 가지는 特定 刑事事件을 合衆國 軍當局에 移送할 수 있다.

最終合意案

合意議事錄 第3項(나)에 關한

1. "特히 重要"하다는 用語는 個個의 特定 事件의 愼重한 調査後 大韓民國이 裁判權을 行使함이 必須的이라고 認定되는 事件에 關係되며 또한 同 用語는 一般的으로 다음 種類의 犯罪에 關係되나 限定的은 아니다.

(가) 大韓民國의 安全에 關한 犯罪,

(나) 사람을 죽음에 이르게 한 犯罪, 強盜罪 및 強姦罪, 다만, 그 犯罪가 合衆國 軍隊의 構成員, 軍屬 또는 家族에 對하여 行하여진 境遇에는 그러하지 아니하다. 및

(다) 前記 各 犯罪의 未遂 또는 共犯.

2. 前項에 規定된 犯罪에 關하여, 關係 當局은 第22條 第6項에 規定된 相互間의 助力을 提供하기 為하여 捜査의 準備 段階부터 特히 緊密히 協力하여야 한다.

0039

非公式合意案

6. (가) 合衆国 軍隊의 構成員, 軍属 또는 家族이 大韓民国 안에서 大韓民国의 利益에 反하여 犯한 犯罪 때문에 合衆国 法院에 訴追되었을 境遇에는, 그 裁判은 大韓民国 안에서 行하여져야 한다.

(1) 다만, 合衆国의 法律이 달리 要求하는 境遇, 또는

(2) 軍事上 緊急事態의 境遇 또는 司法上의 利益을 為한 境遇에 合衆国 軍当局이 大韓民国 領域밖에서 裁判을 行할 意図가 있는 境遇에는 除外된다. 이러한 境遇 合衆国 軍 当局은 大韓民国 当局에 이러한 意図에 対한 意見을 陳述할 수 있는 機会를 適時에 賦与하여야 하며 大韓民国 当局이 陳述하는 意見에 対하여 充分한 考慮를 하여야 한다.

(나) 裁判이 大韓民国 領域 밖에서 行하여질 境遇에는, 合衆国 軍当局은 大韓民国 当局에 裁判의 場所와 日字를 通告하여야 한다. 大韓民国 代表는 그裁判에 立会할 権利를 가진다. 合衆国 当局은 判決과 訴訟의 最終 結果를 大韓民国 当局에 通告하여야 한다.

7. 本条및 本合意議事録의 規定의 施行과 軽微한 犯罪의 迅速한 処理를 為하여, 大韓民国 関係当局과 合衆国 軍当局은 約定을 締結할수있다. 同 約定은 또한 通告없이

合意議事録 第3項 (나) 에関한

合衆国当局의 見地에서 事件이 特히 重要한 것이라는 決定에 関한 疑問이 提起된 境遇에는 合衆国 外交使節은 大韓民国의 関係当局과 相議할수있는 機会가 賦与된 権利를 保有하며 또한 그러한 機会가 賦与되기를 期待한다.

交換公文

親愛하는 大使 貴下

今日 大韓民国政府와 合衆国政府는 大韓民国과 合衆国政府間의 施設과 区域및 大韓民国에서의 合衆国軍隊의 地位에 関한 協定에 正式으로 署名하였읍니다. 同協定의 第22条및 同合意議事録은 大韓民国에 있는 合衆国軍隊 構成員, 軍属및 그들의 家族에 対한 裁判権行使를 規定하고 있읍니다.

이에 関聯하여, 大韓民国政府는 우리 両国家를 結束하는 相互 尊重과 友誼의 強인한 紐帶를 意識하고 또한 合衆国軍隊가 大韓民国의 防衛에 있어서 遂行하는 重大한 役割을 認定하여 (第3項 (나) 에関한 合意議事録) 第4項에 따른 節次上의 約定을 為하여 다음과 같은 諒解事項을 提議하는바입니다:

0040

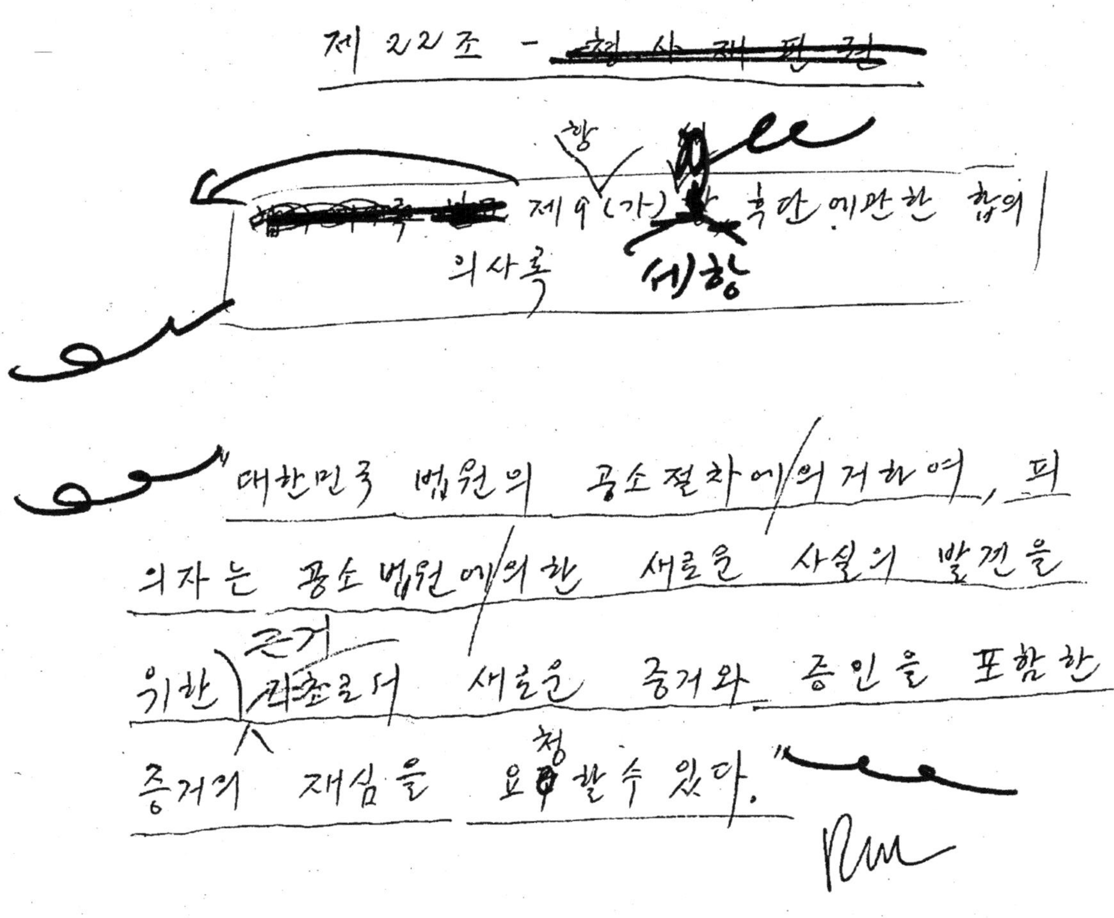

제 22조 - ~~형사재판권~~

[illegible] 제9(가)항 후단에 관한 합의의사록 세항

"대한민국 법원의 공소절차에 의거하여, 피의자는 공소법원에 의한 새로운 사실의 발견을 위한 근거로서 새로운 증거와 증인을 포함한 증거의 재심을 요청할 수 있다."

0041

제 23조

제 12항

한국 노무단원에 의하여 제기된 청구권에 대한 책임의 유무는 대한민국과 합중국간의 별도 협의에 의하여 결정한다.

0042

제25조 보안 조치

제5항

본 협정에 의거하여, 각 정부는 상호 협력함에 있어서 합중국 군대, 그 구성원, 군속, 초청 계약자에 관한 조항에 따라 대한민국에 있는 자, 그들의 가족 및 그들의 재산의 보안과 보호를 보장하기에 필요할 조치를 취할것에 양국정부는 합의한다.

0043

ARTICLE IX ~~[struck out]~~

PARAGRAPH 5

"1. Examination of parcels in the MPO mails in the ROK by ROK customs inspectors will be conducted so as not to damage the contents of the parcels inspected or delay delivery of the mail;

"2. Such examinations will be conducted in U.S. MPO installations in the presence of U.S. officials;

"3. No parcel in the MPO mails will be removed from U.S. postal channels except as mutually agreed;

"4. It is understood that the right of inspection will be exercised on a "sample check" basis so as not to unduly delay delivery or increase the administrative burden of the postal authorities."

0044

ARTICLE IX ~~CUSTOMS AND DUTIES~~

AGREED MINUTE 3

"1. Pertinent information shall include cargo manifests and shipping documents;

"2. In addition to information provided on a routine basis, other pertinent information will be provided on request through the Joint Committee."

0045

ARTICLE XIII ~~NON-APPROPRIATED FUND ORGANIZATIONS~~

AGREED MINUTE

"It is understood that the present use of Non-Appropriated Fund organizations by organizations and persons other than those referred to in items (a), (b), (c), (d), and (e) shall immediately be suspended at the time of the entry into force of this Agreement. The extent of organizations and persons to be granted the use of such organizations under item (f) of this minute shall be left to further negotiations between the appropriate authorities of the two governments."

0046

ARTICLE XV - ~~INVITED CONTRACTORS~~

PARAGRAPH 1

"If the U.S. authorities determine that there would be significant advantage for U.S.-ROK mutual defense to utilize one or more third-country corporations as USFK-invited contractors, the authorities of the Government of the Republic of Korea shall give sympathetic consideration to a U.S. request to extend the benefits of this agreement to such non-U.S. corporations."

0047

ARTICLE XV ~~INVITED CONTRACTORS~~

PARAGRAPH 8

"Unless otherwise agreed in Joint Committee, the privileges provided for in the second sentence of Paragraph 8 of this Article shall be extended only to United States Nationals."

0048

ARTICLE XVII - LABOR

PARAGRAPH 1(b)

"1. Local residents, who are third-country nationals and are also locan-hire USFK employees and local-hire contractor employees paid in won, on the effective date of the agreement, shall be excluded from the application of this provision."

"2. The provisions of Paragraph 1(b) do not preclude the United States armed forces from bringing into Korea, without privileges, third-country contractor employees possessing special skills not available from the Korean labor force."

0049

ARTICLE XVII ~~LABOR~~

PARAGRAPH 3 AND AGREED MINUTE #4

"It is understood that the deviation from Korean labor legislation need not be referred to the Joint Committee in cases when such referral would seriously hamper military operations, in an emergency."

0050

ARTICLE XIX ~~MILITARY PAYMENT CERTIFICATES~~

"The ROK and U.S. negotiators agree that nothing in the Status of Forces Agreement in any way prevents the appropriate authorities of either the Republic of Korea or the United States from raising any appropriate matter at any time with each other. The U.S. negotiators recognize the desire of the ROK authorities to discuss the disposal of Military Payment Certificates under custody of the ROK Government. However, both the ROK and U.S. negotiators have agreed to remove from the SOFA text any any reference to the question of compensation for Military Payment Certificates held by unauthorized persons. This agreement does not prejudice the position of either party in connection with discussion of this question through other channels."

0051

ARTICLE XXII ~~- CRIMINAL JURISDICTION~~

PARAGRAPH 1(b)

"The civil authorities of the Republic of Korea will retain full control over the arrest, investigation and trial of a member of the United States armed forces or civilian component or a dependent."

0052

ARTICLE XXII ~~CRIMINAL JURISDICTION~~

PARAGRAPH 5

"With regard to the custody of the accused in the hands of the Korean authorities in connection with security offenses:

1. There must be mutual ROK-US agreement as to the circumstances in which such custody is appropriate;
2. Korean confinement facilities must be adequate by US standards."

0053

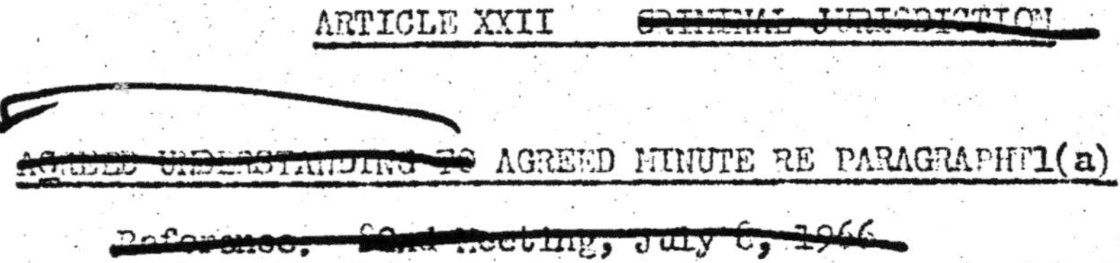

ARTICLE XXII ~~CRIMINAL JURISDICTION~~

~~AGREED UNDERSTANDING TO~~ AGREED MINUTE RE PARAGRAPH 1(a)

~~Reference: 82nd Meeting, July 6, 1966~~

The Government of the Republic of Korea agrees that upon notification under the second sentence of the Agreed Minute Re Paragraph 1(a), the military authorities of the United States may exercise jurisdiction over such persons in accordance with the terms of the Criminal Jurisdiction Article.

0054

ARTICLE XXII ~~CRIMINAL JURISDICTION~~

AGREED MINUTE RE PARAGRAPH 2

"It is understood that the United States authorities shall exercise utmost restraint in requesting waivers of exclusive jurisdiction as provided for in the Agreed Minute Re Paragraph 2 of this Article."

0055

ARTICLE XXII ~~CRIMINAL JURISDICTION~~

AGREED MINUTE 1 RE PARAGRAPH 3(a)

"With regard to the Agreed Minute Re Paragraph 3(a), a substantial departure from the acts a person is required to perform in a particular duty usually will indicate an act outside of his "official duty."

0056

ARTICLE XXII ~~CRIMINAL JURISDICTION~~

AGREED MINUTE RE PARAGRAPH 3(a)

"A duty certificate shall be issued only upon the advice of a Staff Judge Advocate, and the competent authority issuing the duty certificate shall be a General Grade officer."

0057

ARTICLE XXII - ~~CRIMINAL JURISDICTION~~

AGREED MINUTE RE PARAGRAPH 3(a)

"1. The certificate will be conclusive unless modification is agreed upon. The United States authorities shall give due consideration to any objection which may be raised by the Chief Prosecutor for the Republic of Korea."

"2. The accused should not be deprived of his entitlement to a prompt and speedy trial as a result of protracted reconsideration of the duty certificate."

0058

ARTICLE XXII ~~CRIMINAL JURISDICTION~~

~~AGREED UNDERSTANDING TO~~ AGREED MINUTE RE PARAGRAPH /#/ 3(b)

~~Reference: 82nd Meeting, July 8, 1966~~

1. It is understood that the term "of particular importance" has reference to those cases in which, after a careful examination of each specific case, the exercise of jurisdiction by the Republic of Korea is deemed essential and the term has reference, in general but not exclusively, the following types of offense"

(a) security offenses against the Republicof Korea;

(b) offenses causing the death of a human being, robbery, and rape, except where the offenses are directed against a member of the United States armed forces or the civilian component, or a dependent; and

(c) attempts to commit such offenses or participation therein.

2. In respect of the offenses referred to in the above paragraph the authorities concerned shall proceed in particularly close cooperation from the beginning of the preliminary investigation in order to provide the mutual assistance envisaged in paragraph 6 of Article XXII.

0059

ARTICLE XXII ~~CRIMINAL JURISDICTION~~

~~AGREED UNDERSTANDING TO~~ AGREED MINUTE RE PARAGRAPH 3(b)

"In cases where, in the view of the United States authorities, any question arises concerning the determination that a case is one "of particular importance", the U.S. diplomatic mission reserves the right and expects to be afforded an opportunity to confer with the proper authorities of the Republic of Korea."

0060

ARTICLE XXII ~~CRIMINAL JURISDICTION~~

AGREED MINUTE RE PARAGRAPH 9, SUB-PARAGRAPH (a) OF SECOND UNNUMBERED PARAGRAPH

"Under the appellate procedure of the Courts of the Republic of Korea, the accused may request a re-examination of the evidence, including new evidence and witnesses, as a basis for new findings of fact by the appellate court."

0061

ARTICLE XXIII ~~- CLAIMS~~

PARAGRAPH 12 ~~(Understanding relating to deletion of KSC from Paragraph 12)~~

"The liability for claims generated by KSC personnel will be determined by other negotiations between the Republic of Korea and the United States."

0062

ARTICLE XXV ~~- SECURITY MEASURES~~

PARAGRAPH 5

"In cooperating with each other under this Article, the two governments agree that each will take such measures as may be necessary to ensure the security and protection of the U.S. armed forces, the members thereof, the civilian component, the persons who are present in the Republic of Korea pursuant to the Article dealing with Invited Contractors, their dependents and their property.

0063

第 9 條

第5項

1. 大韓民國 稅關檢査官에 의한 大韓民國內 軍事 郵遞局 郵便物에 들어 있는 小包의 檢査는, 檢査를 당하는 小包의 內容物을 損傷시키지 아니하고 또는 郵便物의 配達을 遲延시키지 아니하도록 행한다.

2. 이러한 檢査는 合衆國 官吏의 立會下에 合衆國 軍事 郵遞局 施設 내에서 행한다.

3. 相互 合意된 경우를 除外하고는, 軍事 郵遞局 郵便物의 여하한 小包도 合衆國 郵便經路로부터 除去되지 아니한다.

4. 檢査權은 不當하게 配達을 遲延시키거나 또는 郵遞當局의 行政上의 부담을 증가시키지 아니하도록 하기 위하여 "標本 檢査" 基準에 따라 行使될 것으로 諒解한다.

合意 議事錄 3

1. 關係 情報는 貨物 積貨目錄 및 船積 書類를 포함한다.

2. 定規的으로 提供되는 情報에 追加하여, 기타 關係 情報는 合同 委員會를 通한 要求에 따라 提供된다.

第 13 條

合意 議事錄

(가), (나), (다), (라) 및 (마) 項目에서 言及된 것 이외의 機關 및 人員에 의한 非歲出 資金 機關의 現在의 使用은 本協定의 效力發生時에 即時 停止되는 것으로 諒解한다. 本 議事錄(바) 項目에 따라 이러한 機關의 使用이 許容된 機關과 人員의 範圍는 兩國政府의 關係當局간의 繼續的 協議에 委任한다.

第 15 條

第1項

合衆國 當局이 하나 또는 둘 以上의 第3國 法人을 駐韓 合衆國 軍隊의 招請 契約者로서 使用함이 大韓民國과 合衆國 간의 相互防衛를 위하여 重大한 利益이 될 것이라고 決定할 境遇에는, 大韓民國 政府 當局은 이러한 非合衆國 法人에게 本 協定의 惠擇을 賦與하도록 하는 合衆國의 要請에 對하여 好意的 考慮를 하여야 한다.

0064

第8項

合同委員會에서 別途로 合意되지 아니하는 限, 本 條 第8項의 2段에 規定된 特權은 合衆國 國民에게만 賦與된다.

第 17 條

第1項 (나)

1. 本 協定 效力 發生日字에 第3國 國民이며, 또한 圓貨로서 支給되는 現地 採用 駐韓合衆國 軍隊 雇傭員과 現地 採用 契約者 雇傭員인 現地 居住者는 本 規定의 適用으로부터 除外된다.

2. 第1項 (나)의 規定은 合衆國軍隊가 韓國 勞動力으로부터 獲得할 수 없는 特殊技術을 가지고 있는 第3國 契約者 雇傭員을 特權 없이 韓國으로 데리고 오는 것을 排除하지 않는다.

第3項과 合意 議事錄 第4

韓國 勞動法令으로부터의 離脫은, 合同委員會에의 回附가 非常時에 있어서 軍事作戰을 甚히 妨害할 境遇에는, 同 委員會議에 回附할 必要가 없는 것으로 諒解한다.

第 19 條

大韓民國과 合衆國 交涉 代表는 駐屯軍 地位 協定의 어느 것도 大韓民國과 合衆國의 關係當局이 相互間에 언제든지 如何한 適切한 事項을 提起하는 것을 全혀 防止하지 않는데 合意한다. 合衆國 交涉代表은 大韓民國 政府가 保管하고 있는 軍票 處理 問題를 討議하려는 大韓民國 當局의 要望을 認定한다. 그러나 大韓民國 및 合衆國 兩 交涉 代表은 認可되지 아니한 者에 依하여 保有되고 있는 軍票에 對한 補償問題에 關한 如何한 言及도 駐屯軍 地位協定 條文으로부터 除去하는데 合意하였다. 本 協定은 其他 經路를 通하여 本 問題의 討議와 關聯하여 어느 一方 當事國의 立場을 侵害하지 아니한다.

第 22 條

第1項 (나)

大韓民國 民間當局은 合衆國 軍隊 構成員, 軍屬 또는 家族의 逮捕, 搜査 및 裁判에 對한 完全한 統轄權을 가진다.

0065

第 5 項

安全에 關한 犯罪에 關聯하여 韓國 當局의 手中에 있는 被疑者의 拘禁에 關하여:

1. 여러한 拘禁이 適切할 環境에 關하여 大韓民國과 合衆國間에 相互合意가 있어야 한다.

2. 韓國의 拘禁施設은 合衆國 水準으로 適合하여야 한다.

第 1 項 (가)에 關한 合意 議事錄

大韓民國 政府는 第 1 項 (가)에 關한 合意 議事錄의 後段에 依한 通告가 있으면 合衆國 軍 當局은 刑事裁判權 條項의 規定에 依據하여 여러한 者에 對하여 裁判權을 行使할 수 있다는 것에 合意한다.

第 2 項에 關한 合意 議事錄

合衆國 當局은 本條 第 2 項에 關한 合意議事錄에 規定된 專屬的 裁判權의 抛棄를 要請함에 있어서 最大限으로 自制할 것을 諒解한다.

第 3 項의 關한 合意議事錄 第 1

1. 第 3 項 (가)에 關한 合意 議事錄에 關하여, 어떤 者가 特定 公務에 있어서 行할 것이 要求되는 行爲로부터의 實質的 離脫은, 通常 그의 "公務" 밖의 行爲를 뜻한다.

第 3 項 (가)에 關한 合意 議事錄

2. 公務 證明書는 法務官의 勸告에 따라 발급되며, 公務 證明書를 發給하는 主務 當局者는 將星級 將校라야 한다.

第 3 項 (가)에 關한 合意 議事錄

3. (가) 修正이 合意되지 아니하는 限, 證明書는 決定的이다. 合衆國 當局은 大韓民國을 代身하여 檢察總長이 提起하는 如何한 異議도 正當한 考慮를 해야 한다.

(나) 被疑者는 公務證明書의 遲延된 再考 結果, 即刻的이고도 迅速한 裁判에 對한 그의 權利가 剝奪되어서는 아니된다.

第 3 項 (나)에 關한 合意 議事錄

1. "特히 重要하다"는 用語는 個個의 特定 事件을 愼重히 調査한 後 大韓民國이 裁判權을 行事함이 緊要하다고 생각되는 事件에 關聯되며 또한 이 用語는 一般的으로 다음과 같은 種類의 犯罪에 關聯되나 그와 같은 種類의 犯罪에만 限定되는 것이 아니라고 諒解한다.

(가) 大韓民國의 安全에 關한 犯罪,

(나) 사람을 죽음에 이르게 한 犯罪, 强盜罪 및 强姦罪, 다만, 그 犯罪가 合衆國 軍

0066 ~~0065~~

隊의 構成員, 軍屬 또는 家族에 對하여 行하여진 境遇에는 그러하지 아니하다, 및

(다) 前記 各犯罪의 未遂 또는 共犯.

2. 前項에 規定된 犯罪에 關하여, 關係 當局은 第22條 第6項에 規定된 相互間 助力을 提供하기 爲하여 豫備 搜査를 開始할 때부터 特히 緊密하게 協力하면서 節次를 取하여야 한다.

第3項 (다)에 關한 合意 議事錄

合衆國 當局의 見地에서 事件이 特히 重要한 것이라는 決定에 關한 疑問이 제거될 境遇에는 合衆國 外交 使節은 大韓民國의 關係當局과 相議할 수 있는 機會가 賦與될 權利를 保有하며 또한 그러한 機會가 賦與되기를 期待한다.

第9項 (가) 後段에 關한 合意 議事錄

大韓民國 法院의 抗訴 節次에 依據하여, 被告人은 抗訴 法院에 依한 새로운 事實의 發見을 爲한 根據로서 새로운 證據와 證人을 包含한 證據의 再審을 要請할 수 있다.

第 23 條

第12項

韓國 勞務團員에 依하여 提起된 請求權에 對한 責任은 大韓民國과 合衆國間의 別途 協議에 依하여 決定한다.

第 25 條

本條에 依據하여 相互 協力함에 있어서 各 政府는 合衆國 軍隊, 그 構成員, 軍屬, 招請契約者에 關한 條項에 따라 大韓民國에 있는 자, 그들의 家族 및 그들의 財産의 保安과 保護를 보장하기에 必要할 措置를 取할 것에 兩國 政府는 合意한다.

/이니시알/ /이니시알/

T. W. L. W. G. B.

0067

대한민국과 아메리카 합중국 간의
상호 방위조약 제 4조에 의한 시설과 구역 및
대한민국에서의 합중국 군대의 지위에 관한
협정 및 관계 합의 의사록에 대한
합의 양해 사항

제 9 조

제 5항

1. 대한민국 세관검사관에 의한 대한민국 내 합중국 군사 우체국 우편물에 들어 있는 소포의 검사는, 검사를 당하는 소포의 내용을 손상시키지 아니하고 또는 우편물의 배달을 지연시키지 아니하도록 행한다.

2. 여하한 검사는 합중국 직원의 입회하에 합중국 군사 우체국 시설 내에서 행한다.

3. 상호 합의된 경우를 제외하고는, 군사 우체국 우편물의 여하한 소포도 합중국 우편 경로로부터 제거되지 아니한다.

4. 검사권은 부당하게 배달을 지연시키거나 또는 우체당국의 행정 상의 부담을 증가시키지 아니하도록 하기 위하여 "표본 검사" 기준에 따라 행사될 것으로 양해한다.

합의 의사록 제 3

1. 관계 정보는 화물 적하 목록 및 선적 서류를 포함한다.
2. 정규적으로 제공되는 정보에 추가하여, 기타 관계 정보는 합동 위원회를 통한 요구에 따라 제공된다.

제 13 조

합의 의사록

(가), (나), (다), (라) 및 (마) 항목에서 언급된 것 이외의 기관 및 인원에 의한 비세출 자금기관의 현재의 사용은 본 협정의 효력 발생 시에 즉시 정지되는 것으로 양해한다. 본 의사록 (바)항목에 따라 여하한 기관의 사용이 허용될 기관과 인원의 범위는 양국 정부의 관계 당국 간의 계속적 협의에 위임한다.

0068

-1-

제 15 조

제 1항

합중국 당국이 하나 또는 둘이상의 제 3국 법인을 합중국 군대의 초청 계약자로서 사용함이 대한민국과 합중국 간의 상호 방위를 위하여 중대한 이익이 될 것이라고 결정하는 경우에는, 대한민국 정부 당국은 여하한 비 합중국 법인에게 본 협정의 혜택을 부여하도록 하는 합중국의 요청에 대하여 호의적 고려를 하여야 한다.

제 8항

합동 위원회에서 별도로 합의되지 아니하는 한, 본조 제 8항의 2단에 규정된 특권은 합중국 국민에게만 부여된다.

제 17 조

제 1항(나)

1. 본 협정 효력 발생일자에 제 3국 국민이며, 또한 원화로서 지급되는 현지 채용 합중국 군대 고용원과 현지 채용 계약자 고용원인 현지 거주자는 본 규정의 적용으로부터 제외된다.
2. 제 1항(나)의 규정은 합중국 군대가 한국 노동력으로부터 획득할 수 없는 특수 기술을 가지고 있는 제 3국 계약자 고용원을 특권없이 한국으로 데리고 오는 것을 배제하지 아니한다.

제 3항과 합의 의사록 제 4

한국 노동법령으로부터의 이탈은, 합동위원회에의 회부가 비상시에 있어서 군사 작전을 심히 방해할 경우에는, 동 위원회에 회부할 필요가 없는 것으로 양해한다.

제 19 조

대한민국과 합중국은 주둔군 지위협정의 어느것도 대한민국과 합중국의 관계 당국이 상호간에 언제든지 여하한 적절한 사항을 제기하는 것을 전혀 방지하지 아니하는데 합의한다. 합중국 당국은 대한민국 정부가 보관하고 있는 군표 처리문제를 토의하려는 대한민국 당국의 요망을 인정한다. 그러나 대한민국 및 합중국의 양 당국은 인가되지 아니한 자에 의하여 보유되고 있는 군표에 대한 보상 문제에 관한 여하한 언급도 주둔군 지위협정 조문으로 부터 제거하는데 합의하였다. 본 협정은 다른 경로를 통한 0069

-2-

본 문제의 토의와 관련하여 어느 일방 당사국의 입장을 침해하지 아니한다.

제 22 조

제 1항(가)에 관한 합의 의사록

대한민국 정부는 제 1항(가)에 관한 합의 의사록의 후단에 의한 통고가 있으면 합중국 군 당국은 형사 재판권 조항의 규정에 의거하여 그러한 자에 대하여 재판권을 행사할 수 있다는 것에 합의한다.

제 1항(나)

대한민국 민간당국은 합중국 군대 구성원, 군속 또는 가족의 체포, 수사 및 재판에 대한 완전한 통할권을 보유한다.

제 2항에 관한 합의 의사록

합중국 당국은 본조 제 2항에 관한 합의 의사록에 규정된 전속적 재판권의 포기를 요청함에 있어서 최대한으로 자제하여야 한다는 것을 양해한다.

제 3항(가)에 관한 합의 의사록

1. 제 3항(가)에 관한 합의의사록에 관하여, 어떤 자가 특정 공무에 있어서 행할 것이 요구되는 행위로부터의 실질적 이탈은, 통상 그의 "공무"밖의 행위를 뜻한다.

2. 공무 집행증명서는 법무참모의 권고에 의하여서만 발급되어야 하며, 공무 집행증명서를 발급하는 주무 당국자는 장성급 장교라야 한다.

3. (가) 수정이 합의되지 아니하는 한, 증명서는 결정적이다. 합중국 당국은 대한민국을 대신하여 검찰총장이 제기하는 여하한 이의도 정당한 고려를 하여야한다.

0070

-3-

(나) 피의자는 공무 집행증명서의 지연된 재고의 결과 즉각적이고 신속한 재판에 대한 그의 권리가 박탈되어서는 아니된다.

제 3항(나)에 관한 합의 의사록

1. "특히 중요하다"는 용어는 개개의 특정 사건을 신중히 조사한 후 대한민국이 재판권을 행사함이 긴요하다고 생각되는 사건에 관련되며 또한 이 용어는 일반적으로 다음과같은 종류의 범죄에 관련되나 그와같은 종류의 범죄에만 한정되는 것이 아니라고 양해한다.

(가) 대한민국의 안전에 관한 범죄,

(나) 사람을 죽음에 이르게 한 범죄, 강도죄 및 강간죄, 다만, 그 범죄가 합중국 군대의 구성원, 군속 또는 가족에 대하여 행하여 진 경우에는 그러하지 아니하다. 및

(다) 전기 각 범죄의 미수 또는 공범.

2. 전항에 규정된 범죄에 관하여, 관계 당국은 제 22조 제 6항에 규정된 상호 간의 조력을 제공하기 위하여 예비 수사를 개시할 때부터 특히 긴밀하게 협력하면서 절차를 취하여야 한다.

3. 합중국 당국의 견지에서 사건이 특히 중요한 것이라는 결정에 관한 의문이 제기될 경우에는 합중국 외교 사절은 대한민국의 관계 당국과 상의할 수 있는 기회가 부여될 권리를 보유하며 또한 그러한 기회가 부여되기를 기대한다.

제 5항

안전에 관한 범죄에 관련하여 대한민국 당국의 수중에 있는 피의자의 구금에 관하여 :

1. 그러한 구금 적절한 환경에 관하여 대한민국과 합중국 간에 상호 합의가 있어야 한다.

2. 대한민국의 구금 시설은 합중국 수준의 적합하여야 한다.

-4-

0071

제 9항 (가) 후단에 관한 합의 의사록

대한민국 법원의 항소 절차에 의거하여, 피고인은 항소 법원에 의한 새로운 사실의 발견을 위한 근거로서 새로운 증거와 증인을 포함한 증거의 재조사를 요청할 수 있다.

제 23 조

제 12 항

한국 노무단원에 의하여 제기된 청구권에 대한 책임은 대한민국과 합중국 간의 별도 협의에 의하여 결정된다.

제 25 조

본조에 의거하여 상호 협력함에 있어서 각 정부는 합중국 군대, 그 구성원, 군속, 초청 계약자에 관한 조항에 따라 대한민국에 있는 자, 그들의 가족 및 그들의 재산의 보안과 보호를 보장하기에 필요한 조치를 취할 것에 양국 정부는 합의한다.

-5-

0072

SOFA Text (Korean)

	Page	Line		
①	14.	11.	우편봉인 봉인	봉인 우편봉인
②	50.	16.	본항의 규정,	본항의 규정은,
③	58.	8	90일	3개월.

SOFA Text (English)

④	2.	8.	the United States	United States
⑤	9.	10.	used	used,
⑥	42.	4.	invoaling	involving
⑦	42.	8.	form	from
⑧	53.	8	consituted	constituted
⑨	54.	21-22	in so far	insofar
⑩	57.	11.	shall distributed	shall be distributed
⑪	57.	19.	wames	maives
⑫	58	2.	paragraph	paragraphs

Agreed Minute (Korean)

⑬	9	11	제14조	제16조
⑭	10	7	제14조	제16조
⑮	24	1	폭행 협박	폭행, 협박

Agreed Minute (English)

⑯	12	7	Article XIV	Article XVI
⑰	13	7	Article XIV	Article XVI
⑱	34	8	a civilian component	civilian component

0073

AGREED UNDERSTANDINGS TO THE AGREEMENT UNDER ARTICLE IV OF THE MUTUAL DEFENSE TREATY BETWEEN THE REPUBLIC OF KOREA AND THE UNITED STATES OF AMERICA, REGARDING FACILITIES AND AREAS AND THE STATUS OF UNITED STATES ARMED FORCES IN THE REPUBLIC OF KOREA AND RELATED AGREED MINUTES

0074

AGREED UNDERSTANDINGS TO THE AGREEMENT UNDER ARTICLE IV OF THE MUTUAL DEFENSE TREATY BETWEEN THE REPUBLIC OF KOREA AND THE UNITED STATES OF AMERICA, REGARDING FACILITIES AND AREAS AND THE STATUS OF UNITED STATES ARMED FORCES IN THE REPUBLIC OF KOREA AND RELATED AGREED MINUTES

ARTICLE IX

PARAGRAPH 5

1. Examination of parcels in the MPO mails in the ROK by ROK customs inspectors will be conducted so as not to damage the contents of the parcels inspected or delay delivery of the mail;
2. Such examinations will be conducted in U.S. IMPO installations in the presence of U.S. officials;
3. No parcel in the MPO mails will be removed from U.S. postal channels except as mutually agreed;
4. It is understood that the right of inspection will be exercised on a "sample check" basis so as not to unduly delay delivery or increase the administrative burden of the postal authorities.

AGREED MINUTE 3

1. Pertinent information shall include cargo manifests and shipping documents;
2. In addition to information provided on a routine basis, other pertinent information will be provided on request through the Joint Committee.

ARTICLE XIII

AGREED MINUTE

It is understood that the present use of Non-appropriated Fund organizations by organizations and persons other than those referred to in items (a), (b), (c), (d), and (e) shall immediately be suspended at the time of the entry into force of this Agreement. The extent of organizations and persons to be granted the use of such organizations under item (f) of this minute shall be left to further negotiations between the appropriate authorities of the two Governments.

ARTICLE XV

PARAGRAPH 1

If the U.S. authorities determine that there would be significant advantage for ROK-U.S. mutual defense to utilize one or more third-country corporations as USFK-invited contractors, the authorities of the Government of the Republic of Korea shall give sympathetic consideration to a U.S. request to extend the benefits of this agreement to such non-U.S. corporations.

PARAGRAPH 8

1. Unless otherwise agreed in Joint Committee, the privileges provided for in the second sentence of paragraph 8 of this Article shall be extended only to United States Nationals.

ARTICLE XVII

PARAGRAPH 1(b)

1. Local residents, who are third-country nationals and are also local-hire USFK employees and local-hire contractor employees paid in won, on the effective date of the agreement, shall be excluded from the application of this provision.
2. The provisions of paragraph 1(b) do not preclude the United States armed forces from bringing into Korea, without privileges, third-country contractor employees possessing special skills not available from the Korean labor force.

PARAGRAPH 3 AND AGREED MINUTE 4

It is understood that the deviation from Korean labor legislation need not be referred to the Joint Committee in cases when such referral would seriously hamper military operations in an emergency.

ARTICLE XIX

The ROK and U.S. negotiators agree that nothing in the Status of Forces Agreement in anyway prevents the appropriate authorities of either the Republic of Korea or the United States from raising any appropriate matter at any time with each other. The U.S. negotiators recognize the desire of the ROK authorities to discuss the disposal of Military Payment Certificates under custody of the ROK Government. However, both the ROK and U.S. negotiators have agreed to remove from the SOFA text any reference to the question of compensation for Military Payment Certificates held by unauthorized persons. This agreement does not prejudice the position of either party in connection with discussion of this question through other channels.

0076

ARTICLE XXII

PARAGRAPH 1(b)

The civil authorities of the Republic of Korea will retain full control over the arrest, investigation and trial of a member of the United States armed forces or civilian component or a dependent.

PARAGRAPH 5

With regard to the custody of the accused in the hands of the Korean authorities in connection with security offenses:

1. There must be mutual ROK-U.S. agreement as to the circumstances in which such custody is appropriate;

2. Korean confinement facilities must be adequate by U.S. standards.

AGREED MINUTE RE PARAGRAPH 1(a)

The Government of the Republic of Korea agrees that upon notification under the second sentence of the Agreed Minute Re Paragraph 1(a), the military authorities of the Unites States may exercise jurisdiction over such persons in accordance with the terms of the Criminal Jurisdiction Article.

AGREED MINUTE RE PARAGRAPH 2

It is understood that the United States authorities shall exercise utmost restraint in requesting waivers of exclusive jurisdiction as provided for in the Agreed Minute Re Paragraph 2 of this Article.

AGREED MINUTE (1) RE PARAGRAPH 3(a)

With regard to the Agreed Minute Re Paragraph 3(a), a substantial departure from the acts a person is required to perform in a particular duty usually will indicate an act outside of his "official duty".

AGREED MINUTE RE PARAGRAPH 3(a)

A duty certificate shall be issued only upon the advice of a Staff Judge Advocate, and the competent authority issuing the duty certificate shall be a General Grade officer.

AGREED MINUTE RE PARAGRAPH 3(a)

(1) The certificate will be conclusive unless modification is agreed upon. The United States authorities shall give due consideration to any objection which may be raised by the Chief Prosecutor for the Republic of Korea.

(2) The accused should not be deprived of his entitlement to a prompt and speedy trial as a result of protracted reconsideration of the duty certificate.

0077

AGREED MINUTE RE PARAGRAPH 3(b)

1. It is understood that the term "of particular importance" has reference to those cases in which, after a careful examination of each specific case, the exercise of jurisdiction by the Republic of Korea is deemed essential, and the term has reference, in general but not exclusively, to the following types of offense:

(a) security offenses against the Republic of Korea;

(b) offenses causing the death of a human being, robbery, and rape, except where the offenses are directed against a member of the United States armed forces, or the civilian component, or a dependent; and

(c) attempts to commit such offenses or participation therein.

2. In respect of the offenses referred to in the above paragraph, the authorities concerned shall proceed in particularly close cooperation from the beginning of the preliminary investigation in order to provide the mutual assistance envisaged in paragraph 6 of Article XXII.

AGREED MINUTE RE PARAGRAPH 3(b)

3. In cases where, in the view of the United States authorities, any question arises concerning the determination that a case is one "of particular importance", the U.S. diplomatic mission reserves the right and expects to be afforded an opportunity to confer with the proper authorities of the Republic of Korea.

AGREED MINUTE RE PARAGRAPH 9, SUBPARAGRAPH (a) OF SECOND UNNUMBERED PARAGRAPH

Under the appellate procedure of the Courts of the Republic of Korea, the accused may request a re-examination of the evidence, including new evidence and witnesses, as a basis for new findings of fact by the appellate court.

ARTICLE XXIII

PARAGRAPH 12

The liability for claims generated by KSC personnel will be determined by other negotiations between the Republic of Korea and the United States.

ARTICLE XXV

In cooperating with each other under this Article, the two Governments agree that each will take such measures as may be necessary to ensure the security and protection of the U.S. armed forces, the members thereof, the civilian component, the persons who are present in the Republic of Korea pursuant to the Article dealing with Invited Contractors, their dependents and their property.

0078

AGREED UNDERSTANDINGS TO THE
AGREEMENT UNDER ARTICLE IV
OF THE MUTUAL DEFENSE TREATY
BETWEEN THE UNITED STATES OF AMERICA
AND THE REPUBLIC OF KOREA,
REGARDING FACILITIES AND AREAS AND
THE STATUS OF UNITED STATES ARMED
FORCES IN THE REPUBLIC OF KOREA
AND RELATED AGREED MINUTES

ARTICLE IX

PARAGRAPH 5

1. Examination of parcels in the United States military post office mails in the Republic of Korea by customs inspectors of the Republic of Korea will be conducted so as not to damage the contents of the parcels inspected or delay delivery of the mail.

2. Such examinations will be conducted in United States military post office installations in the presence of United States officials.

3. No parcel in the military post office mails will be removed from United States postal channels except as mutually agreed.

4. It is understood that the right of inspection will be exercised on a "sample check" basis so as not to unduly delay delivery or increase the administrative burden of the postal authorities.

0079

AGREED MINUTE 3

1. Pertinent information shall include cargo manifests and shipping documents.

2. In addition to information provided on a routine basis, other pertinent information will be provided on request through the Joint Committee.

ARTICLE XIII

AGREED MINUTE

It is understood that the present use of non-appropriated fund organizations by organizations and persons other than those referred to in items (a), (b), (c), (d), and (e) shall immediately be suspended at the time of the entry into force of this Agreement. The extent of organizations and persons to be granted the use of such organizations under item (f) of this Minute shall be left to further negotiations between the appropriate authorities of the two Governments.

ARTICLE XV

PARAGRAPH 1

If the United States authorities determine that there

would be significant advantage for United States-Republic of Korea mutual defense to utilize one or more third-country corporations as United States ~~Forces Korea~~ armed forces invited contractors, the authorities of the Government of the Republic of Korea shall give sympathetic consideration to a United States request to extend the benefits of this Agreement to such non-United States corporations.

PARAGRAPH 8

Unless otherwise agreed in the Joint Committee, the privileges provided for in the second sentence of paragraph 8 of this Article shall be extended only to United States nationals.

ARTICLE XVII

PARAGRAPH 1 (b)

1. Local residents, who are third-country nationals and are also local-hire United States ~~Forces Korea~~ armed forces employees, and local-hire invited contractor employees paid in won, on the effective date of the Agreement, shall be excluded from the application of this provision.

2. The provisions of paragraph 1(b) do not preclude the United States armed forces from bringing into the Republic of Korea, without privileges, third-country contractor employees possessing special skills not available from the Kore~~a~~n labor force.

PARAGRAPH 3 AND AGREED MINUTE 4

It is understood that the deviation from ~~Korean~~ labor legislation of the Republic of Korea need not be referred to the Joint Committee in

0081

cases when such referral would seriously hamper military operations in an emergency.

ARTICLE XIX

The Republic of Korea and the United States agree that nothing in this Agreement in any way prevents the appropriate authorities of either the Republic of Korea or the United States from raising any appropriate matter at any time with each other. The United States authorities recognize the desire of the authorities of the Republic of Korea to discuss the disposal of military payment certificates under custody of the Government of the Republic of Korea. However, both the Republic of Korea and United States authorities have agreed to remove from the text of the Status of Forces Agreement any reference to the question of compensation for military payment certificates held by unauthorized persons. This agreement does not prejudice the position of either Party in connection with discussion of this question through other channels.

ARTICLE XXII

AGREED MINUTE RE PARAGRAPH 1 (a)

The Government of the Republic of Korea agrees that, upon notification under the second sentence of the Agreed Minute Re Paragraph 1(a),

0082

the military authorities of the United States may exercise jurisdiction over such persons in accordance with the terms of the Criminal Jurisdiction Article.

PARAGRAPH 1 (b)

The civil authorities of the Republic of Korea will retain full control over the arrest, investigation and trial of a member of the United States armed forces or civilian component or a dependent.

AGREED MINUTE RE PARAGRAPH 2

It is understood that the United States authorities shall exercise utmost restraint in requesting waivers of exclusive jurisdiction as provided for in the Agreed Minute Re Paragraph 2 of this Article.

AGREED MINUTE RE PARAGRAPH 3 (a)

1. With regard to the Agreed Minute Re Paragraph 3 (a), a substantial departure from the acts a person is required to perform in a particular duty usually will indicate an act outside of his "official duty."

2. A duty certificate shall be issued only upon the advice of a Staff Judge Advocate, and the competent authority issuing the duty certificate shall be a general grade officer.

3. (a) The certificate will be conclusive unless modification is agreed upon. The United States authorities

0083

shall give due consideration to any objection which may be raised by the Chief Prosecutor for the Republic of Korea.

(b) The accused should not be deprived of his entitlement to a prompt and speedy trial as a result of protracted reconsideration of the duty certificate.

AGREED MINUTE RE PARAGRAPH 3 (b)

1. It is understood that the term "of particular importance" has reference to those cases in which, after a careful examination of each specific case, the exercise of jurisdiction by the Republic of Korea is deemed essential, and the term has reference, in general but not exclusively, to the following types of offense:

(a) security offenses against the Republic of Korea;

(b) offenses causing the death of a human being, robbery, and rape, except where the offenses are directed against a member of the United States armed forces, the civilian component, or a dependent; and

(c) attempts to commit such offenses or participation therein.

2. In respect of the offenses referred to in the above paragraph, the authorities concerned shall proceed in particularly close cooperation from the beginning of the preliminary investigation in order to provide

0084

the mutual assistance envisaged in paragraph 6 of Article XXII.

3. In cases where, in the view of the United States authorities, any question arises concerning the determination that a case is one "of particular importance," the United States diplomatic mission reserves the right and expects to be afforded an opportunity to confer with the proper authorities of the Republic of Korea.

PARAGRAPH 5

With regard to the custody of the accused in the hands of the authorities of the Republic of Korea in connection with security offenses:

6 1. There must be mutual Republic of Korea-United States agreement as to the circumstances in which such custody is appropriate.

2. Confinement facilities of the Republic of Korea must be adequate by United States standards.

AGREED MINUTE RE PARAGRAPH 9, SUB-PARAGRAPH (a) OF SECOND UN-NUMBERED PARAGRAPH

Under the appellate procedure of the courts of the Republic of Korea, the accused may request a re-examination of the evidence, including new evidence and witnesses, as a basis for new findings of fact by the appellate court.

ARTICLE XXIII

0085

PARAGRAPH 12

The liability for claims generated by Korean Service Corps personnel will be determined by other negotiations between the Republic of Korea and the United States.

ARTICLE XXV

In cooperating with each other under this Article, the two Governments agree that each will take such measures as may be necessary to ensure the security and protection of the United States armed forces, the members thereof, the civilian component, the persons who are present in the Republic of Korea pursuant to the Article dealing with invited contractors, their dependents and their property.

0086

AGREED UNDERSTANDINGS TO THE AGREEMENT UNDER ARTICLE IV OF THE MUTUAL DEFENSE TREATY BETWEEN THE REPUBLIC OF KOREA AND THE UNITED STATES OF AMERICA, REGARDING FACILITIES AND AREAS AND THE STATUS OF UNITED STATES ARMED FORCES IN THE REPUBLIC OF KOREA AND RELATED AGREED MINUTES

ARTICLE IX

略字는 풀어쓴다.

PARAGRAPH 5

the United States

1. Examination of parcels in the MPO mails in the ROK by ROK customs inspectors will be conducted so as not to damage the contents of the parcels inspected or delay delivery of the mail;. 句讀點을 整理한다.

2. Such examinations will be conducted in U.S. MPO installations in the presence of U.S. officials;.

3. No parcel in the MPO mails will be removed from U.S. postal channels except as mutually agreed;.

4. It is understood that the right of inspection will be exercised on a "sample check" basis so as not to unduly delay delivery or increase the administrative burden of the postal authorities.

AGREED MINUTE 3

1. Pertinent information shall include cargo manifests and shipping documents;.

2. In addition to information provided on a routine basis, other pertinent information will be provided on request through the Joint Committee.

ARTICLE XIII

AGREED MINUTE

小文字로 한다.

It is understood that the present use of Non-appropriated Fund organizations by organizations and persons other than those referred to in items (a), (b), (c), (d), and (e) shall immediately be suspended at the time of the entry into force of this Agreement. The extent of organizations and persons to be granted the use of such organizations under item (f) of this minute shall be left to further negotiations between the appropriate authorities of the two Governments.

M 頭文字로 한다.

0087

118

ARTICLE XV

PARAGRAPH 1 略字는 좋이 있다.

If the U.S. authorities determine that there would be significant advantage for ROK-U.S. mutual defense to utilize one or more third-country corporations as USFK-invited contractors, the authorities of the Government of the Republic of Korea shall give sympathetic consideration to a U.S. request to extend the benefits of this agreement to such non-U.S. corporations.

A 頭文字로 한다.

PARAGRAPH 8

the 挿入한다.

1 Unless otherwise agreed in Joint Committee, the privileges provided for in the second sentence of paragraph 8 of this Article shall be extended only to United States Nationals.

削除한다.

小文字로 한다.

ARTICLE XVII

PARAGRAPH 1(b)

i.e. 挿入한다.

1. Local residents, who are third-country nationals and are also local-hire USFK employees and local-hire contractor employees paid in won, on the effective date of the agreement, shall be excluded from the application of this provision.

頭文字로 한다.

2. The provisions of paragraph 1(b) do not preclude the United States armed forces from bringing into Korea, without privileges, third-country contractor employees possessing special skills not available from the Korean labor force.

削除한다.

PARAGRAPH 3 AND AGREED MINUTE 4

It is understood that the deviation from Korean labor legislation need not be referred to the Joint Committee in cases when such referral would seriously hamper military operations in an emergency.

ARTICLE XIX

this

The ROK and U.S. negotiators agree that nothing in the Status of Forces Agreement in anyway prevents the appropriate authorities of either the Republic of Korea or the United States from raising any appropriate matter at any time with each other. The U.S. negotiators recognize the desire of the ROK authorities to discuss the disposal of Military Payment Certificates under custody of the ROK Government. However, both the ROK and U.S. negotiators have agreed to remove from the SOFA text any reference to the question of compensation for Military Payment Certificates held by unauthorized persons. This agreement does not prejudice the position of either party in connection with discussion of this question through other channels.

authorities, of the

削除한다.

authorities

0088

項目의 개정등의 說明을 계관한다. ARTICLE XXII

② PARAGRAPH 1(b)

The civil authorities of the Republic of Korea will retain full control over the arrest, investigation and trial of a member of the United States armed forces or civilian component or a dependent.

⑤ PARAGRAPH 5

With regard to the custody of the accused in the hands of the (Korean) authorities in connection with security offenses: of the Republic of Korea

1. There must be mutual ROK-U.S. agreement as to the circumstances in which such custody is appropriate(;) ,

2. (Korean) confinement facilities must be adequate by U.S. standards.

of the Republic of Korea

① AGREED MINUTE RE PARAGRAPH 1(a)

The Government of the Republic of Korea agrees that, upon notification under the second sentence of the Agreed Minute Re Paragraph 1(a), the military authorities of the Unites States may exercise jurisdiction over such persons in accordance with the terms of the Criminal Jurisdiction Article.

③ AGREED MINUTE RE PARAGRAPH 2

It is understood that the United States authorities shall exercise utmost restraint in requesting waivers of exclusive jurisdiction as provided for in the Agreed Minute Re Paragraph 2 of this Article.

削除한다.

④ AGREED MINUTES RE PARAGRAPH 3(a)

1. With regard to the Agreed Minute Re Paragraph 3(a), a substantial departure from the acts a person is required to perform in a particular duty usually will indicate an act outside of his "official duty".

削除한다.

AGREED MINUTE RE PARAGRAPH 3(a)

2. A duty certificate shall be issued only upon the advice of a Staff Judge Advocate, and the competent authority issuing the duty certificate shall be a General Grade officer.

AGREED MINUTE RE PARAGRAPH 3(a)

3. (a) 1. The certificate will be conclusive unless modification is agreed upon. The United States authorities shall give due consideration to any objection which may be raised by the Chief Prosecutor for the Republic of Korea.

(b) 2. The accused should not be deprived of his entitlement to a prompt and speedy trial as a result of protracted reconsideration of the duty certificate.

0089

AGREED MINUTE RE PARAGRAPH 3(b)

1. It is understood that the term "of particular importance" has reference to those cases in which, after a careful examination of each specific case, the exercise of jurisdiction by the Republic of Korea is deemed essential and the term has reference, in general but not exclusively, to the following types of offense:

(a) security offenses against the Republic of Korea;

(b) offenses causing the death of a human being, robbery, and rape, except where the offenses are directed against a member of the United States armed forces or the civilian component, or a dependent; and

(c) attempts to commit such offenses or participation therein.

2. In respect of the offenses referred to in the above paragraph, the authorities concerned shall proceed in particularly close cooperation from the beginning of the preliminary investigation in order to provide the mutual assistance envisaged in paragraph 6 of Article XXII.

AGREED MINUTE RE PARAGRAPH 3(b)

In cases where, in the view of the United States authorities, any question arises concerning the determination that a case is one "of particular importance", the U.S. diplomatic mission reserves the right and expects to be afforded an opportunity to confer with the proper authorities of the Republic of Korea.

AGREED MINUTE RE PARAGRAPH 9, SUBPARAGRAPH (a) OF SECOND UNNUMBERED PARAGRAPH

Under the appellate procedure of the Courts of the Republic of Korea, the accused may request a re-examination of the evidence, including new evidence and witnesses, as a basis for new findings of fact by the appellate court.

ARTICLE XXIII

PARAGRAPH 12

The liability for claims generated by KSC personnel will be determined by other negotiations between the Republic of Korea and the United States.

ARTICLE XXV

In cooperating with each other under this Article, the two Governments agree that each will take such measures as may be necessary to ensure the security and protection of the U.S. armed forces, the members thereof, the civilian component, the persons who are present in the Republic of Korea pursuant to the Article dealing with Invited Contractors, their dependents and their property.

AGREED UNDERSTANDINGS TO THE AGREEMENT UNDER ARTICLE IV OF THE MUTUAL DEFENSE TREATY BETWEEN THE UNITED STATES OF AMERICA AND THE REPUBLIC OF KOREA, REGARDING FACILITIES AND AREAS AND THE STATUS OF UNITED STATES ARMED FORCES IN THE REPUBLIC OF KOREA AND RELATED AGREED MINUTES

ARTICLE IX

~~Customs and Duties~~

PARAGRAPH 5

1. Examination of parcels in the United States military post office mails in the Republic of Korea by (Republic of Korea) customs inspectors will be conducted so as not to damage the contents of the parcels inspected or delay delivery of the mail.

2. Such examinations will be conducted in United States military post office installations in the presence of United States officials.

3. No parcel in the military post office mails will be removed from United States postal channels except as mutually agreed.

4. It is understood that the right of inspection will be exercised on a "sample check" basis so as not to unduly delay delivery or increase the administrative burden of the postal authorities.

0091

AGREED MINUTE 3

1. Pertinent information shall include cargo manifests and shipping documents.

2. In addition to information provided on a routine basis, other pertinent information will be provided on request through the Joint Committee.

ARTICLE XIII

~~Non-appropriated Fund Organizations~~

AGREED MINUTE

It is understood that the present use of non-appropriated fund organizations by organizations and persons other than those referred to in items (a), (b), (c), (d), and (e) shall immediately be suspended at the time of the entry into force of this Agreement. The extent of organizations and persons to be granted the use of such organizations under item (f) of this Minute shall be left to further negotiations between the appropriate authorities of the two Governments.

ARTICLE XV

~~Invited Contractors~~

PARAGRAPH 1

If the United States authorities determine that there would be significant advantage for United States-Republic of Korea mutual defense to utilize one or more third-country corporations as United

0092

States Forces Korea invited contractors, the authorities of the Government of the Republic of Korea shall give sympathetic consideration to a United States request to extend the benefits of this Agreement to such non-United States corporations.

PARAGRAPH 8

Unless otherwise agreed in the Joint Committee, the privileges provided for in the second sentence of paragraph 8 of this Article shall be extended only to United States nationals.

ARTICLE XVII

~~Labor~~

PARAGRAPH 1 (b)

1. Local residents, who are third-country nationals and are also local-hire United States Forces Korea employees, and local-hire invited contractor employees paid in won, on the effective date of the Agreement, shall be excluded from the application of this provision.

2. The provisions of paragraph 1(b) do not preclude the United States armed forces from bringing into Korea, without privileges, the Republic of third-country contractor employees possessing special skills not available from the Korean labor force.

PARAGRAPH 3 AND AGREED MINUTE 4

It is understood that the deviation from Korean labor legislation of the Republic of Korea

0093

need not be referred to the Joint Committee in cases when such referral would seriously hamper military operations in an emergency.

ARTICLE XIX

~~Military Payment Certificates~~

The Republic of Korea and the United States agree that nothing in this Agreement in any way prevents the appropriate authorities of either the Republic of Korea or the United States from raising any appropriate matter at any time with each other. The United States authorities recognize the desire of the authorities of the Republic of Korea to discuss the disposal of military payment certificates under custody of the Republic of Korea Government. However, both the Republic of Korea and United States authorities have agreed to remove from the text of the Status of Forces Agreement any reference to the question of compensation for military payment certificates held by unauthorized persons. This agreement does not prejudice the position of either Party in connection with discussion of this question through other channels.

ARTICLE XXII

~~Criminal Jurisdiction~~

AGREED MINUTE RE PARAGRAPH 1 (a)

The Government of the Republic of Korea agrees that, upon notification under the second sentence of the Agreed Minute Re Paragraph 1(a),

0034

the military authorities of the United States may exercise jurisdiction over such persons in accordance with the terms of the Criminal Jurisdiction Article.

PARAGRAPH 1 (b)

The civil authorities of the Republic of Korea will retain full control over the arrest, investigation and trial of a member of the United States armed forces or civilian component or a dependent.

AGREED MINUTE RE PARAGRAPH 2

It is understood that the United States authorities shall exercise utmost restraint in requesting waivers of exclusive jurisdiction as provided for in the Agreed Minute Re Paragraph 2 of this Article.

AGREED MINUTE RE PARAGRAPH 3 (a)

1. With regard to the Agreed Minute Re Paragraph 3 (a), a substantial departure from the acts a person is required to perform in a particular duty usually will indicate an act outside of his "official duty."

2. A duty certificate shall be issued only upon the advice of a Staff Judge Advocate, and the competent authority issuing the duty certificate shall be a general grade officer.

3. (a) The certificate will be conclusive unless modification is

agreed upon. The United States authorities shall give due consideration to any objection which may be raised by the Chief Prosecutor for the Republic of Korea.

(b). The accused should not be deprived of his entitlement to a prompt and speedy trial as a result of protracted reconsideration of the duty certificate.

AGREED MINUTE RE PARAGRAPH 3 (b)

1. It is understood that the term "of particular importance" has reference to those cases in which, after a careful examination of each specific case, the exercise of jurisdiction by the Republic of Korea is deemed essential, and the term has reference, in general but not exclusively, to the following types of offense:

(a) security offenses against the Republic of Korea;

(b) offenses causing the death of a human being, robbery, and rape, except where the offenses are directed against a member of the United States armed forces, the civilian component, or a dependent; and

(c) attempts to commit such offenses or participation therein.

2. In respect of the offenses referred to in the above paragraph, the authorities concerned shall proceed in particularly close cooperation from the beginning of the preliminary investigation in order to provide

0096

the mutual assistance envisaged in paragraph 6 of Article XXII.

3. In cases where, in the view of the United States authorities, any question arises concerning the determination that a case is one "of particular importance", the United States diplomatic mission reserves the right and expects to be afforded an opportunity to confer with the proper authorities of the Republic of Korea.

PARAGRAPH 5

With regard to the custody of the accused in the hands of the authorities of the Republic of Korea in connection with security offenses:

1. There must be mutual Republic of Korea-United States agreement as to the circumstances in which such custody is appropriate.

2. Korean Confinement facilities of the Republic of Korea must be adequate by United States standards.

AGREED MINUTE RE PARAGRAPH 9, SUB-PARAGRAPH (a) OF SECOND UNNUMBERED PARAGRAPH

Under the appellate procedure of the Courts of the Republic of Korea, the accused may request a re-examination of the evidence, including new evidence and witnesses, as a basis for new findings of fact by the appellate court.

ARTICLE XXIII

0097

~~Claims~~

PARAGRAPH 12

The liability for claims generated by Korean Service Corps personnel will be determined by other negotiations between the Republic of Korea and the United States.

ARTICLE XXV

~~Security Measures~~

In cooperating with each other under this Article, the two Governments agree that each will take such measures as may be necessary to ensure the security and protection of the United States armed forces, the members thereof, the civilian component, the persons who are present in the Republic of Korea pursuant to the Article dealing with Invited Contractors, their dependents and their property.

0098

대한민국과 아메리카 합중국 간의

상호 방위조약 제4조에 의한 시설과 구역 및

대한민국에서의 합중국 군대의 지위에 관한

협정 및 관계 합의 의사록에 대한

합의 양해 사항

제 9 조

제5항

1. 대한민국 세관 검사관에 의한 대한민국내 합중국 군사 우체국 우편물에 들어 있는 소포의 검사는, 검사를 당하는 소포의 내용물을 손상 시키지 아니하고 또는 우편물의 배달을 지연시키지 아니하도록 행한다.

2. 이러한 검사는 합중국 직원의 입회하에 합중국 군사 우체국 시설 내에서 행한다.

3. 상호 합의된 경우를 제외하고는, 군사 우체국 우편물의 여하한 소포도 합중국 우편 경로로부터 제거되지 아니한다.

4. 검사관은 부당하게 배달을 지연시키거나 또는 우체국의 행정상의 부담을 증가시키지 아니하도록 하기 위하여 "표본 검사" 기준에 따라 행사될 것으로 양해한다.

합의 의사록 3

1. 관계 정보는 화물 적하목록 및 선적 서류를 포함한다.

2. 정규적으로 제공되는 정보에 추가하여, 기타 관계 정보는 합동위원회를 통한 요구에 따라 제공된다.

0099

제 13 조

합의 의사록

(가),(나),(다),(라) 및 (마) 항목에서 언급된 것 이외의 기관 및 인원에 의한 비세출자금 기관의 현재의 사용은 본협정의 효력 발생시에 즉시 정지되는 것으로 양해한다. 본 의사록(바) 항목에 따라 이러한 기관의 사용이 허용된 기관과 인원의 범위는 양국 정부의 관계 당국간의 계속적 협의에 위임한다.

제 15 조

제 1 항

합중국 당국이 하나 또는 둘 이상의 제3국 법인을 합중국 군대의 초청 계약자로서 사용함이 대한민국과 합중국 간의 상호 방위를 위하여 중대한 이익이 될 것이라고 결정하는 경우에는, 대한민국 정부 당국은 이러한 법인에게 본 협정의 혜택을 부여하기 위한 합중국의 요청에 대하여 호의적 고려를 하여야 한다.

제 8 항

합동위원회에서 달리 합의되지 아니하는 한, 본 조 제8항의 2단에 규정된 특권은 합중국 국민에게만 부여된다.

제 17 조

0100

제 1 항 (나)

1. 본 협정 효력 발생일 자에 제3국 국민이며, 또한 현재로서 지금되는

현지 채용 합중국 군대 고용원과 현지 채용 초청계약자 고용원인 현지 거주자는 본 규정의 적용으로 부터 제외된다.

2. 제1항 (나)의 규정은 합중국 군대가 한국 노동력으로 부터 획득될 수 없는 특수기술을 가지고 있는 제3국 계약자 고용원을 특권 없이 대한민국으로 데리고 오는 것을 배제하지 아니한다.

제 3 항과 합의 의사록 제4

대한민국 노동법령으로 부터의 이탈은, 합동위원회에의 회부가 비상시에 있어서 군사 작전을 심히 방해할 경우에는, 동 위원회에 회부할 필요가 없는 것으로 양해한다.

제 19 조

대한민국과 합중국은 본 협정의 어느 것도 대한민국과 합중국의 관계 당국이 상호 간에 언제든지 여하한 적절한 사항을 제기하는 것을 결코 방지하지 아니하는데 합의한다. 합중국 당국은 대한민국 정부가 보관하고 있는 군표 처리 문제를 토의하려는 대한민국 당국의 요망을 인정한다. 그러나 대한민국 및 합중국의 양 당국은 인가되지 아니한 자에 의하여 보유되고 있는 군표에 대한 보상 문제에 관한 여하한 언급도 주둔군 지위협정 조문으로 부터 제거하는데 합의하였다. 이 합의는 다른 경로를 통한 본 문제의 토의와 관련하여 어느 일방 당사국의 입장을 침해하지 아니한다.

제 22 조

② 제 1 항 (나) 0101

대한민국 민간 당국은 합중국 군대 구성원, 군속 또는 가족의 제도,

수사 및 재판에 대한 일권한 동[illegible]권을 보유한다.

(6) 제 5 항

인권에 관한 범죄에 관련하여 대한민국 당국의 수중에 있는 피의자의 구금에 관하여 :

1. 이러한 구금이 적절한 환경에 관하여 대한민국과 합중국 간에 상호 합의가 있어야 한다.

2. 대한민국의 구금시설은 합중국 수준으로 적합하여야 한다.

(1) 제 1 항 (가)에 관한 합의 의사록

대한민국 정부는 제1항 (가)에 관한 합의 의사록의 후단에 의한 통고가 있으면 합중국 군 당국은 형사재판권 조항의 규정에 의거하여 이러한 자에 대하여 재판권을 행사할 수 있다는 것에 합의한다.

(3) 제 2 항에 관한 합의 의사록

합중국 당국은 본조 제2항에 관한 합의의사록에 규정된 전속적 재판권의 포기를 요청함에 있어서 최대한으로 자제 하여야 한다는 것을 양해한다.

(4) 제 3 항 (가)에 관한 합의 의사록

1. 제 3 항 (가)에 관한 합의 의사록에 관하여, 어떤 자가 특정 공무에 있어서 행한 것이 요구되는 행위로 부터의 실질적 이탈은, 통상 그의 "공무" 밖의 행위를 뜻한다.

2. 공무 집행 증명서는 법무참모의 권고에 의하여 발급되어야하며, 공무집행 증명서를 발급하는 주무 당국자는 장성급 장교여야 한다.

0102

3. (가) 수정이 합의되지 아니하는 한, 증명서는 결정적이다. 합중국 당국은 대한민국을 대신하여 검찰총장이 제기하는 이러한 이의에 대하여 정당한 고려를 하여야 한다.

(나) 피의자는 공무집행 증명서의 기재된 사고의 결과로서 추가적이고도 신속한 재판에 대한 그의 권리가 박탈되어서는 아니된다.

⑤ 제 3 항 (나)에 관한 합의 의사록

1. "특히 중요하다"는 용어는 개개의 특정 사건을 신중히 조사한 후 대한민국이 재판권을 행사함이 긴요하다고 생각되는 사건에 관련되며 또한 이 용어는 일반적으로 다음과 같은 종류의 범죄에 관련되나 그와 같은 종류의 범죄에만 한정되는 것이 아니라고 양해한다.

(가) 대한민국의 안전에 관한 범죄,

(나) 사람을 죽음에 이르게 한 범죄, 강도죄 및 강간죄. 다만, 그 범죄가 합중국 군대의 구성원, 군속 또는 가족에 대하여 행하여진 경우에는 그러하지 아니하다. 및

(다) 전기 각범죄의 미수 또는 공범.

2. 전항에 규정된 범죄에 관하여, 관계 당국은 제22조 제6항에 규정된 상호간의 의무를 제공하기 위하여 이러한 수사를 개시한 때부터 특히, 긴밀하게 협력하면서 절차를 취하여야 한다.

3. 합중국 당국의 견지에서 사건이 특히 중요한 것이라는 결정에 관한 의문이 제기된 경우에는 합중국 외교 사절은 대한민국의 관계당국과 상의할 수 있는 기회가 부여될 권리를 보유하며 또한 그러한 기회가 부여되기를 기대한다.

0103

제 9 항 (가) 후단에 관한 합의 의사록

대한민국 법원의 항소 절차에 의거하여, 피고인은 항소 법원에 의한 새로운 사실의 발견을 위한 근거로서 새로운 증거와 증인을 포함한 증거의 재조사를 요청할 수 있다.

제 23 조

제 12 항

한국 노무단 원에 의하여 제기된 청구권에 대한 책임은 대한민국과 합중국 간의 별도 협의에 의하여 결정한다.

제 25 조

본조에 의거하여 상호 협력함에 있어서 각 정부는 합중국 군대, 그 구성원, 군속, 초청 계약자에 관한 조항에 따라 대한민국에 있는 자, 그들의 가족 및 그들의 재산의 보안과 보호를 보장하기에 필요한 조치를 취할 것에 양국 정부는 합의한다.

0104

ARTICLE XVII LABOR

(b) Employees or any employee organization shall have the right of further collective action in the event a labor dispute is not resolved by the foregoing procedures except in cases where the Joint Committee determines such action seriously hampers military operations of the United States armed forces for the joint defense of the Republic of Korea. In the event an agreement cannot be reached on this question in the Joint Committee, it may be made the subject of review through discussions between appropriate officials of the Government of the Republic of Korea and the diplomatic mission of the United States of America.

AGREED MINUTES

4. When employers cannot conform with provisions of labor legislation of the Republic of Korea applicable under this Article on account of the military requirements of the United States armed forces, the matter shall be referred, in advance, to the Joint Committee for consideration and appropriate action. In the event mutual agreement cannot be reached in the Joint Committee regarding appropriate action, the issue may be made the subject of review through discussions between appropriate officials of the Government of the Republic of Korea and the diplomatic mission of the United States of America.

0105

제 17 조 노 무

④ (나) 고용원 또는 고용원 단체는 노동쟁의가 전기 절차에 의하여 해결되지 아니하는 경우에는 계속 단체 행동권을 가진다. 다만, 합동위원회가 이러한 행동이 대한민국의 공동방위를 위한 합중국 군대의 군사작전을 심히 방해한다고 결정하는 경우에는 제외한다. 합동위원회에서 이 문제에 관하여 합의에 도달할수 없을 경우에는 그 문제는 대한민국 정부의 관계관과 아메리카 합중국 외교 사절간의 토의를 통한 재 검토의 대상이 될수 있다.

합의의사록

④ 고용주가 합중국 군대의 군사상 필요 때문에 본 조에 따라 적용되는 대한민국 노동 법령을 따를수 없을 때에는, 그 문제는 사전에 검토와 적당한 조치를 위하여 합동위원회에 회부되어야한다. 합동위원회에서 적당한 조치에 관하여 상호 합의가 이루어질 수 없을 경우에는, 그 문제는 대한민국 정부의 관계관과 아메리카 합중국의 외교 사절 간의 토의를 통한 재 검토의 대상이 될 수 있다.

0106

제 17 조 노 무

4. (나) 고용원 또는 고용원 단체는 노동 쟁의가 전기 절차에 의하여 해결되지 아니하는 경우에는 계속 단체 행동권을 가진다. 다만, 합동위원회가 이러한 행동이 대한민국의 공동 방위를 위한 합중국 군대의 군사 작전을 심히 방해한다고 결정하는 경우에는 제외한다. 합동위원회에서 이 문제에 관하여 합의에 도달할 수 없을 경우에는 그 문제는 대한민국 정부의 관계관과 아메리카 합중국 외교 사절 간의 토의를 통한 재검토의 대상이 될수 있다.

합의의사록

4. 고용주가 합중국 군대의 군사상 필요 때문에 본 조에 따라 적용되는 대한민국 노동 법령을 따를 수 없을 때에는, 그 문제는 사전에 검토와 적당한 조치를 위하여 합동위원회에 회부되어야 한다. 합동위원회에서 적당한 조치에 관하여 상호 합의가 이루어질 수 없을 경우에는, 그 문제는 대한민국 정부의 관계관과 아메리카 합중국의 외교 사절 간의 토의를 통한 재검토의 대상이 될 수 있다.

0107

Dear Mr. Ambassador:

Today the Governments of the Republic of Korea and the United States have formally signed the Agreement between the United States of America and the Republic of Korea regarding facilities and areas and the status of United States armed forces in the Republic of Korea. Article XXII of that Agreement and its Agreed Minutes provide for the exercise of jurisdiction over members of the United States armed forces, the civilian component, and their dependents in the Republic of Korea. In this regard, the Government of the Republic of Korea, conscious of the strong ties of mutual respect and friendship which bind our two countries, and recognizing the vital role which United States armed forces play in the defense of the Republic of Korea, proposes the following understandings for procedural arrangements pursuant to Paragraph 4 of the Agreed Minute Re Paragraph 3(b):

That, to facilitate the processing of cases resulting from the presence of United States armed forces deployed in the Republic of Korea for mutual defense purposes, in implementation of the provisions of the Agreed Minute Re Paragraph 3(b), the Government of the Republic of Korea will not require the military authorities of the United States to make a request for a waiver in each particular case, and the military authorities of the United States shall have jurisdiction unless the Government of the Republic of Korea determines in a specific case that it is of particular importance that jurisdiction be exercised therein by the authorities of the Republic of Korea;

0108

That, in the interest of expediting the administration of justice, any such determination by the Government of the Republic of Korea shall be provided in writing by the Minister of Justice to the appropriate military authorities of the United States within fifteen days after the Republic of Korea is notified or is otherwise apprised of the commission of an offense falling within its primary jurisdiction, or such shorter period as may be mutually agreed upon pursuant to Paragraph 4 of the Agreed Minute in Paragraph 3(b). The military authorities of the United States shall not exercise jurisdiction before the expiration of the fifteen days or other agreed period. I would be grateful for your confirmation of the above understandings.

Sincerely yours,

0109

親愛하는 大使 貴下,

今日 大韓民國 政府와 合衆國 政府는 大韓民國과 合衆國 政府 間의 施設과 區域 및 大韓民國에서의 合衆國 軍隊의 地位에 關한 ~~地位에 關한~~ 協定에 正式으로 署名하였읍니다. 同 協定의 第22條 및 同 合意議事錄은 大韓民國에 있는 合衆國 軍隊 構成員, 軍屬 및 그들의 家族에 對한 裁判權 行使를 規定하고 있읍니다. 그에 關聯하여, 大韓民國 政府는 우리 兩國家를 結束하는 相互 尊重과 友誼의 强韌한 紐帶를 意識하고 또한 合衆國 軍隊가 大韓民國의 防衛에 있어서 遂行하는 重大한 役割을 認定하여 第3項(나)에 關한 合意議事錄 第4項에 따른 節次上의 約定을 爲하여 다음과 같은 諒解事項을 提議하는 바 입니다.

相互防衛目的을 爲하여, 大韓民國에 派遣된 合衆國 軍隊의 [illegible] 발생하는 事件의 處理를 신속히 하기 위하여, 第三項(나)에 關한 合意議事錄의 規定을 施行함에 있어서 大韓民國政府는 合衆國軍當局이 個個의 特定事件에 있어서 포기를 요청할 것을 要求하지 않으며, 大韓民國政府가 特定事件에 있어서 大韓民國當局이 裁判

權을 行使할 特別히 重要하다고 決定하지 아니하는 限, 合衆國 軍當局은 裁判權을 가진다

韓國政府가 신속히 할 경우에, 大韓民國 政府에 依한 그와 같은 決定은 大韓民國이 그의 第一次的 裁判權에 屬하는 犯罪發生을 通告받거나 또는 알게 된 後 15日 內에 또는 第二項(나)에 規定된 合意議事錄 第4項에 따라 相互合意될 수 있는 그보다 短期間 內에 書面으로 合衆國의 關係 軍當局에 通告하여야 한다.

合衆國 軍當局은 15日 또는 보다 合意된 期間이 滿了되기 前에는 裁判權을 行使하여서는 아니된다.

本人은 上記 條項 3項에 對한 貴下의 承認을 要請하여 마지 않습니다

경구

July 7, 1966

His Excellency
Winthrop G. Brown
Ambassador of the United States of America
Seoul, Korea

Dear Mr. Ambassador (Excellency):

Today the Governments of the Republic of Korea and the United States have formally signed the Agreement between the United States of America and the Republic of Korea regarding facilities and areas and the status of United States armed forces in the Republic of Korea. Article XXII of that Agreement and its Agreed Minutes provide for the exercise of jurisdiction over members of the United States armed forces, the civilian component, and their dependents in the Republic of Korea. In this regard, the Government of the Republic of Korea, conscious of the strong ties of mutual respect and friendship which bind our two countries, and recognizing the vital role which United States armed forces play in the defense of the Republic of Korea, proposes the following understandings for procedural arrangements pursuant to Paragraph 4 of the Agreed Minute Re Paragraph 3(b):

That, to facilitate the processing of cases resulting from the presence of United States armed forces deployed in the Republic of Korea for mutual defense purposes, in implementation of the provisions of the Agreed Minute Re Paragraph 3(b), the Government of the Republic of Korea will not require the military authorities of the United States to make a request for a waiver in each particular case, and the

0112

military authorities of the United States shall have jurisdiction unless the Government of the Republic of Korea determines in a specific case that it is of particular importance that jurisdiction be exercised therein by the authorities of the Republic of Korea;

That, in the interest of expediting the administration of justice, any such determination by the Government of the Republic of Korea shall be provided in writing by the Minister of Justice to the appropriate military authorities of the United States within fifteen days after the Republic of Korea is notified or is otherwise apprised of the commission of an offense falling within its primary jurisdiction, or such shorter period as may be mutually agreed upon pursuant to Paragraph 4 of the Agreed Minute in Paragraph 3(b). The military authorities of the United States shall not exercise jurisdiction before the expiration of the fifteen days or other agreed period. I would be grateful for your confirmation of the above understandings.

Sincerely yours,

~~(Tong Won Lee)~~

~~Foreign~~ Minister of Foreign Affairs

0113

(2)

미합중국 대사
윈드롭 지. 브라운
대한민국, 서울

1966년 7월 9일

각하,

금일 대한민국 정부와 합중국 정부는 대한민국과 합중국 정부간의 시설과 구역 및 대한민국에서의 합중국 군대의 지위에 관한 협정에 정식으로 서명하였읍니다. 동 협정의 제 22조 및 동 합의 의사록은 대한민국에 있는 합중국 군대 구성원, 군속 및 그들의 가족에 대한 재판권 행사를 규정하고 있읍니다. 이에 관련하여, 대한민국 정부는 우리 양국가를 결속하는 상호 존중과 우의의 강인한 유대를 의식하고 또한 합중국 군대가 대한민국의 방위에 있어서 수행하는 중대한 역활을 인정하여 제 3조(나) 에 관한 합의 의사록 제 4항에 따른 절차상의 약정을 위하여 다음과 같은 양해 사항을 제의하는 바입니다.

상호 방위 목적을 위하여, 대한민국에 배치된 합중국 군대의 주둔으로 말미암아 발생하는 사건의 처리를 신속히 하기 위하여, 제 3항(나)에 관한 합의 의사록의 규정을 시행함에 있어서 포기를 요청할것을 요구하지 아니하며, 대한민국

대한민국 정부는
합중국 당국이 개개의
특정사건에 있어서

0114

정부가 특정사건에 있어서 대한민국 당국이 재판권을 행사함이 특히 중요하다고 결정하지 아니하는한, 합중국 군당국은 재판권을 가진다.

사법행정의 신속화를 위하여 대한민국 정부에 의한 그와같은 결정은 대한민국이 그의 제 1차 재판권에 속하는 범죄 발생을 통고받거나 또는 알게된후 15일내에 또는 제 3항(나) 에 관한 합의 의사록 제 4항에 따라 상호합의 될수 있는 그보다 단기간내에 법무부 장관이 서면으로 합중국의 관계 군당국에 통고하여야 한다.

합중국 군당국은 15일 또는 달리 합의된 기간이 만료되기 전에는 재판권을 행사하여서는 아니된다.

본인은 상기 양해사항에 대한 귀하의 확인을 감사히 여기는 바입니다.

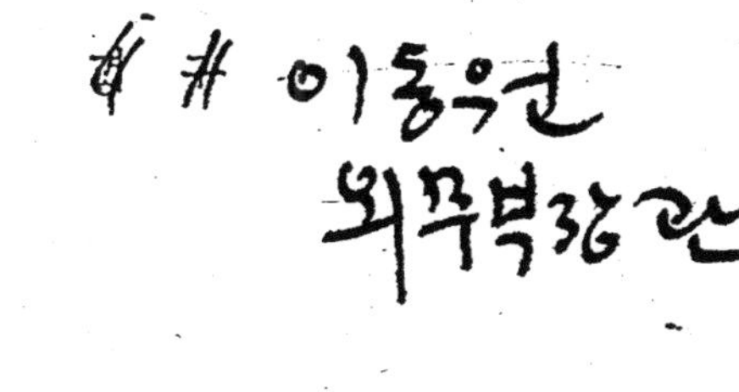

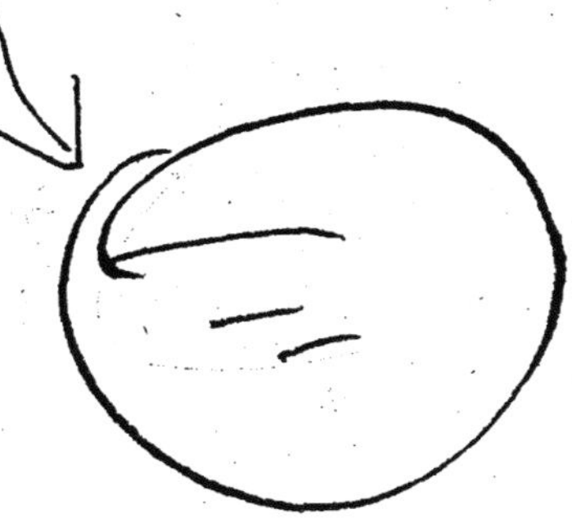

0115

(3) 제4호

July 9, 1966

His Excellency
Tong Won Lee
Minister of Foreign Affairs
of the Republic of Korea
Seoul, Korea

Dear Mr. Minister:

I have received your letter of this date on the subject of the Agreement signed today between the Republic of Korea and the United States of America regarding facilities and areas and the status of United States armed forces in the Republic of Korea, and confirm the following understandings contained therein with respect to the exercise of jurisdiction over members of the United States armed forces, the civilian component, and their dependents:

That, to facilitate the processing of cases resulting from the presence of United States armed forces deployed in the Republic of Korea for mutual defense purposes, in implementation of the provisions of the Agreed Minute Re Paragraph 3(b), the Government of the Republic of Korea will not require the military authorities of the United States to make a request for a waiver in each particular case, and the military authorities of the United States shall have jurisdiction unless the Government of the Republic of Korea determines in a specific case that it is of particular importance that jurisdiction be exercised therein by the authorities of the Republic of Korea;

0116

That, in the interest of expediting the administration of justice, any such determination by the Government of the Republic of Korea shall be provided in writing by the Minister of Justice to the appropriate military authorities of the United States within fifteen days after the Republic of Korea is notified or is otherwise apprised of the commission of an offense falling within its primary jurisdiction, or such shorter period as may be mutually agreed upon pursuant to Paragraph 4 of the Agreed Minute Re Paragraph 3(b). The military authorities of the United States shall not exercise jurisdiction before the expiration of the fifteen days or other agreed period.

Very sincerely yours,

Winthrop G. Brown
Ambassador

0117

(4)

1966년 7월 9일

대한민국 외무부장관
이 동 원 각하
서 울.

각 하,

본인은 금일 대한민국과 합중국 간에 서명된 시설과 구역 및 대한민국에서의 합중국 군대의 지위협정에 관한 각하의 금일자 공한을 접수하였으며, 합중국 군대의 구성원, 군속 및 그들의 가족에 대한 재판권의 행사에 관하여 동 공한에 포함된 다음과 같은 양해사항을 확인하는 바입니다.

상호 방위목적을 위하여, 대한민국에 배치된 합중국 군대의 주둔으로 말미아마 발생하는 사건의 처리를 신속히 하기 위하여 제3항(나)에 관한 합의의사록의 규정을 시행함에 있어서 포기를 요청할 것을 요구하지 아니하며, 대한민국 정부가 특정사건에 있어서 대한민국 당국이 재판권을 행사함이 특히 중요하다고 결정하지 아니하는한, 합중국 군 당국은 재판권을 가진다.

사법행정의 신속화를 위하여 대한민국 정부에 의한 그와같은 결정은 대한민국이 그의 제1차 재판권에 속하는 범죄발생을 통고받거나 또는 알게된후 15일내에 또는 제3항 (나)에 관한 합의의사록 제4항에

0118

따라 상호합의 될수 있는, 그보다 단기간내에 법무부 장관이 서면으로 합중국의 관계군 당국에 통고하여야 한다.

합중국 군당국은 15일 또는 달리 합의된 기간이 만료되기 전에는 재판권을 행사하여서는 아니된다.

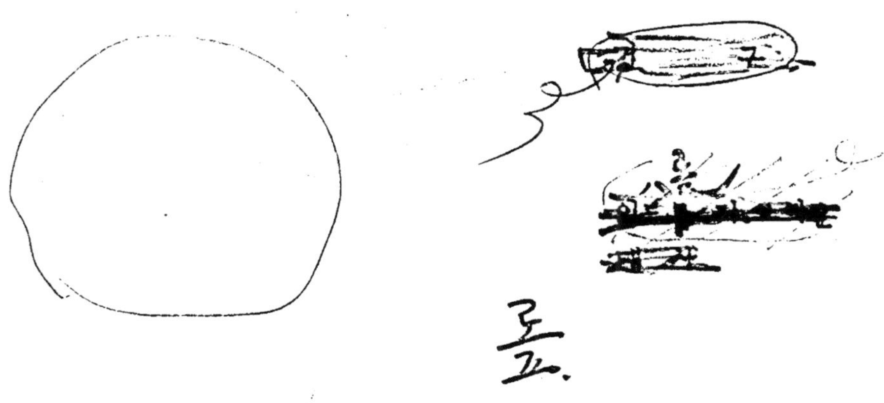

0119

1966년 7월 9일

각 하,

금일 대한민국 정부와 합중국 정부는 대한민국과 합중국 정부간의 시설과 구역 및 대한민국에서의 합중국 군대의 지위에 관한 협정에 정식으로 서명하였읍니다. 동 협정의 제 22조 및 동 합의 의사록은 대한민국에 있는 합중국 군대 구성원, 군속 및 그들의 가족에 대한 재판권 행사를 규정하고 있읍니다. 이에 관련하여, 대한민국 정부는 우리 양국가를 결속하는 상호 존중과 우의의 강인한 유대를 의식하고 또한 합중국 군대가 대한민국의 방위에 있어서 수행하는 중대한 역활을 인정하여 제 3항 (나)에 관한 합의 의사록 제 4항에 따른 절차상의 약정을 위하여 다음과 같은 양해 사항을 제의하는 바입니다.

상호 방위 목적을 위하여, 대한민국에 배치된 합중국 군대의 주둔으로 말미암아 발생하는 사건의 처리를 신속히 하기 위하여, 제3항 (나)에 관한 합의 의사록의 규정을 시행함에 있어서 대한민국 정부는 합중국 당국이 개개의 특정 사건에 있어서 포기를 요청할것을 요구하지 아니하며, 대한민국 정부가 특정사건에 있어서 대한민국 당국이 재판권을 행사함이 특히 중요하다고 결정하지 아니하는한, 합중국 군당국은 재판권을 가진다.

사법행정의 신속화를 위하여 대한민국 정부에 의한 그와

/.. 0120

같은 결정은 대한민국이 그의 제 1차 재판권에 속하는 범죄 발생을 통고받거나 또는 알게된후 15일내에 또는 제3항(나)에 관한 합의 의사록 제4항에 따라 상호 합의될 수 있는 그보다 단 기간내에 법무부 장관이 서면으로 합중국의 관계 군 당국에 통고하여야 한다.

합중국 군 당국은 15일 또는 달리 합의된 기간이 만료되기 전에는 재판권을 행사하여서는 아니된다.

본인은 상기 양해사항에 대한 각하의 확인을 감사히 여기는 바입니다.

아메리카합중국 대사

윈드롭.지.브라운

대한민국, 서울

0121

July 9, 1966

His Excellency
Tong Won Lee
Minister of Foreign Affairs
of the Republic of Korea
Seoul, Korea

Dear Mr. Minister:

I have received your letter of this date on the subject of the Agreement signed today between the Republic of Korea and the United States of America regarding facilities and areas and the status of United States armed forces in the Republic of Korea, and confirm the following understandings contained therein with respect to the exercise of jurisdiction over members of the United States armed forces, the civilian component, and their dependents:

That, to facilitate the processing of cases resulting from the presence of United States armed forces deployed in the Republic of Korea for mutual defense purposes, in implementation of the provisions of the Agreed Minute Re Paragraph 3(b), the Government of the Republic of Korea will not require the military authorities of the United States to make a request for a waiver in each particular case, and the military authorities of the United States shall have jurisdiction unless the Government of the Republic of Korea determines in a specific case that it is of particular importance that jurisdiction be exercised therein by the authorities of the Republic of Korea;

0122

That, in the interest of expediting the administration of justice, any such determination by the Government of the Republic of Korea shall be provided in writing by the Minister of Justice to the appropriate military authorities of the United States within fifteen days after the Republic of Korea is notified or is otherwise apprised of the commission of an offense falling within its primary jurisdiction, or such shorter period as may be mutually agreed upon pursuant to Paragraph 4 of the Agreed Minute Re Paragraph 3(b). The military authorities of the United States shall not exercise jurisdiction before the expiration of the fifteen days or other agreed period.

Very sincerely yours,

Winthrop G. Brown
Ambassador

0123

1966년 7월 9일

각 하.

본인은 금일 대한민국과 아메리카합중국 간에 서명된 시설과 구역 및 대한민국에서의 합중국 군대의 지위 협정에 관한 각하의 금일자 공한을 접수하였으며, 합중국 군대의 구성원, 군속 및 그들의 가족에 대한 재판권의 행사에 관하여 동 공한에 포함된 다음과 같은 양해사항을 확인하는 바입니다.

상호 방위목적을 위하여, 대한민국에 배치된 합중국 군대의 주둔으로 말미암아 발생하는 사건의 처리를 신속히 하기 위하여 제 3항 (나)에 관한 합의 의사록의 규정을 시행함에 있어서 포기를 요청할 것을 요구하지 아니하며, 대한민국 정부가 특정사건에 있어서 대한민국 당국이 재판권을 행사함이 특히 중요하다고 결정하지 아니하는한, 합중국 군 당국은 재판권을 가진다.

사법행정의 신속화를 위하여 대한민국 정부에 의한 그와 같은 결정은 대한민국이 그의 제1차 재판권에 속하는 범죄발생을

/ ..

0124

통고받거나 또는 알게된후 15일내에 또는 제3항 (나)에 관한 합의 의사록 제4항에 따라 상호 합의될 수 있는. 그보다 단 기간내에 법무부 장관이 서면으로 합중국의 관계 군 당국에 통고하여야 한다.

합중국 군 당국은 15일 또는 달리 합의된 기간이 만료 되기 전에는 재판권을 행사하여서는 아니된다.

대한민국 외무부장관
이 동 원 각 하
서 울.

0125

AGREED MINUTE RE PARAGRAPH 3(b) OF ARTICLE XXII: CRIMINAL JURISDICTION

1. The authorities of the Republic of Korea, recognizing that it is the primary responsibility of the United States military authorities to maintain good order and discipline where persons subject to United States military laws are concerned, will, upon the request of the military authorities of the United States pursuant to paragraph 3(c), waive their primary right to exercise jurisdiction under paragraph 3(b) except when they determine that it is of particular importance that jurisdiction be exercised by the authorities of the Republic of Korea. In cases where any question concerning such determination as may be made by the authorities of the Republic of Korea in accordance with the foregoing provisions cannot be resolved in discussions between the authorities concerned, the United States diplomatic mission will be afforded an opportunity to confer with the proper authorities of the Republic of Korea.

2. With the consent of the competent authorities of the Republic of Korea, the military authorities of the United States may transfer to the courts or authorities of the Republic of Korea for investigation, trial and decision, particular criminal cases in which jurisdiction rests with the United States.

6/30 10:30 a.m 미국측 대안

0126

With the consent of the military authorities of the United States, the competent authorities of the Republic of Korea may transfer to the military authorities of the United States for investigation, trial and decision, particular criminal cases in which jurisdiction rests with the Republic of Korea.

3. (a) Where a member of the United States armed forces or civilian component, or a dependent, is arraigned before a court of the United States, for an offense committed in the Republic of Korea against Korean interests, the trial shall be held within the Republic of Korea

(i) except where the law of the United States requires otherwise, or

(ii) except where, in cases of military exigency or in the interests of justice, the military authorities of the United States intend to hold the trial outside the Republic of Korea. In this event they shall afford the authorities of the Republic of Korea timely opportunity to comment on such intention and shall give due consideration to any comments the latter may make.

(b) Where the trial is held outside of the Republic of Korea the military authorities of the United States shall inform the authorities of the Republic of Korea of the place and date of the trial. A representative of the Republic of Korea shall be entitled to be present at the trial. The authorities of the United States shall inform the authorities of the Republic of Korea of the judgment and the final outcome of the proceedings.

4. In the implementation of the provisions of this Article, and to facilitate the expeditious disposal of offenses, arrangements may be made between the military authorities of the United States and the competent authorities of the Republic of Korea.

0128

AGREED UNDERSTANDING IN AGREED JOINT SUMMARY REGARDING AGREED MINUTE RE PARAGRAPH 3(b), OF ARTICLE XXII - CRIMINAL JURISDICTION

1. It is understood that the term "of particular importance" has reference to those cases in which, after a careful examination of each specific case, the exercise of jurisdiction by the Republic of Korea is deemed ~~imperative~~ essential and is limited, in general, but not exclusively, to the following types of offenses:

(a) security offenses against the Republic of Korea;

(b) offenses causing the death of a human being, robbery, and rape, except where the offenses are directed against a member of the United States armed forces, the civilian component, or a dependent; and

(c) attempts to commit such offenses or participation therein.

2. In respect of the offenses referred to in the above paragraph, the authorities concerned shall proceed in particularly close cooperation from the beginning of the preliminary investigation in order to provide the mutual assistance envisaged in paragraph 6 of Article XXII.

in general but not exclusively

Such case re... refer to the following types of offenses ~~are~~

~~above cases afore mentioned~~

It is understood also that the ROKG intends, to the extent possible, to confine its determination of particular importance, to the following types of offenses.

0129

LETTER FROM THE AMERICAN AMBASSADOR TO THE FOREIGN MINISTER

Dear Mr. Minister:

Today the Governments of the United States of America and the Republic of Korea have formally signed the Agreement between the United States of America and the Republic of Korea regarding Facilities and Areas and the Status of United States Armed Forces in the Republic of Korea.

Article XXII of that Agreement and its Agreed Minutes provide for the exercise of jurisdiction over members of the United States armed forces, the civilian component, and their dependents in the Republic of Korea. In this regard, I would be grateful for your confirmation of the following understandings:

That, to facilitate the processing of cases resulting from the presence of United States armed forces deployed in Korea for mutual defense purposes, in implementation of the provisions of Agreed Minute Re Paragraph 3(b), it shall not be necessary for the United States to make a request for waiver in each particular case, and it shall be taken for granted that the Republic of Korea has waived its primary right to exercise jurisdiction thereunder except where the Government of the Republic of Korea determines in a specific case that it is of particular importance that jurisdiction be exercised therein by the authorities of the Republic of Korea;

That, in the interest of expediting the administration of justice, any such determination by the Government of the Republic of Korea shall be provided in writing by the Minister of Justice to the appropriate United States authorities within fifteen days (or such shorter period as may be mutually agreed upon pursuant to paragraph 4 of the Agreed Minute Re Paragraph 3(b)) after the Republic of Korea is notified or is otherwise apprised of the commission of an offense falling within its primary jurisdiction. The authorities of the United States may not exercise jurisdiction before the expiration of the fifteen day or other agreed period.

Sincerely yours,

/s/

0130

LETTER FROM THE FOREIGN MINISTER TO THE AMERICAN AMBASSADOR

Dear Mr. Ambassador:

As requested in your letter of ___________, I am pleased to confirm our understandings:

That, to facilitate the processing of cases resulting from the presence of United States armed forces deployed in Korea for mutual defense purposes, in implementation of the provisions of Agreed Minute Re Paragraph 3(b), it shall not be necessary for the United States to make a request for waiver in each particular case, and it shall be taken for granted that the Republic of Korea has waived its primary right to exercise jurisdiction thereunder except where the Government of the Republic of Korea determines in a specific case that it is of particular importance that jurisdiction be exercised therein by the authorities of the Republic of Korea;

That, in the interest of expediting the administration of justice, any such determination by the Government of the Republic of Korea shall be provided in writing by the Minister of Justice to the appropriate United States authorities within fifteen days (or such shorter period as may be mutually agreed upon pursuant to paragraph 4 of the Agreed Minute Re Paragraph 3(b)) after the Republic of Korea is notified or is otherwise apprised of the commission of an offense falling within its primary jurisdiction. The authorities of the United States may not exercise jurisdiction before the expiration of the fifteen day or other agreed period.

Sincerely yours,

/s/

0131

PARAGRAPH 4. (b) OF ARTICLE XVII: LABOR

4. (b) Employees or any employee organization shall have the right of further collective action in the event a labor dispute is not resolved by the foregoing procedures except in cases where the Joint Committee determines such action seriously hampers military operations of the United States armed forces for the joint defense of the Republic of Korea. In the event an agreement cannot be reached on this question in the Joint Committee, it may be made the subject of review through discussions between appropriate officials of the Government of the Republic of Korea and the diplomatic mission of the United States of America.

0132

ARTICLE XXII CRIM — JURISDICTION

AGREED UNDERSTANDING TO AGREED MINUTE RE PARAGRAPH/#/ 3(b)

Reference: 82nd Meeting, July 8, 1966

~~U.S.-ROK SOFA ARTICLE-AGREED UNDERSTANDING RE AGREED MINUTE PARA 3 (b).~~

IT IS UNDERSTOOD THAT THE TERM "OF PARTICULAR IMPORTANCE" HAS REFERENCE TO THOSE CASES IN WHICH, AFTER A CAREFUL EXAMINATION OF EACH SPECIFIC CASE, THE EXERCISE OF JURISDICTION BY THE REPUBLIC OF KOREA IS DEEMED ESSENTIAL AND THE TERM HAS REFERENCE. IN GENERAL BUT NOT EXCLUSIVELY, THE FOLLOWING TYPES OF OFFENSE"

(a) security offenses against the Republic of Korea;

(b) offenses causing the death of a human being, robbery, and rape, except where the offenses are directed against a member of the United States armed forces or the civilian component, or a dependent; and

(c) attempts to commit such offenses or participation therin.

— In respect of the offenses referred to in the above paragraph the authorities concerned shall proceed in particularly close cooperation from the beginning of the preliminary investigation in order to provide themutual assistance envisaged in paragraph 6 of —ticle XXII.

0133

ARTICLE XXII CRIMINAL JURISDICTION

~~AGREED UNDERSTANDING TO AGREED MINUTE RE PARAGRAPH 3(b)~~

~~U.S.-ROK SOFA-CJ ARTICLE AGREED UNDERSTANDING AGREED MINUTE~~

Reference: 82nd Meeting, July 8, 1966

~~RE PARA 3 (b)~~

"IN CASES WHERE ANY QUESTION arises CONCERNING THE DETERMINATION THAT A CASE IS ONE "OF PARTICULAR IMPORTANCE", ~~CANNOT BE RESOLVED IN DISCUSSIONS BETWEEN THE AUTHORITIES CONCERNED~~, THE U.S. DIPLOMATIC MISSION RESERVES THE RIGHT AND EXPECTS TO BE AFFORDED AN OPPORTUNITY TO CONFER WITH THE PROPER AUTHORITIES OF THE REPUBLIC OF KOREA."

(82nd meeting

(Agreed understanding)

, in the view of the United States authorities,

0134

US-ROK SOFA CJ ARTICLE - AGREED MINUTE RE PARAGRAPH 3(b):

"1. The authorities of the Republic of Korea, recognizing that it is the primary responsibility of the United States military authorities to maintain good order and discipline where persons subject to United States military laws are concerned, will, upon the request of the military authorities of the United States pursuant to Paragraph 3(c), waive their primary right to exercise jurisdiction under Paragraph 3(b) except when they determine that it is of particular importance that jurisdiction be exercised by the authorities of the Republic of Korea.

"2. With the consent of the competent authorities of the Republic of Korea, the military authorities of the United States may transfer to the courts or authorities of the Republic of Korea for investigation, trial and decision, particular criminal cases in which jurisdiction rests with the United States.

With the consent of the military authorities of the United States, the competent authorities of the Republic of Korea may transfer to the military authorities of the United States for investigation, trial and decision, particular criminal cases in which jurisdiction rests with the Republic of Korea.

"3. (a) Where a member of the United States armed forces or civilian component, or a dependent, is arraigned before a court of the United States, for an offense committed in the Republic of Korea against Korean interests, the trial shall be held within the Republic of Korea

(i) except where the law of the United States requires otherwise, or

(ii) except where, in cases of military exigence or in the interests of justice, the military authorities of the United States intend to hold the trial outside the Republic of Korea. In this event they shall afford the authorities of the Republic of Korea timely opportunity to comment on such intention and shall give due consideration to any comments the latter may make.

0135

(b) Where the trial is held outside of the Republic of Korea the military authorities of the United States shall inform the authorities of the Republic of Korea of the place and date of the trial. A representative of the Republic of Korea shall be entitled to be present at the trial. The authorities of the United States shall inform the authorities of the Republic of Korea of the judgment and the final outcome of the proceedings.

"4. To facilitate the expeditious disposal of offenses under this Article, arrangements may be made between the United States military authorities and the competent authorities of the Republic of Korea to dispense with notification."

0136

LABOR ARTICLE - ROK REPLY TO US STATEMENT

(To be presented at 82nd session)

1. Turning to Labor Article, the Korean negotiators appreciate the US negotiators' acceptance of the revised ROK draft, tabled at 81st session. The Korean side accepts, with certain remarks, the US modifications effected in Paragraph 1(b) and Agreed Minutes No. 4 and No. 5, as well as the three understandings, as proposed today by the US negotiators.

2. In agreeing to this Article the Korean negotiators would like to reiterate following three points for the record in the Joint Summary Records:

a. First, the Korean side has come to accept the phrase "military requirements" provided for in Paragraph 3 and Agreed Minutes No. 2 and No. 4, which provides that employers, if required, may deviate from Korean labor legislation without referring the matter in advance to the Joint Committee. We still believe the phrase "military requirements" is broad and ambiguous, and could sometimes lead to undesirable controversy over interpretation during implementation of the Agreement. Whenever such controversy arises in the future, the Korean side would like to have it settled in the light of the text of the Article and Agreed Minutes as well as statements made by the US negotiators for the Agreed Joint Summary. Specifically, the Korean side expects that, as the US Chief Negotiator stated that the 73rd session, "the US armed forces only rarely, if ever, will not be able to conform to ROK labor legislation applicable under this Article, except in emergency situations."

0137

3. Secondly, the Korean side has accepted the phrase "for considera-tion and appropriate action" in place of the phrase "for mutual agreement" in Agreed Minute No. 4. In accepting this phrase, the Korean side takes the view that the "appropriate action" will be taken as a result of consideration by the Joint Committee, or of diplomatic consultation in the event mutual agree-ment cannot be reached in the Joint Committee regarding appropriate action.

4. Thirdly, the Agreed Minute No. 4 provides that deviation from Korean labor legislation shall be referred, in advance whenever possible, to the Joint Committee for consideration and appropriate action. While this provision states that deviation from ROK labor legislation shall be referred whenever possible in advance, it implies that such deviation shall be referred to the Joint Committee as soon as such referral becomes possible. Whenever the matter is referred to the Joint Committee after the deviation had already been made on account of military requirements, it is presumed that the Korean side could raise objection in the Joint Committee to the action taken by the employer and request that appropriate action, i.e., corrective action or measures for remedy, be taken. It is understood that such corrective action will be taken as and when the Joint Committee so directs. In the event that mutual agreement cannot be reached in the Joint Committee regarding appropriate action, the matter may be discussed between officials of the Government of the Republic of Korea and the US diplomatic mission. The foregoing remarks are not intended to introduce any new understanding, but rather are intended to provide guidance to the members of the Joint Committee in their interpretation and implementation of the Article.

LABOR ARTICLE - ROK REPLY TO US STATEMENT

(To be presented at 82nd session)

1. Turning to Labor Article, the Korean negotiators appreciate the US negotiators' acceptance of the revised ROK draft, tabled at 81st session. The Korean side accepts, with certain remarks, the US modifications effected in Paragraph 1 (b) and Agreed Minutes No. 4 and No. 5, as well as the three understandings, as proposed today by the US negotiators.

2. In agreeing to this Article the Korean negotiators would like to reiterate following three points for the record in the Joint Summary Records:

a. First, the Korean side has come to accept the phrase "military requirements" provided for in Paragraph 3 and Agreed Minutes No. 2 and No. 4, which provides that employers, if required, may deviate from Korean labor legislation without referring the matter in advance to the Joint Committee. We still believe the phrase "military requirements" is broad and ambiguous, and could sometimes lead to undesirable controversy over interpretation during implementation of the Agreement. Whenever such controversy arises in the future, the Korean side would like to have it settled in the light of the text of the Article and Agreed Minutes as well as statements made by the US negotiators for the Agreed Joint Summary. Specifically, the Korean side expects that, as the US Cheif Negotiator stated at the 73rd session, "the US armed forces only rarely, if ever, will not be able to conform to ROK labor legislation applicable under this Article, except in emergency situations."

b. Similarly, the Korean negotiators would like to clarify that the provisions of Agreed Minute #4 is understood to apply to the proviso of Para. 3 and, therefore, any

0139

deviation from Korean labor legislation on account of military requirements as stated in Paragraph 3 and Agreed Minutes #2 and #4, shall be subject of referral to the Joint Committee for consideration and appropriate action, in advance or afterword as the case may be.

3. Secondly, the Korean side has accepted the phrase "for consideration and appropriate action" in place of the phrase "for mutual agreement" in Agreed Minute No. 4. In accepting this phrase, the Korean side takes the view that the "appropriate action" will be taken as a result of consideration by the Joint Committee, or of diplomatic consultation in the event mutual agreement cannot be reached in the Joint Committee regarding appropriate action.

4. Thirdly, the Agreed Minute No. 4 provides that deviation from Korean labor legislation shall be referred, in advance whenever possible, to the Joint Committee for consideration and appropriate action. While this provision states that deviation from ROK labor legislation shall be referred whenever possible in advance, it implies that such deviation shall be referred to the Joint Committee as soon as such referral becomes possible. Whenever the matter is referred to the Joint Committee after the deviation had already been made on account of military requirements, it is presumed that the Korean side could raise objection in the Joint Committee to the action taken by the employer and requests that appropriate action, i.e., corrective action or measures for remedy, be taken. It is understood that such corrective action will be taken as and when the Joint Committee so directs. In the event that mutual agreement cannot be reached in the Joint Committee regarding appropriate action,

0140

the matter may be discussed between officials of the Government of the Republic of Korea and the US diplomatic mission. The foregoing remarks are not intended to introduce any new understanding, but rather are intended to provide guidance to the members of the Joint Committee in their interpretation and implementation of the Article.

0141

Under Para. 3, employer may deviate, if required, from Korean labor legislation on account of the military requirements of USFK. In Agreed Minute #4, it provides that when employer cannot conform to the Korean labor legislation applicable under this Article on account of the military requirements, deviation may be made upon consultation at the Joint Committee. The latter provision may possibly lead to an interpretation that the proviso "to the extent not in-consistent with the military requirements" provided for in Para. 3 may not be applicable by the Agreed Minute #4, on the ground that the proviso accordes discretionary authority to employer not to conform Korean labor legislation and, therefore, the phrase "applicable under this Article" is not related with that proviso of Para. 3. We belief that this is not the intension of the U.S. negotiators in proposing the phrase in the Para. 3. In order to prevent such a mis-interpretation, the Korean negotiators would like to have clarified from U.S. side that the provisions of Agreed Minute #4 is understood to apply to the proviso of Para. 3 and, therefore, any matter of deviation from Korean labor legislation on account of military requirements shall be subject of referral to the Joint Committee for consideration and appropriate action, in advance or afterword as the case may be.

17-17

0142

LABOR ARTICLE

(To be presented at 82nd session)

1. Turning to Labor Article, the Korean negotiators would like to announce that Korean side accepts the revised Paragraph 3 and Agreed Minutes #4 together with certain understandings and we understand that full agreement has been reached on this contraversial Article.

2. It is recalled that in negotiating the Labor Article, the both sides had wide differences in their positions with regard to inclusion of invited contractors, the Korean service Corps, domestic, direct hiring of employees, conformance of Korean labor legislation, dispute procedures, employee's right to collective action, deferment of skilled employees from military service, termination of employment, recognition of labor union, and so forth. It is grutifying to note that such differences have been finally narrowed as a result of our earnest deliberations through 18 sessions since their 41st session held on February 6, 1964. In the belief that this successful agreement owes very much to those who participated directly or indirectly in this negotiation in the past and at present, I would like to take this opportunity to renew to all of them for their tireless and valuable contributions toward the conclusion of this Article, which was one of the most hard working tasks before us to be achieved by our negotiating teams.

3. On this last occasion to discuss on this Article, the Korean negotiators would like to state the followings for record of our final session. At first place, the Korean side has come to accept the phrase "military requirements" provided for in Paragraph 3 and Agreed Minutes

0143

1314

#2 and #4, on account of which the employers may deviate from the provisions of Korean labor legislation. As all of us recognize, the phrase "military requirements" is too broad and ambiguous, which would sometimes lead to undesirable controversies over interpretation and in their implementation. For the convenience of reference by both parties in the future, the Korean side would like to extract, <u>inter alia</u>, some statements made by the U.S. negotiators in the past in relation to the definition of the "military requirements". At the 68th session, the U.S. chief negotiator stated that "under the present conditions of Armistice, the U.S. armed forces must be prepared to meet any military contingencies, including developments which are unforeseable." He continued that "military requirements were those requirements which contributed to the accomplishment of the military mission of the U.S. armed forces". At that session, in replying to the doubts by Korean side that if the phrase "military requirements" were accepted, the Korean employees would be denied their rights, Mr. Habib answered that "this was not the intent nor did the language have this meaning." Again, at the 71st session, the U.S. negotiators reiterated that the "United States forces in Korea must have the authority to vary from the ROK labor laws when necessary to satisfy the military requirements..... The failure to do so could seriously hamper military operations in an emergency." At the 73rd session, Mr. Habib pointed out that "the U.S. armed forces only rarely, if ever, will not be able to conform to ROK labor legislation applicable under this Article, except in emergency situations."

1715

0144

The Korean side wishes to have the above statements by the U.S. negotiators as guidelines and criteria in interpretation and implementation of the phrase "military requirements" which are provided for in this Article.

4. As for second instance, the Korean side has accept the phrase "for consideration and appropriate action" in place of the phrase "for mutual agreement" in Agreed Minute #4. In accepting this phrase, the Korean side takes it a matter of course that the appropriate action by the employer can only be taken upon mutual agreement at the Joint Committee, as it is implicit in the text of Agreed Minute #4.

12-16

0145

LABOR ARTICLE

(To be presented at 82nd session)

1. Turning to Labor Article, the Korean negotiators would like to appreciate the U.S. negotiators for their acceptance of our revised draft tabled at 81st session and to announce that the Korean side accepts, with certain remarks, the U.S. modifications effected in Para.1(b) and Agreed Minutes #4 and #5 as well as three understandings, as proposed today.

2. In agreeing to this Article, the Korean negotiators would like to reiterate the following three remarks for record in the Joint Summary Records. At first place, the Korean si e has come to accept the phrase "military requirements" provided for in Paragraph 3 and Agreed Minutes #2 and #4, on account of which the employers, if required, may deviate from Korean labor legislation without referring the matter in advance to the Joint Committee. As all of us recognise, the phrase "military requirements" is too broad and ambiguous, which would sometimes lead to undesirable controbersy over interpretation and in implementation. Whenever such controversy arises in the future, the Korean side would like to have it settled in the light of certain statements made in that regard by the U.S. negotiators at the past negotiating sessions. In any case, the Korean side expects that, as the U.S. negotiator stated at the 73rd session, "the U.S. armed forces only rerely, if ever, will not be able to conform to ROK labor legislation applicable under this Article, escept in emergency situations." Similarly, the Korean negotiators would
6. like to have clarified from U.S. side that the provisions

17-11 0146

of Agreed Minute #4 is understood to apply to the proviso of Para. 3 and, therefore, any deviation from Korean labor legislation on account of military requirements shall be subject of referral to the Joint Committee for consideration and appropriate action, in advance or afterword as the case may be.

3. Secondly, the Korean side has accepted the phrase "for consideration and appropriate action" in place of the phrase "for mutual agreement" in Agreed Minute #4.

Therefore, the Agreed Minute #4 now provides that deviation from Korean labor legislation shall be referred, in advance whenever possible, to the Joint Committee for appropriate action. This provision implies that such deviation, whenever possible, shall be referred in advance and, whenever impossible, shall be referred at the time such referral becomes possible. The Korean side taken the view that whenever the matter referred in advance, the "appropriate action" will be taken by the employer upon mutual agreement at the Joint Committee or following diplomatic consultation, as it is implied in the text of Agreed Minute #4.

Whenever the matter is referred after the deviation had already been made on account of military requirements, it is presumed that the Korean side, if any case may be, would raise objection to the action taken by employer and request him to take appropriate action, i.e., corrective action or measures for remedy. It is understood that such corrective action can only be taken as and when the Joint Committee directs to that effect. These sorts of interpretation in this regard are strictly based on the spirit of the present provisions

(7-12) 0147

and on the exchange of views at the informal meeting. These remarks are not intended to introduce any new understanding, but rather intended to provide guidance to the members of the Joint Committee for their easy interpretation and smooth implementation of the Article.

0148

17-13

노 무 조 항

1. 개 요

노무조항은 미국 군대가 한국인 고용을 직접 고용하는 제도를 지속하되 모집에 있어서 가능한 한 한국정부의 모집 기관을 이용한다고 규정하고 있다. 이 조항은 고용조건, 보상 및 노사관계에 있어서 한국 노동관계 법령을 준수함을 원칙으로 하였으며 군사상 필요로 한국 법령을 준수치 못할 경우에는 가능한 한 사전에 합동 위원회에 회부하여 해결방안을 강구하기로 되어 있다. 고용주인 미군은 한국 소득세 법령에 의거하여 고용원의 임금중에서 원천 과세액을 공제하여 한국 정부에 납부하기로 되어 있다.

본 조항에 의하여 고용주와 고용인간의 분쟁은 우선 불평처리의 노동관계 절차에 의하여 해결하되 해결되지 않을 경우에는 다음과 같은 세 단계로 해결하기로 되어 있다.

첫째, 노동청에 회부하여 조정하고

둘째, 합동위원회에 회부하고 그는 특별분과 위원회에 조정을 의뢰하여

셋째, 합동 위원회가 직접 해결한다.

이 합동 위원회의 결정은 구속력을 가지되 제 2 단계인 합동 위원회에 회부된후 70일의 기간이 경과된 후에도 노동쟁의가 해결되지 않은 경우에는 고용원이나 고용원 단체(노동조합)는 정상 업무를 방해 행위(파업을 포함한 단체 행동권의 행사)를 할수 있도록 되어 있다. 그리고 단체 행동권은 원칙적으로 모든 고용원이 향유하지만 합동 위원회는 한국의 국방상 또는 한국의 관계법령의 규정을 참작하여 단체 행동권을 행사하여서는 안될 긴요한 고용원의 범위를 결정하기로 되어 있다.

끝으로 고용원 단체 즉 노동조합은 한국 법령에 의하여 조직되면 당연히 고용주에 의하여 승인된다. 그러나 그러한 노동조합의 목적이 한.미 공동 이익에 배반할 경우에는 승인되지 않기로 되어 있다.

0149

II. 중요 문제별 내용

1. 고용원의 직접 고용제도

가. 문제점

미군, 비세출 자금기관, 초청계약자인 고용주는 한국인 고용원을 직접 모집하고 고용한다.

나. 이 유

(1) 고용주가 고용원을 직접 고용함은 우리 법령이나 다른 모든 나라에서 통용되는 일반 원칙이다.

(2) 일본이나 독일에서 간접 고용제를 채용하고 있는바 이는 전후 패전국으로서 노무자를 전쟁배상의 일환으로 제공하였던 역사적 연유로 확립된 제도이며 패전국이 아닌 아국은 해방후부터 직접 고용제를 채택, 전통화된 것이다.

(3) 이러한 직접 고용제 하에서 정부는 제 3 자의 입장에서 공정하게 고용원의 이익을 추구하는데 개입함으로서 성과를 올릴수 있다.

(4) 간접 고용제 하에서는 고용인 단체 (노동조합) 의 단체 교섭권과 단체 행동권의 행사에 있어서 그 상대가 고용주가 아닌 고용인들의 자국 정부가 된다. 이 경우 만약 아국에서 그러한 제도를 채용하게 된다면 고용인들은 국군의 고용인과 동일한 취급과 대우를 받게 될것이다. 그들은 대체로 노동운동에 종사할수 없게 되어 있음으로 본 조항에 의한 간접 고용제하의 단체 행동권은 확보할수 없었을 것이다. 일본이나 독일에서는 그 군대의 고용원들이 단체 행동권을 갖고 있음으로 미군 고용원에도 동일한 적용을 하는데 지장이 없었다.

(5) 본 협정에서 원칙적으로 직접 고용제를 채택하였지만 고용주는 가능한 한 한국 정부의 모집 기관을 통하여 고용원을 모집하기로 하였으며 그 경우 모집에 소요된 직접 경비를 한국 정부에게 판상하기로 하였다.

0150

2. 고용원의 적용범위

가. 문제점

고용원은 미국 군속, 초청 계약자의 비한국인 고용원, 한국 노무 근무 단원 및 가사 사용인을 제외한 고용주가 고용한 모든 한국 국적을 가진 민간인으로 한다.

나. 이 유

(1) 이중 문제가 되는 한국 노무 근무 단원의 제외는 정부가 그들을 6. 25 동란중에는 전시 동원법에 의하여 미군에게 제공하였고 그후는 자유 모집에 의하여 제공하여 왔음으로 그 고용방법이 미군의 다른 일반 고용원과 상이 하였다.

(2) 따라서 한국 노무 근무단의 지위는 종래 다른 미군 고용원과 동일하지 않았으며 그들의 지위에 관하여는 별도로 교섭하기로 되어 있다.

(3) 이들의 지위협정을 체결함에 있어서 정부는 과거에도 물의를 일으킨 바를 충분히 참작하여 그들의 기본권을 확보하는 동시에 최대한의 이익을 추구하도록 미국 당국과 교섭 에 임할 작정이다.

3. 한국 노동 법령의 준수

가. 문제점

고용주는 고용의 조건, 보상 및 노사관계에 있어서 미군의 군사상 필요에 배치되지 않는한 한국의 노동관계 법 령을 준수한다.

나. 이 유

(1) 여기서 노동조건, 보상 및 노사관계란 모든 고용주와 고용인 간의 관계를 의미하여 그를 한국 법명에 따르기로 한 원칙은 당연한 규정이나 미군의 군사상 필요에 배치되는 경우 한국 노동법령을 준수하지 않을수 있는 여지를 마련한 것이문제가 된다. 그러나 이와 같은 군사상 필요에 따라 한국 법령을 준수하지 못하는 것은 미군의 군사상의 임무와 전시등과 같은 비상시에

0151

한국 법령을 그대로 지키지 못할 것임으로 마련한 구정이다.

(2) 다른 협정에도 이와 흡사한 구정이 있는바 예컨데 일본의 경우에는 "별도 상호 합의하는 한도내에서" 란 구정으로 합의만 하면 어떠한 경우에도 (군사상 필요시만 한정하지 않고) 접수국의 법령을 준수하지 않으며 "리비아" 협정에는 "일반적으로.....준수한다"는 구정으로 준수 할 것을 고용주인 미군에게 일방적으로 결정할수 있는 재량을 주었다.

(3) 우리협정에는 군사상 필요시 한국 법령을 준수하지 못할 경우를 인정하였지만 합의의사록 제 4 항에서 군사상 필요로 한국법을 준수치 못할시는 가능한 한 사전에 합동 위원회에 회부하여 적절한 조치를 강구하고 적절한 조치에 관하여 합동 위원회에서 합의되지 않을 경우에는 외교경로를 통하여 재 검토 하기로 하였다.
시간적 여유가 없어 합동 위원회에 사전에 회부하지 못한 것은 사후에 라도 회부하여야 함은 당연한 일이다. 사후에 회부한 것중에서 정당한 이유없이 한국 법령을 준수하지 않은 것에 대하여 한국측은 의의를 제기할수 있으며 그러한 경우의 손해에 대하여 고정조치를 요구할수 있게 되어 있다.

4. 쟁의 조정 절차

가. 문제점

고용주와 고용원간의 쟁의는 (1) 노동 위원회, (2) 합동 위원회와 그의 특별 분과 위원회, (3) 합동 위원회에 회부하여 조정하되, 제 2 단계인 합동 위원회에 회부된후 70일이 경과하여도 쟁의가 해결되지 않은 경우 고용원은 단체 행동권을 행사할수 있다.

나. 이 유

(1) 이 경우 조정기간이 너무 길기 때문에 고용원의 단체 행동권 행사를 너무 장기간 속박한다는 이론이 있을 것이나, 한국의 노동쟁의법에 의하여도 조정기간에 20일 (일반사업) 혹은 30일 (공익사업) 중재기간에 20일, 그리고 긴급 조정시 30일간

0152

21-6

도합 70일 혹은 80일간은 쟁의 행위를 할수 없도록 규정되어 있음으로 한국 법령의 규정과 거의 비슷하다. 다만 노동청에 회부된 날로 부터 냉각기간은 가산하지 않은 것이 문제가 되나 이는 노동청에서 10일 이상 조정을 할 경우에만 한국법과 차이가 생기게 되지만 한국 고용원의 권익을 옹호한 노동청이 10일 이상 문제를 장악하고 있지 않을수 있음으로 문제가 되지 않는다.

5. 단체 행동권의 행사

가. 문제점

단체 행동권은 원칙적으로 모든 고용원이 향유하되 합동 위원회는 단체 행동권을 행사하지 못할 긴요한 고용원의 범위를 결정한다.

나. 이 유

(1) 일부 긴요한 고용원의 단체 행동권 행사를 합동 위원회가 제한 한다는 것이 문제가 되나 이는 미군이 한국의 방위를 위하여 주둔 하므로 그 군무 수행상 막대한 지장을 초래할 특정 고용원의 단체 행동권의 행사를 제한 하자는 것이며 한국 법령에도 단순한 노무에 종사하는 자는 노동 운동을 할수 있으나 그들중에서 중요한 기밀사무, 서무, 인사, 물품출납, 경리 또는 노무자의 감독 사무에 종사하는 자는 노동 운동을 위한 집단적 행동을 하지 못하게 되어 있다. (공무원 복무규정 제 27 조)

(2) 미군의 군무 수행상 불가결한 자란 고도의 기술을 가진 숙련 기술자 등으로서 전시등 위급시 임전태세에 지장이 있는 단체 행동권의 행사만을 제한 하자는 것이며 일반적인 고용원의 권리를 제한 하자는 것이 아니다.

노무조합

노무조합에서는 노동자의 기본권인 단결권, 단체교섭권, 단체행동권을 확보했으며 대체적인 문제점은 다음과 같다.

문 제 점

1. 고용원의 직접 고용제도

미군, 비세출자금 기관, 초청계약자인 고용주는 한국인 고용원을 직접 모집하고 고용한다.

이 유

가. 고용주가 고용원을 직접 고용함은 우리 법령이나 다른 모든나라에서 통용되는 일반 원칙이다.

나. 일본이나 독일에서 간접 고용제를 채용하고 있는바 이는 전후 패전국으로서 노무자를 전쟁배상의 일환으로 제공하였던 역사적 연유로 확립된 제도이며 패전국이 아닌 아국은 해방후 부터 직접 고용제를 채택, 전통화된 것이다.

다. 이러한 직접 고용제 하에서 정부는 제 3 자의 입장에서 공정하게 고용원의 이익을 추구하는데 개입함으로서 성과를 올릴수 있다.

라. 본 협정에서 원칙적으로 직접 고용제를 채택하였지만 고용주는 가능한 한 한국 정부의 모집 기관을 통하여 고용원을 모집하기로 하였으며 그 경우 모집에 소오된 직접 경비를 한국 정부에게 보상하기로 하였다.

문 제 점

2. 고용원의 적용범위

고용원은 미국 군속, 초청 계약자의 비한국인 고용원, 한국 노무 근무 단원 및 가사 사용인을 제외한 고용주가 고용한 모든 한국 국적을 가진 민간인으로 한다.

이 유

가. 이중 문제가 되는 한국 노무 근무단원의 제외는 정부가 그들을

21-6

0154

6. 25 동란중에는 전시 동원법에 의하여 미군에게 제공하였고 그후는 자유 모집에의하여 제공하여 왔음으로 그 고용방법이 미군의 다른 일반 고용원과 상이 하였다.

나. 따라서 한국 노무 근무단의 지위는 종래 다른 미군 고용원과 동일하지 않았으며 그들의 지위에 관하여는 별도로 교섭하기로 되어 있다.

다. 이들의 지위협정을 체결함에 있어서 정부는 과거에도 물의를 일으킨바를 충분히 참작하여 그들의 기본권은 확보하는 동시에 최대한의 이익을 추구하도록 미국당국과 교섭에 임할 작정이다.

문 제 점

3. 한국 노동 법령의 준수

고용주는 고용의 조건, 보상 및 노사관계에 있어서 미군의 군사상 필요에 배치되지 않는한 한국의 노동관계 법령을 준수한다.

이 유

가. 여기서 노동조건, 보상 및 노사관계란 모든 고용주와 고용인 간의 관계를 의미하여 그를 한국 법령에 따르기로 한 원칙은 당연한 규정이나 미군의 군사상 필요에 배치되는 경우 한국 노동법령을 준수하지 않을수 있는 여지를 마련한 것이 문제가 된다.

그러나 이와 같은 군사상 필요에 따라 한국 법령은 준수하지 못하는 것은 미군의 군사상의 임무와 전시등과 같은 비상시에 한국 법령을 그대로 지키지 못할 것임으로 타면한 규정이다.

나. 다른 협정에도 이와 흡사한 규정이 있는바 예컨대 일본의경우에는 "별도 상호 합의하는 한도내에서" 란 규정으로 합의만 하면 어떠한 경우에도 (군사상 필요시만 한정하지 않고) 접수국의 법령을 준수하지 않으며 "리비아" 협정에는 "일반적으로...... 준수한다" 는 규정으로 준수 한계를 고용주인 미군에게 일방적으로 결정할수 있는 재량을 주었다.

2-7

0155

다. 우미협정에는 군사상 필요시 한국 법령을 준수하지 못할 경우를 인정하였지만 합의 의사록 제 4 항에서 군사상 필요로 한국법을 준수치 못할시는 가능한 한 사전에 합동 위원회에 회부하여 적절한 조치를 강구하고 적절한 조치에 관하여 합동 위원회에서 합의되지 않은 경우에는 외교경로를 통하여 재 검토 하기로 하였다. 시간적 여유가 없어 합동 위원회에 사전에 회부하지 못한 것은 사후에라도 회부하여야 함은 당연한 일이다. 사후에 회부한 것중에서 정당한 이유없이 한국 법령을 준수하지 않은 것에 대하여 한국측은 의의를 제기할수 있으며 그러한 경우의 손해에 대하여 고정조치를 요구할수 있게 되어 있다.

문 제 점

4. 쟁의 조정 절차

고용주와 고용원 간의 쟁의는 (1) 노동 위원회, (2) 합동 위원회와 그의 특별 분과위원회, (3) 합동 위원회에 회부하여 조정하되, 제 2 단계인 합동 위원회에 회부된후 70일이 경과하여도 쟁의가 해결되지 않은 경우 고용원은 단체 행동권을 행사할수 있다.

이 유

가. 이 경우 조정기간이 너무 길기 때문에 고용원의 단체 행동권 행사를 너무 장기간 속박한다는 이론이 있을 것이나, 한국의 노동쟁의법에 의하여도 조정기간에 20일 (일반사업) 혹은 30일 (공익사업) 중재기간에 20일, 그리고 긴급 조정시 30일간 도합 70일 혹은 80일 간은 쟁의 행위를 할수 없도록 규정되어 있음으로 한국 법령의 규정과 거의 비슷하다. 다만 노동청에 회부된 날로 부터 냉각기간을 가산하지 않은 것이 문제게 되나 이는 노동청에서 10일 이상 조정을 할 경우에만 한국법과 차이가 생기며 한국 고용원의 권익을 옹호할 노동청이 10일 이상 문제를 장악하고 있지 않을 것임으로

2-8 0156

문제가 되지 않는다.

나. 일본 협정의경우 이와 유사한 해고에 관한 조정규정이 있는바 여기에서는 일본측이 미측에 의의를 제기한후 7일후 합동위원회에서 심의하게 되는바 30일 이내에 합동 위원회에서 합의 되지 않으면 해고는 확정되어 버림으로서 일본측은 재론할수 없으며 고용원들도 단체 행동권을 포함한 일체의 다른 조치를 취할수 없게 되어 있다.

문 제 점

5. 단체 행동권의 행사

, 단체 행동권은 원칙적으로 모든 고용원이 향유하되 합동 위원회는 단체 행동권을 행사하지 못할 긴요한 고용원의 범위를 결정한다.

이 유

가. 일부 긴요한 고용원의 단체 행동권 행사를 합동 위원회가 제한한다는 것이 문제가 되나 이는 미군이 한국의 방위를 위하여 주둔하므로 그 군무 수행상 막대한 지장을 초래할 특정고용원의 단체 행동권의 행사를 제한 하자는 것이며 한국 법령에도 단순한 노무에 종사하는 자중에서 중요한 기밀사무, 서무, 인사, 물품출납, 경비 또는 노무자의 감독 사무에 종사하는 자는 노동 운동을 위한 집단적 행동을 하지 못하게 되어 있다. (공무원 복무규정 제 27 조)

나. 미군의 군무 수행상 불가결한 자란 고도의 기술을 가진 숙련 기술자 등으로서 전시등 위급시 임전태세에 지장이 있는 단체 행동권의 행사만을 제한 하자는 것이며 일반적인 고용원의 권리를 제한 하자는 것이 아니다.

문 제 점

6. 노동 조합의 승인

노동조합은 그 목적이 한.미 공동 이익에 배반되지 않는한 고용주가 승인하여야 한다.

0157

가. 노동조합은 고용원이 모여 합법적 절차에 의하여 설립하면 자동적으로 협의권을 갖게 됨으로 문제가 되나 이 경우 한.미 공동 이익에 배반되는 경우란 노동조합이 공산당 혹은 좌익 분자에 의하여 조정되거나 운영될 경우를 가상할수 있는바 이러한 경우 그러한 단체를 인정하는 것은 우리나라의 이익에 반할 뿐만 아니라 미국의 이익에도 반하는 것임으로 승인하지 않도록 하려는 규정이다. 이러한 단체는 우리의 반공법과 같은 법령에도 배반됨으로 당연히 해산되며 그 주도자들은 해당 규정에 의하여 처벌을 받게 될것임으로 당연하고 필요한 규정이다.

0158

노 무 조 항

우리의 노무조항은 그 체제상 일본이나 "나또" 제국의 주둔군 지위협정이 채택한 "간접 고용제" 와는 다른 "직접 고용제" 를 토대로 제규정이 마련되게 되어있다. 이러한 제도의 차이는 일본이나 독일의 경우 주둔군에 대한 노동자의 제공이 전쟁배상의 일환으로 그 접수국 당국에 의하여 이루어 졌음에 반하여 우리나라는 미군이 이땅에 진주부터 그들의 필요에 따라 직접 노동자를 채용하였던 관용에 따라 이룩된 것이다. 따라서 각 협정에 있어서 우리나라의 노무조항은 다른 나라와 근본적으로 상이하다.

이러한 "직접 고용제" 의 토대에서 우리 조항은 고용주가 미군과 그 기관 및 미군에 의한 초청계약자로 확정되었으며 고용인은 KSC 및 가사 사용인을 제외한 한국 국적을 가진 민간인으로 정하였다. 이러한 고용주는 그들 한국인 고용인을 직접 고용하고 관리하게 된다. 그 고용과 관리에 있어서 고용주와 고용인은 특별한 경우를 제외하고는 한국 노동법령을 준수하여야할 것을 규정하고 있다. 미군은 주지하는 바와 같이 한국의 방위 목적을 위하여 주둔하고 있음으로 한국 노동법령을 준수함에 있어서 특별한 경우 예컨대 군사 작전상 불가피한 경우에는 한국 노동법령을 준수할수 없을때가 있을 것이다. 이러한 경우를 예상하고 노동조항은 그러한 경우에는 한국 법령을 그대로 준수하지 않아도 무방하다고 규정하였다. 그러나 그러한 특별한 경우를 제외하고 한국 법령을 준수치 못할 경우에는 한국측의 사전합의를 얻어서만 가능하도록 규정하고 있다.

한편, 노동쟁의 절차, 단체 행동권의 비행사자, 비상시의 노동력 배정, 비상시의 기술자 병역 연기, 고용인의 소득세 납부, 노동조합의 승인등 문제에 관하여 별도의 규정을 마련하였다. 그 내용을 대체로 다음과 같다.

1. 노동쟁의 해결절차로서 쟁의가 발생하면 한국 노동청, 합동위원회 혹 그가 지정하는 특별 분과위원회, 합동 위원회의

0153

21-16

순으로 회부되어 조정되며 제 2 단계에 회부 된 날로부터 70 일이 경과되지 않는한 단체 행동권을 행사할수 없도록 규정되어 있다.

2. 단체 행동권에 있어서 합동 위원회에서 미군의 사명 수행과 한국의 관계법령을 참작하여 파업등 단체 행동권을 행사하지 못할자의 범위를 결정하기로 되어 있다. 이 경우 파업권 행사를 미리 제한 받지 아니한 모든 고용인은 단체 행동권을 향유하는 것이 된다.

3. 한국 정부가 노동력을 배정하게 될 경우 미군에게도 한국군에게 주는 배정 특권을 동일하게 부여하도록 규정하였으며 비상시 미군 임무 수행에 불가결한 기술을 습득한 긴요한 자에 대하여는 미군이 요청하면 상호 합의하에 병역 의무를 연기하여 주기로 되어 있다.

4. 미군 고용인의 소득세 납부에 있어서 본 협정발효 후 부터 고용주는 고용인에게 지불한 급료중에서 한국 소득세법에 규정된 원천 과세액을 공제하여 한국 정부에 납부하기로 되었다.

5. 노동 조합은 한국법에 의하여 설립되면 승인되도록 되었다. 그러나 한미 공동 이익에 배치하는 조합은 인정하지 않기로 하였다. 그리고 고용인이 조합에 가입하였다거나 가입하지 않았다고 해서 고용에 있어서 차별대우를 하는등과 같은 부당 노동행위를 금하고 있다.

현재까지 이상과 같은 내용으로 노무조항은 대부분 합의에 도달하였다.

0160

-21-

ARTICLE XVII LABOR

(Underlined parts are modifications.)

(proposed on June 9, 1966 to Amb. Brown)

Present Draft	New Draft
4. (b) The Joint Committee, taking into consideration the role of the employees of the United States armed forces in the defense of the Republic of Korea and pertinent provisions of legislation of the Republic of Korea, shall determine those categories of essential employees who shall not exercise the right of further collective action in the event a labor dispute is not resolved by the foregoing procedures. In the event an agreement cannot be reached on this question in the Joint Committee, it may be made the subject of review through discussions between appropriate officials of the Government of the Republic of Korea and the diplomatic mission of the United States of America.	4. Employees or any employee organization shall have the right of further collective action in the event a labor dispute is not resolved by the foregoing procedures, except in cases where the Joint Committee determines such action seriously hampers military operations of the United States armed forces for the joint defense of the Republic of Korea. In the event an agreement cannot be reached on this question in the Joint Committee, it may be made the subject of review through discussions between appropriate officials of the Government of the Republic of Korea and the diplomatic mission of the United States of America.

AGREED MINUTES

Present Draft	New Draft
4. When employers cannot conform ith provisions of labor legislation f the Republic of Korea applicable	4. When employers cannot confo[rm] with provisions of labor legislation of the Republic of Korea applicable

0161

under this Article on account of the military requirements of the United States armed forces, the matter shall be referred, in advance whenever possible, to the Joint Committee for consideration and appropriate action. In the event mutual agreement can not be reached in the Joint Committee regarding appropriate action, the issue may be made the subject of review through discussions between rppropriate officials of the Government of the Republic of Korea and the diplomatic mission of the United States of America.

under this Article on account of the military requirements of the United States armed forces, the matter shal be referred, <u>in advance</u>, to the Joint Committee <u>for mutual agreement</u>. In the event mutual agreement cannot be reached in the Joint Committee regarding appropriate action, the issue may be made the subject of review through discussions between appropriate officials of the Government of the Republic of Korea and the diplomatic mission of the United States of America.

0162

PARAGRAPH 4(b) OF ARTICLE XVII: LABOR
(Proposal by U.S. side)

June 30, 1966

4. (b) Employees or any employee organization shall have the right of further collective action in the event a labor dispute is not resolved by the foregoing procedures except in cases where the Joint Committee determines such action seriously hampers military operations of the United States armed forces for the joint defense of the Republic of Korea. In the event an agreement cannot be reached on this question in the Joint Committee, it may be made the subject of review through discussions between appropriate officials of the Government of the Republic of Korea and the diplomatic mission of the United States of America.

1. 韓國案과 同一 (受諾)
2. 但 合意議事錄 第4項 不受諾

0163

LABOR ARTICLE

It would be difficult to qualify the nature and scope of the military requirements and as a result, the US authorities would be actually free to ~~in~~ deviate from our labor legislation at any time. This would lead to unnecessary ~~many~~ labor disputes which could seriously harm good friendly relations between both countries. Accordingly, the Korean Government hope to revise that provisions along the lines we proposed to the effect that such deviations from our law on account of military requirements be referred in advance to the Joint Committee for mutual agreement. We could do every possible effort to meet the US military requirments at the Joint Committee. On the other hand, there are concrete provisions in seperate paragraph to cover emergency situations.

0164

노무조항

1. 우리측은 합의의사록 제4항에 "고용주가 합중국군대의 군사상 필요 때문에 본조에 따라 적용되는 대한민국노동법령을 따를 수 없을 때에는, 그 문제는 사전에 상호합의를 위하여 합동위원회에 회부되어야 한다 ----"로 수정할 것을 제의하였는바,

2. 이 안을 미측이 반대하여 원안대로 "---가능한 한 사전에 검토와 적당한 조치를 위하여 ---"로 낙착하게 되면 사실상 본조 제3항의 규정에 따라 미국군의 한국인 고용원에 대한 노동조건, 보상 및 노사관계 등은 한국노동법령을 따르기 보다 미군의 군사상 필요라는 이유로 자의 또는 그들에게 편리한 대로 변경시킬 우려가 있으며

3. 이러한 한국노동법 불준수 또는 변경에 대하여 우리측이 막을 방법이 없는 것으로, 다만 현재 우리측이 제안하고 있는 바와 같이 그러한 변경은 미 CONFIDENTIAL 합동위원회에

0165

회복하여 한국측의 합의를 얻도록 하는 것
만이 유일한 방법임. 또한 이 구절은
노무조항에 있어서 가장 중요한 조항이며
이것이 수락되지 않는다면 남어지 노무조항도
유명무실한 것이 될 우려가 있음.

0166

(D) July 2, 1966

That, in the interests of expediting the administration of justice, the determination by the Government of the Republic of Korea under the provisions of Agreed Minute Re Paragraph 3 (b) will be provided by the Minister of Justice in writing to the appropriate military authorities of the United States within fifteen days (or such shorter period as may be mutually agreed upon pursuant to paragraph 4 of the Agreed Minute Re Paragraph 3 (b)) after the Republic of Korea is notified by the military authorities of the United States or is otherwise apprised of the commission of an offense falling within its primary jurisdiction. The above notification from the military authorities of the United States may be regarded as a request for waiver of primary jurisdiction of the Republic of Korea. In case the Government of the Republic of Korea is apprised of the commission of an offense falling within its primary jurisdiction, the Minister of Justice shall notify such determination to exercise or waive its primary jurisdiction.

0167

ARTICLE XXII CRIMINAL JURISDICTION

UNDERSTANDING

1. It is understood that offenses falling under the categories of cases in which after a careful examination of each specific case ~~it is determined that exercise of jurisdiction by the~~ Republic of Korea is of particular importance include, in particular, the following:

(i) security offenses against the Republic of Korea;

(ii) offenses causing the death of a human being, robbery, and rape, except where the offenses are directed against a member of the United States armed forces or the civilian component, or a dependent; and

(iii) attempts to commit such offenses or participation therein.

2. In respect of the offenses referred to in the above paragraph, the authorities concerned shall proceed in particularly close cooperation from the beginning of the preliminary investigation in order to provide the mutual assitance in paragraph 6 of Article XXII.

0168

ARTICLE XVII LABOR
(2nd Amendment)

July 2, 1966

AGREED MINUTE

4. When employers cannot conform with provisions of labor legislation of the Republic of Korea applicable under this Article on account of the military requirements of the United States armed forces, the matter shall be referred to the Joint Committee for consultation (and appropriate action). In the event mutual agreement can not be reached in the Joint Committee, the issue may be made the subject of further consultation for mutual agreement between appropriate officials of the Government of the Republic of Korea and the diplomatic mission of the United States of America.

Agreed Understanding

The deviation from Korean labor legislation shall be referred to the Joint Committee for mutual agreement in advance, except in the case when reaching advance agreement by the Joint Committee would seriously hamper military operations in an emergency. (Proposed by the Korean side at the 81st Meeting)

0163

ARTICLE XXII CRIMINAL JURISDICTION

July 3, 1966

1. It is understood that offenses falling under the categories of cases in which it is determined that exercise of jurisdiction by the Republic of Korea is of particular importance include, in particular, the following:

(i) security offenses against the Republic of Korea;

(ii) offenses causing the death of a human being, robbery, rape and any other offenses of malicious nature, except where the offenses are directed against a member of the United States armed forces or the civilian component, or a dependent; and

(iii) attempts to commit such offenses or participation therein.

2. In respect of the offenses referred to in the above paragraph, the authorities concerned shall proceed in particularly close cooperation from the beginning of the preliminary investigation in order to provide the mutual assistance in paragraph 6 of Article XXII.

0170

ARTICLE XVII LABOR

(3rd amendment)

Julu 3, 1966

AGREED MINUTES

4. When employers cannot conform with provisions of labor legislation of the Republic of Korea applicable under this Article on account of the military requirements of the United States armed forces, the matter shall be referred to the Joint Committee for consideration and decision for appropriate action. In the event a decision is not made in the Joint Committee, the issue may be made the subject of further consultation for mutual agreement between appropriate officials of the Government of the Republic of Korea and the diplomatic mission of the United States of America.

Agreed Understanding

The deviation from Korean labor legislation shall be referred to the Joint Committee for mutual agreement in advance, except in the case when such referral to by the Joint Committee would seriously hamper military operations in an emergency. (Proposed by Korean side at the 81st Meeting.)

0171

ARTICLE XXII CRIMINAL JURISDICTION

(July 4, 1966)

UNDERSTANDING (I)

1. It is understood that the term "of particular importance" has reference to those cases in which, after a careful examination of each specific case, the exercise of jurisdiction by the Republic of Korea is deemed essential and is limited, in general, but not exclusively, to the following types of offense:

ALTERNATIVE UNDERSTANDING (II)

It is understood also that the Government ofthe Republic of Korea intends,to the extent possible, to confine its determination of particular importance, to the following types of offense:

UNDERSTANDING (III)

It is understood that the term "of particular importance" has reference to those cases in which, after a careful examination of each specific case, the exercise of jurisdiction bu the Republic of Korea is deemdd essential and the term ~~. It is also understood that the term "of particular importance"~~ has reference, in general but not exclusively, to the following types of offenses:

0172

ARTICLE XXII CRIMINAL JURISDICTION
(July 4, 1966)

UNDERSTANDING

1. It is understood that the term "of particular importance" has reference to those cases in which, after a careful examination of each specific case, the exercise of jurisdiction by the Republic of Korea is deemed essential and offenses falling under the categories of particular importance include, but are not limited to, the following:

(i) security offenses against the Republic of Korea;

(ii) offenses causing the death of a human being, robbery and rape, except where the offenses are directed against a member of the United States armed forces or the civilian component, or a dependent; and

(iii) attempts to commit such offenses or participation therein.

2. In respect of the offenses referred to in the above paragraph, the authorities concerned shall proceed in particularly close cooperation from the beginning of the preliminary investigation in order to provide the mutual assistance in paragraph 6 of Article XXII.

0173

Understanding

It is understood that the illustration of offenses in the above understanding is not definitive but illustrative. Therefore, the authorities of the Republic of Korea will be able to exercise jurisdiction over cases involving offenses not specifically provided for in the above understanding, provided the authorities of the Republic of Korea determines that it is of particular importance that jurisdiction be exercised by the authorities of the Republic of Korea.

0174

DRAFT I

ARTICLE XXII CRIMINAL JURISDICTION

July 4, 1966

AGREED MINUTE RE PARAGRAPH 2

The Republic of Korea, recognizing the effectiveness in appropriate cases of the administrative and disciplinary sanctions which may be imposed by the United States military authorities over members of the United States armed forces or civilian component, and their dependents, may, at the request of the military authorities of the United States, waive its right to exercise jurisdiction under paragraph 2.

0175

O.K.

DRAFT II

ARTICLE XXII CRIMINAL JURISDICTION

July 4, 1966

AGREED MINUTE RE PARAGRAPH 1(a)

It is understood that under the present state of United States law, the military authorities of the United States have no effective criminal jurisdiction in peacetime over members of the civilian component or dependents. If the scope of United States military jurisdiction changes as a result of subsequent legislation, constitutional amendment for decision by appropriate authorities of the United States, the Government of the United States shall inform the Government of the Republic of Korea through diplomatic channels.

Agreed Understanding Re Agreed Minute Re Para 1(a):

O.K.

The Government of the Republic of Korea agrees that, upon notification under the second sentence of the Agreed Minute Re Paragraph 1(a), the military authorities of the United States may exercise —

- - - - . . ."

0176

DRAFT III

ARTICLE XVII LABOR
(4th Amendment)

July 4, 1966

AGREED MINUTES

4. When employers cannot conform with provisions of labor legislation of the Republic of Korea applicable under this Article on account of the military requirements of the United States armed forces, the matter shall be referred, in advance, to the Joint Committee for consideration and appropriate action. In the event mutual agreement cannot be reached in the Joint Committee regarding appropriate action, the issue may be made the subject of review through discussions between appropriate officials of the Government of the Republic of Korea and the diplomatic mission of the United States of America.

Understanding

"It is understood that the deviation from Korean labor legislation need not be referred to the Joint Committee in cases when such referral would seriously hamper military operations in an emergency." ((Proposed by the United States side at the eighty second meeting.))

0177

DRAFT VI

ARTICLE XXII CRIMINAL JURISDICTION

AGREED MINUTE RE PARAGRAPH 3(b)

1. The authorities of the Republic of Korea, recognizing that it is the primary responsibility of the United States military authorities to maintain good order and discipline where persons subject to United States military laws are concerned, will, upon the request of the military authorities of the United States pursuant to paragraph 3(c), waive their primary right to exercise jurisdiction under paragraph 3(b) except when they determine that it is of particular importance that jurisdiction be exercised by the authorities of the Republic of Korea.

2. With the consent of the competent authorities of the Republic of Korea, the military authorities of the United States may transfer to the courts or authorities of the Republic of Korea for investigation, trial and decision, particular criminal cases in which jurisdiction rests with the United States.

With the consent of the military authorities of the United States, the competent authorities of the Republic of Korea may transfer to the military authorities of the United States for investigation, trial and decision, particular criminal cases in which jurisdiction rests with the Republic of Korea.

3. (a) Where a member of the United States armed forces or civilian component, or a dependent, is arraigned before a court of the United States, for an offense committed in the Republic of Korea against

0178

Korean interests, the trial shall be held within the Republic of Korea

(i) except where the law of the United States requires otherwise, or

(ii) except where, in cases of military exigency or in the interests of justice, the military authorities of the United States intend to hold the trial outside the Republic of Korea. In this event they shall afford the authorities of the Republic of Korea timely opportunity to comment on such intention and shall give due consideration to any comments the latter may make.

(b) Where the trial is held outside of the Republic of Korea the military authorities of the United States shall inform the authorities of the Republic of Korea of the place and date of the trial. A representative of the Republic of Korea shall be entitled to be present at the trial. The authorities of the United States shall inform the authorities of the Republic of Korea of the judgment and the final outcome of the proceedings.

4. In the implementation of the provisions of this Article, and to facilitate the expeditious disposal of offenses, arrangements may be made between the military authorities of the United States and the competent authorities of the Republic of Korea.

0179

DRAFT V

ARTICLE XXII CRIMINAL JURISDICTION

July 4, 1966

UNDERSTANDING

1. It is understood that offenses falling under the categories of cases in which, after a careful examination of each specific case, it is determined that exercise of jurisdiction by the Republic of Korea is of particular importance include, in particular, the following:

(i) security offenses against the Republic of Korea;

(ii) offenses causing the death of a human being, robbery and rape, except where the offenses are directed against a member of the United States armed forces or the civilian component, or a dependent; and

(iii) attempts to commit such offenses or participation therein.

2. In respect of the offenses referred to in the above paragraph, the authorities concerned shall proceed in particularly close cooperation from the beginning of the preliminary investigation in order to provide the mutual assistance in paragraph 6 of Article XXII.

0180

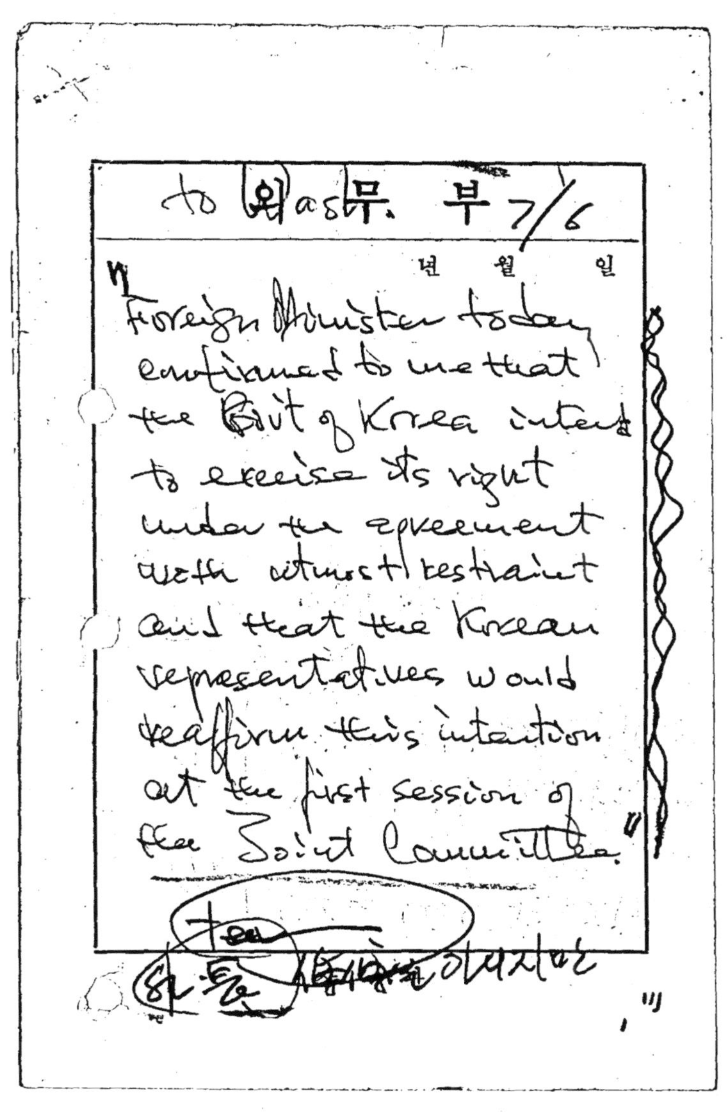

to 외무부 7/6

년 월 일

"Foreign Minister today confirmed to me that the Govt of Korea intends to exercise its right under the agreement with utmost restraint and that the Korean representatives would reaffirm this intention at the first session of the Joint Committee."

0181

ARTICLE XXII CRIMINAL JURISDICTION

July 5, 1966

AGREED MINUTE RE PARAGRAPH 1(a)

It is understood that under the present state of United States law, the military authorities of the United States have no effective criminal jurisdiction over members of the civilian component or dependents. If the scope of United States military jurisdiction changes as a result of subsequent legislation, constitutional amendment or decision by appropriate authorities of the United States, the Government of the United States shall inform the Government of the Republic of Korea through diplomatic channels.

1966.7.5. 미측에 수교한 대안. Lee

0182

ARTICLE XXII CRIMINAL JURISDICTION

July 5, 1966

AGREED MINUTE RE PARAGRAPH 2

The Republic of Korea, recognizing the effectiveness in appropriate cases of the administrative and disciplinary sanctions which may be imposed by the United States military authorities over members of the United States armed forces or civilian component, and their dependents, may, at the request of the military authorities of the United States, waive its right to exercise jurisdiction under paragraph 2.

0183

DRAFT VI

ARTICLE XXII CRIMINAL JURISDICTION

(July 5, 1966)

AGREED MINUTE RE PARAGRAPH 3(b)

1. The authorities of the Republic of Korea, recognizing that it is the primary responsibility of the United States military authorities to maintain good order and discipline where persons subject to United States military laws are concerned, will, upon the request of the military authorities of the United States pursuant to paragraph 3(c), waive their primary right to exercise jurisdiction under paragraph 3(b) except when they determine that it is of particular importance that jurisdiction be exercised by the authorities of the Republic of Korea.

2. With the consent of the competent authorities of the Republic of Korea, the military authorities of the United States may transfer to the courts or authorities of the Republic of Korea for investigation, trial and decision, particular criminal cases in which jurisdiction rests with the United States.

With the consent of the military authorities of the United States, the competent authorities of the Republic of Korea may transfer to the military authorities of the United States for investigation, trial and decision, particular criminal cases in which jurisdiction rests with the Republic of Korea.

3. (a) Where a member of the United States armed forces or civilian component, or a dependent, is arraigned before a court of the United States, for an offense committed in the Republic of Korea against

0184

Korean interests, the trial shall be held within the Republic of Korea

(i) except where the law of the United States requires otherwise, or

(ii) except where, in cases of military exigency or in the interests of justice, the military authorities of the United States intend to hold the trial outside the Republic of Korea. In this event they shall afford the authorities of the Republic of Korea timely opportunity to comment on such intention and shall give due consideration to any comments the latter may make.

(b) Where the trial is held outside of the Republic of Korea the military authorities of the United States shall inform the authorities of the Republic of Korea of the place and date of the trial. A representative of the Republic of Korea shall be entitled to be present at the trial. The authorities of the United States shall inform the authorities of the Republic of Korea of the judgment and the final outcome of the proceedings.

4. In the implementation of the provisions of this Article, and to facilitate the expeditious disposal of offenses, arrangements may be made between the military authorities of the United States and the competent authorities of the Republic of Korea.

0185

ARTICLE XXII CRIMINAL JURISDICTION
(July 5, 1966)

UNDERSTANDING

1. It is understood that the term "of particular importance" has reference to those cases in which, after a careful examination of each specific case, the exercise of jurisdiction by the Republic of Korea is deemed essential and offenses falling under the categories of particular importance include, but are not limited to, the following:

(i) security offenses against the Republic of Korea;

(ii) offenses causing the death of a human being, robbery and rape, except where the offenses are directed against a member of the United States armed forces or the civilian component, or a dependent; and

(iii) attempts to commit such offenses or participation therein.

2. In respect of the offenses referred to in the above paragraph, the authorities concerned shall proceed in particularly close cooperation from the beginning of the preliminary investigation in order to provide the mutual assistance in paragraph 6 of Article XXII.

0186

ARTICLE XVII LABOR

July 5, 1966

AGREED MINUTES

4. When employers cannot conform with provisions of labor legislation of the Republic of Korea applicable under this Article on account of the military requirements of the United States armed forces, the matter shall be referred, in advance, to the Joint Committee for consideration and appropriate action. In the event mutual agreement cannot be reached in the Joint Committee regarding appropriate action, the issue may be made the subject of review through discussions between appropriate officials of the Government of the Republic of Korea and the diplomatic mission of the United States of America.

UNDERSTANDING

"It is understood that the deviation from Korean labor legislation need not be referred to the Joint Committee in cases when such referral would seriously hamper military operations in an emergency."

0187

제 23조 청구권 —

Handed to U.S. side 7/7/65

합의의사록

1. 달리 규정하는 경우를 제외하고는, 본조의 제5항, 제6항, 제7항 및 제8항의 규정은, 서울특별시의 지역에서 일어난 사건으로부터 발생한 청구권에 관하여는 본 협정의 효력 발생일 후 6개월만에, 그리고 대한민국 안 다른 곳에서 발생한 청구권에 관하여는 본 협정의 효력 발생일 후 1년만에, 효력이 발생하게 된다.

0188

ARTICLE XXIII CLAIMS

AGREED MINUTE NO. 1

Reference: 82nd Meeting, July 8, 1966

".Unless otherwise provided, the provisions of paragraphs 5,6,7 and 8 of this Article will become effective six months from the date of entry into force of this Agreement with respect to claims arising from incidents in the Seoul Special City area, and one year from that date with respect to claims arising elsewhere in the Republic of Korea."

1

0189

US-ROK CLAIMS ARTICLE - AGREED MINUTE NO. 1

"1. Unless otherwise provided, the provisions of paragraphs 5,6,7 and 8 of this Article will become effective six months from the date of entry into force of this Agreement with respect to claims arising from incidents in the Seoul Special City area, and one year from that date with respect to claims arising elsewhere in the Republic of Korea."

0190

SOFA Negotiations

July 2, 1966.

We highly appreciate the Embassy's efforts and cooperation in pursuading Washington to take forward position on our proposal. However, we regret to find the counter-proposal of the U.S. unacceptabl for the following reasons:

1. Our request for continued negotiations for the revised drafts on those major Articles is made largely with the political consideration, rather than from technical point of views.

2. Whatever arrangement or agreement which is distinctively different from and inferior to the versions for Japan and the Philippines, is bound to be the subject of harsh criticism and is utterly unacceptable by the National Assembly.

3. The U.S. response to the key issues, namely, waiver formula, still retains automatic waiver formula in letters to be exchanged. (These letters must go to the National Assembly .) This arrangement is bound to be interpretted as a substantial differences from the versions U.S. gave to most of the NATO countries as well as to the Philippines. To the eyes of critics, this differences would be regarded as dicisively inferior formula.

4. The provisions and the written arraggements that have to be submitted to the National Assembly for its perusal and ratification should not contain any version inferior to these given to other countries, particularly to the Philippines.

5. The U.S. response does not touch upon other important items we proposed to revise. They are:

a. U.S. Criminal Jurisdiction over civilian component and their dependents.

b. U.S. request for waiver for our exclusive jurisdiction.

0191

c. U.S. deviation from Korean labor legislation on account of military requirement.

Those important points left out in the U.S. response have been targets of severe criticism in the past and will continue to be subject to criticism, if they are not amended as we proposed.

6. If we accept the U.S. draft as proposed on June 30, then our press and the National Assembly will assail us as well as the U.S. for treating the Korean people worse than the Japanese or the Philippinos.

Their discrimination will be utilized by certain quarters with a view to stimulating our people, emotional as ever in politics, domestic or otherwise, for increasingly antagonistic feelings towards the U,S. not to speak of our own Government.

7. Any discriminatory arramgements by the U.S. on the problem of SOFA, however, slight it may be, will seriously hurt the pride of our people who are gaining confidence in their fledgling ability for viable and independent nationhood.

8. The U.S. side is seriously concerned with odd experiences in implementing the waiver formula they gave to the Philippines. They harbor doubt and suspicion in our case in the light of their unfavorable experiences with the Philippines.

However, the U.S. doubt and suspicion are entirely unwarranted in our case.

Our people firmly believe that Korea is the only country truly friendly to the United States and their friendly feeling and attitude towards the U.S. soldiers are unmatched.

0192

The U.S. cannot afford to lose this true friendship with our people by giving us inferior arrangements in SOFA.

9. From the view point of our international standing, rapidly improving in the wake of the settlement of the Korea-Japan problem, deployment of our troops to Vietnam, and successful sponsoring of the ASPAC Conference, our people simply cannot stand any SOFA arrangements inferior to those given to other countries by the United States.

本 note 는 통령 님의 presentation 用으로 作成(Card)한 것임. Card는 Brown大使 7/2 10:45 a.m. 통령실에서 讀되였음.

0193

LETTER FROM FOREIGN MINISTER FOR AMBASSADOR

Dear Mr. Ambassador:

Today the Governments of the United States and the Republic of Korea have formally signed the Agreement between the United States of America and the Republic of Korea regarding Facilities and Areas and the Status of United States Armed Forces in the Republic of Korea. Article XXII of that Agreement and its Agreed Minutes provide for the exercise of jurisdiction over members of the United States armed forces, the civilian component, and their dependents in the Republic of Korea. In this regard, the Government of the Republic of Korea, conscious of the strong ties of mutual respect and friendship which bind our two countries, and recognizing the vital role which large numbers of United States armed forces must play in the defense of the Republic of Korea, proposes the following understandings for procedural arrangements pursuant to Paragraph 4 of the Agreed Minute Re Paragraph 3(b):

That, to facilitate the processing of cases resulting from the presence of United States armed forces deployed in Korea for mutual defense purposes, in implementation of the provisions of the Agreed Minute Re Paragraph 3(b), the Government of the Republic of Korea will not require the United States to make a request for a waiver in each particular case and jurisdiction thereunder shall be exercised

0194

The military authorities of
by the United States unless the Government of the Republic of Korea determines in a specific case that it is of particular importance that jurisdiction be exercised therein by the authorities of the Republic of Korea;

That, in the interest of expediting the administration of justice, any such determination by the Government of the Republic of Korea shall be provided in writing by the Minister of Justice to the appropriate military authorities of the United States ~~authorities~~ within fifteen days [or such shorter period as may be mutually agreed upon pursuant to Paragraph 4 of the Agreed Minute Re Paragraph 3(b)] after the Republic of Korea is notified or is otherwise apprised of the commission of an offense falling within its primary jurisdiction. The military authorities of the United States shall not exercise jurisdiction before the expiration of the fifteen day or other agreed period unless notified otherwise by the Government of the Republic of Korea. I would be grateful for your confirmation of the above understandings.

0195

by the military authorities of the United States unless the Government of the Republic of Korea determines in a specific case that it is of particular importance that jurisdiction be exercised therein by the authorities of the Republic of Korea;

That, in the interest of expediting the administration of justice, any such determination by the Government of the Republic of Korea shall be provided in writing by the Minister of Justice to the appropriate military authorities of the United States within fifteen days (or such shorter period as may be mutually agreed upon pursuant to Paragraph 4 of the Agreed Minute Re Paragraph 3(b)) after the Republic of Korea is notified or is otherwise apprised of the commission of an offense falling within its primary jurisdiction. The military authorities of the United States shall not exercise jurisdiction before the expiration of the fifteen day or other agreed period unless notified otherwise by the Government of the Republic of Korea.
The military authorities of the United States shall not exercise jurisdiction before the expiration of fifteen day or other agreed period unless notified otherwise of the Republic of Korea Government.
If the Republic of Korea Government, however, notifies the military authorities of the United States that for special reasons it desires to reserve decision with respect to the exercise of jurisdiction, the military authorities of the United States shall not exercise its jurisdiction until notice is received that the Republic of Korea Government will not exercise jurisdiction or until the expiration of an additional

0196

period of fifteen days, whichever is sooner. I would be grateful for your confirmation of the above understandings.

Sincerely yours,

0197

DRAFT IV

LETTER FROM FOREIGN MINISTER FOR AMBASSADOR

Dear Mr. Ambassador: July 4, 1966

Today the Governments of the United States and the Republic of Korea have formally signed the Agreement between the United States of America and the Republic of Korea regarding Facilities and Areas and the Status of United States Armed Forces in the Republic of Korea. Article XXII of that Agreement and its Agreed Minutes provide for the exercise of jurisdiction over members of the United States armed forces, the civilian component, and their dependents in the Republic of Korea. In this regard, the Government of the Republic of Korea, conscious of the strong ties of mutual respect and friendship which bind our two countries, and recognising the vital role which large numbers of United States armed forces must play in the defense of the Republic of Korea, proposes the following understandings for procedural arrangements pursuant to Paragraph 4 of the Agreed Minute Re Paragraph 3(b):

That, to facilitate the processing of cases resulting from the presence of United States armed forces deployed in the Republic of Korea for mutual defense purposes, in implementation of the provisions of the Agreed Minute Re Paragraph 3(b), the Government of the Republic of Korea will not require the military authorities of the United States to make a request for a waiver in each particular case and jurisdiction thereunder shall be exercised by the military authorities of the

0198

United States unless the Government of the Republic of Korea determines in a specific case that it is of particular importance that jurisdiction be exercised therein by the authorities of the Republic of Korea;

That, in the interest of expediting the administration of justice, any such determination by the Government of the Republic of Korea shall be provided in writing by the Minister of Justice to the appropriate military authorities of the United States within fifteen days after the Republic of Korea is notified or is otherwise apprised of the commission of an offense falling within its primary jurisdiction. The military authorities of the United States shall not exercise jurisdiction before the expiration of the fifteen day period unless notified otherwise by the Government of the Republic of Korea.

I would be grateful for your confirmation of the above understandings.

Sincerely yours,

0199

by the military authorities of the United States unless the Government of the Republic of Korea determines in a specific case that it is of particular importance that jurisdiction be exercised therein by the authorities of the Republic of Korea;

That, in the interest of expediting the administration of justice, any such determination by the Government of the Republic of Korea shall be provided in writing by the Minister of Justice to the appropriate military authorities of the United States within fifteen days (or such shorter period as may be mutually agreed upon pursuant to Paragraph 4 of the Agreed Minute Re Paragraph 3(b)) after the Republic of Korea is notified or is otherwise apprised of the commission of an offense falling within its primary jurisdiction. The military authorities of the United States shall not exercise jurisdiction before the expiration of the fifteen day or other agreed period unless notified otherwise by the Government of the Republic of Korea.

The military authorities of the United States shall not exercise jurisdiction before the expiration of fifteen day or other agreed period unless notified otherwise of the Republic of Korea Government.

If the Republic of Korea Government, however, notifies the military authorities of the United States that for special reasons it desires to reserve decision with respect to the exercise of jurisdiction, the military authorities of the United States shall not exercise its jurisdiction until notice is received that the Republic of Korea Government will not exercise jurisdiction or until the expiration of an additional

0200

LETTER FROM FOREIGN MINISTER FOR AMBASSADOR

July 5, 1966

Dear Mr. Ambassador:

Today the Governments of the United States and the Republic of Korea have formally signed the Agreement between the United States of America and the Republic of Korea regarding Facilities and Areas and the Status of United States armed forces in the Republic of Korea. Article XXII of that Agreement and its Agreed Minutes provide for the exercise of jurisdiction over members of the United States armed forces, the civilian component, and their dependents in the Republic of Korea. In this regard, the Government of the Republic of Korea, conscious of the strong ties of mutual respect and friendship which bind our two countries, and recognizing the vital role which large numbers of United States armed forces must play in the defense of the Republic of Korea, proposes the following understandings for procedural arrangements pursuant to Paragraph 4 of the Agreed Minute Re Paragraph 3(b):

That, to facilitate the processing of cases resulting from the presence of United States armed forces deployed in the Republic of Korea for mutual defense purposes, in implementation of the provisions of the Agreed Minute Re Paragraph 3(b), the Government of the Republic of Korea will not require the military authorities of the United States to make a request for a waiver in each particular case and jurisdiction thereunder shall be exercised by the military authorities of the

0201

United States unless the Government of the Republic of Korea determines in a specific case that it is of particular importance that jurisdiction be exercised therein by the authorities of the Republic of Korea;

That, in the interest of expediting the administration of justice, any such determination by the Government of the Republic of Korea shall be provided in writing by the Minister of Justice to the appropriate military authorities of the United States within fifteen days after the Republic of Korea is notified or is otherwise apprised of the commission of an offense falling within its primary jurisdiction. The military authorities of the United States shall not exercise jurisdiction before the expiration of the fifteen day period unless notified otherwise by the Government of the Republic of Korea.

I would be grateful for your confirmation of the above understandings.

Sincerely yours,

0202

July 9, 1966

His Excellency
Winthrop G. Brown
Ambassador of the United States of America
Seoul, Korea

Excellency:

Today the Governments of the United States and the Republic of Korea have formally signed the agreement between the United States of America and the Republic of Korea regarding facilities and areas and the status of United States Armed Forces in the Republic of Korea. l.c.
Article XXII of that agreement and its agreed minutes provide for the exercise of jurisdiction over members of the United States armed forces, the civilian component, and their dependents in the Republic of Korea. In this regard, the Government of the Republic of Korea, conscious of the strong ties of mutual respect and friendship which bind our two countries, and recognizing the vital role which United States armed forces play in the defense of the Republic of Korea, proposes the following understandings for procedural arrangements pursuant to Paragraph 4 of the Agreed Minute Re Paragraph 3 (b):

0203

That, to facilitate the processing of cases resulting from the presence of United States armed forces deployed in Korea for mutual defense purposes, in implementation of the provisions of the Agreed Minute Re Paragraph 3 (b), the Government of the Republic of Korea will not require the military authorities of the United States to make a request for a waiver in each particular case, and the military authorities of the United States shall have jurisdiction unless the Government of the Republic of Korea determines in a specific case that it is of particular importance that jurisdiction be exercised therein by the authorities of the Republic of Korea;

That, in the interest of expediting the administration of justice, any such determination by the Government of the Republic of Korea shall be provided in writing by the Minister of Justice to the appropriate military authorities of the United States within fifteen days after the Republic of Korea is notified or is otherwise apprised of the commission of an offense falling

0204

within its primary jurisdiction, or such shorter period as may be mutually agreed upon pursuant to Paragraph 4 of the Agreed Minute Re Paragraph 3 (b). The military authorities of the United States shall not exercise jurisdiction before the expiration of the fifteen days or other agreed period.

I would be grateful for your confirmation of the above understandings.

Sincerely yours,

0205

CONFIDENTIAL

Dear Mr. Ambassador:

Today the Governments of the United States and the Republic of Korea have formally signed the agreement between the United States of America and the Republic of Korea regarding facilities and areas and the status of United States Armed Forces in the Republic of Korea. Article XXII of that agreement and its agreed minutes provide for the exercise of jurisdiction over members of the United States Armed Forces, the civilian component, and their dependents in the Republic of Korea. In this regard, the Government of the Republic of Korea, conscious of the strong ties of mutual respect and friendship which bind our two countries, and recognizing the vital role which United States Armed Forces play in the defense of the Republic of Korea, proposes the following understandings for procedural arrangements pursuant to paragraph 4 of the agreed minute re paragraph 3 (B):

That, to facilitate the processing of cases resulting from the presence of United States Armed Forces deployed in Korea for mutual defense purposes, in implementation of the provisions of the agreed minute re paragraph 3 (B), the Government of the Republic of Korea will not require the military authorities of the United States to make a request for a waiver in each particular case, and the military authorities of the United States shall have jurisdiction unless the Government of the Republic of Korea determines in a specific case that it is of particular importance that jurisdiction be exercised therein by the authorities of the Republic of Korea;

That, in the interest of expediting the administration of justice, any such determination by the Government of the Republic of Korea shall be provided in writing by the Minister of Justice to the appropriate military authorities of the United States within fifteen days after the Republic of Korea is notified or is otherwise apprised of the

0206

commission of an offense falling within its primary jurisdiction, or such shorter period as may be mutually agreed upon pursuant to Paragraph 4 of the Agreed Minute in Paragraph 3 (B). The military authorities of the United States shall not exercise jurisdiction before the expiration of the fifteen days or other agreed period.

I would be grateful for your confirmation of the above understandings.

Sincerely yours,

0207

LETTER FROM FOREIGN MINISTER FOR AMBASSADOR

Dear Mr. Ambassador:

Today the Governments of the United States and the Republic of Korea have formally signed the Agreement between the United States of America and the Republic of Korea regarding Facilities and Areas and the Status of United States Armed Forces in the Republic of Korea.

Article XXII of that Agreement and its Agreed Minutes provide for the exercise of jurisdiction over members of the United States armed forces, the civilian component, and their dependents in the Republic of Korea. In this regard, the Government of the Republic of Korea, conscious of the strong ties of mutual respect and friendship which bind our two countries, and recognizing the vital role which large numbers of United States armed forces must play in the defense of the Republic of Korea, proposes the following understandings for procedural arrangements pursuant to Paragraph 4 of the Agreed Minute , Re Paragraph 3(b):

That, to facilitate the processing of cases resulting from the presence of United States armed forces deployed in Korea for mutual defense purposes, in implementation of the provisions of the Agreed Minute ,Re

0208

Paragraph 3(b), the Government of the Republic of Korea (has decided that

it) shall not require the United States to make a request for a waiver in

each particular case, and

/1. it may be assumed that the Republic of Korea has waived its primary right to exercise jurisdiction thereunder./

/2. it may be assumed that jurisdiction thereunder rests with (or remains with, or shall be exercised by) the United States./

/3. the United States may assume the right to exercise jurisdiction thereunder./

/4. the United States may proceed to exercise jurisdiction thereunder./

except where the Government of the Republic of Korea determines in a specific case that it is of particular importance that jurisdiction be exercised therein by the authorities of the Republic of Korea;

That, in the interest of expediting the administration of justice, any such determination by the Government of the Republic of Korea shall be provided in writing by the Minister of Justice to the appropriate United States authorities within fifteen days ~~(or such shorter period as may be mutually agreed upon pursuant to Paragraph 4 of the Agreed Minute Re Paragraph 3(b)~~ after the Republic of Korea is notified or is otherwise apprised of the commission of an offense falling within its primary jurisdiction. The

0209

authorities of the United States shall not exercise jurisdiction before the

expiration of the fifteen day unless notified by the ROK otherwise.

I would be grateful for your confirmation of the above understandings.

Sincerely yours,

/s/

0210

July 9, 1966

His Excellency
Tong Won Lee
Minister of Foreign Affairs
of the Republic of Korea
Seoul

~~Dear Mr. Minister:~~ Excellency:

I have received your letter of this date on the subject of the Agreement signed today between the Republic of Korea and the United States of America regarding facilities and areas and the status of United States Armed Forces in the Republic of Korea, and confirm the following understandings contained therein with respect to the exercise of jurisdiction over members of the United States armed forces, the civilian component, and their dependents:

That, to facilitate the processing of cases resulting from the presence of United States armed forces deployed in the Republic of Korea for mutual defense purposes, in implementation of the provisions of the Agreed Minute Re Paragraph 3 (b), the Government of the Republic of Korea will not require the military authorities of the United States to make a request for a waiver in each particular case, and the military

0211

approved by Mr. Ericson

authorities of the United States shall have jurisdiction unless the Government of the Republic of Korea determines in a specific case that it is of particular importance that jurisdiction be exercised therein by the authorities of the Republic of Korea;

That, in the interest of expediting the administration of justice, any such determination by the Government of the Republic of Korea shall be provided in writing by the Minister of Justice to the appropriate military authorities of the United States within fifteen days after the Republic of Korea is notified or is otherwise apprised of the commission of an offense falling within its primary jurisdiction, or such shorter period as may be mutually agreed upon pursuant to Paragraph 4 of the Agreed Minute Re Paragraph 3 (b). The military authorities of the United States shall not exercise jurisdiction before the expiration of the fifteen days or other agreed period.

Very sincerely yours,

Winthrop G. Brown
Ambassador

0212

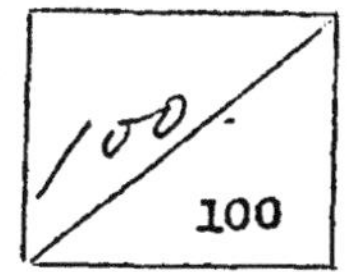

韓・美間駐屯軍地位協定案対比表

(労務, 刑事裁判権, 請求権, 条項)

1966. 7. 7.

1966, 12, 31에 예고문에
의거 일반문서로 재분류됨

外 務 部

0213

第22条 刑事裁判権

非公式合意案	最終合意案
第一項 (가) 1. 本条의 規定에따를것을 条件으로, (가) 合衆国軍当局은 合衆国軍隊의 構成員, 軍属및 그들의 家族에対하여 合衆国法令이 賦与한 모든 刑事裁判権및 懲戒権을 行使할 権利를 가진다.	第一項 (가) 左同 合意議事録第1項 (가) 合衆国法律의 現状態下에서 合衆国軍当局은 平和時에는 軍属및 家族에 対하여 有効한 刑事裁判権을 가지지 아니한다. 追後의立法, 憲法改正, 또는 合衆国関係当局에 依한 決定의 結果로서 合衆国 軍事裁判権의 範囲가 変更된다면, 合衆国政府는 外交経路를 通하여 大韓民国政府에 通告하여야 한다. 合意議事録第1項 (가) 에関한 諒解事項 大韓民国政府는 第一項 (가) 에 関한 合意議事録의 後段에 依한 通告가 있으면 合衆国軍当局은 刑事裁判権条項의 規定에 依拠하여 그러한 者에 対하여 裁判権을 行使할수도 있다. 0214

— 1 —

非公式合意案	最終合意案
<u>合意議事録 第2項</u> 大韓民国은 合衆国当局이 適当한 境遇에 合衆国軍隊의 構成員, 軍属 및 그들의 家族에 対하여 課할 수 있는 行政的 및 懲戒的인 制裁의 有効性을 認定하여 合同委員会에서 第2項에 따라 裁判権을 行使할 權利의 抛棄를 要請하는 境遇에는 이 要請에 対하여 好意的 考慮를 한다.	<u>合意議事録 第2項</u> 大韓民国은 合衆国当局이 適当한 境遇에 合衆国軍隊의 構成員, 軍属및 그들의 家族에 対하여 課할수있는 行政的및 懲戒的 判裁의 有効性을 認定하여, 合衆国軍当局의 要請에 依하여 第2項에 따라 裁判権을 行使할 権利를 抛棄할수도 있다.
<u>合意議事録 第3項 (나)</u> 1. 大韓民国政府는 裁判権이 競合하는 境遇에는 本条第3項 (나)에 依하여 大韓民国当局에 賦与된 第一次的権利를 本合意議事録 第2項, 第3項, 第4項, 第5項, 第6項 및 第7項에 따라 合衆国을 為하여 抛棄한다. 2. 本 合意議事録 第7項에 依하여 締結될 수 있는 特別한 約定에 따를것을 条件으로, 合衆国 軍 当局은 本合意議事録 第1項에 規定된 権利抛棄에 該当하는 個別的事件을 大韓民国 関係当局에 通報하여야 한다. 3. 大韓民国 関係当局이 特定事件에 있어서 特殊한 事情을 理由로하여 大韓民国의 司法上의 重大한 利益이 大韓民国의 裁判権의 行使를 不可避하게 한다는 意見을 가지는 境遇에는, 本合意議事録 第2項에 規定된 通告를 받	<u>合意議事録 第3項 (나)</u> 1. 大韓民国当局은, 合衆国軍法에 服하는 者에 関하여 秩序와 規律을 維持함이 合衆国軍当局의 主된 責任임을 認定하여, 第3項 (다)에 依한 合衆国軍当局의 要請이 있으면 大韓民国当局이 裁判権을 行使함이 特히 重要하다고 決定하는 境遇를 除外하고, 第3項 (나)에 依한 裁判権을 行使할 그들의 第一次的 権利를 抛棄한다. 2. 合衆国 軍当局은 大韓民国 関係当局의 同意를얻어 捜査審理및 裁判을 為하여 合衆国이 裁判権을 가지는 特定刑事 事件을 大韓民国의 法院이나 当局에 移送할수 있다. 大韓民国 関係当局은 合衆国 軍当局의 同意를얻어 捜査審理및 裁判을 為하여 大韓民国이 裁判権을 가지는 特定刑事事件을 合衆国 軍当局에 移送할수있다.

0215

非 公 式 合 意 案	最 終 合 意 案
은 날로부터 21日 以內에 또는 本合意議事錄 第7項에 따라 締結되는 約定에서 規定된 수 있는 그보다 短期間內에 合衆国의 関係軍当局에 通告함으로써 本合意議事錄 第1項에서 賦与된 權利 抛棄를 撤回할 수 있다. 大韓民国 当局은 또한 이러한 通告를 받기에 앞서 通告書를 提出할 수도 있다。 (가) 個個의 特定事件의 愼重한 調査와 이러한 調査의 結果에 따를것을 条件으로, 特히 다음과 같은 事件에 있어서 前記第3項의 趣旨內에서 大韓民国의 司法上의 重大한 利益이 大韓民国의 裁判權行使를 不可避하게 할 수 있는 것으로 한다。 (1) 大韓民国의 安全에 関한 犯罪, (2) 사람을 죽음에 이르게 한 犯罪, 強盜罪 및 強姦罪, 다만,· 그 犯罪가 合衆国 軍隊의 構成員, 軍屬 또는 家族에 対하여 行하여진 境遇에는 그러하지 아니하다。 및 (3) 前記 各 犯罪의 未遂 또는 共犯, (나) 本項(가)에 規定된 犯罪에 関하여, 関係当局은 本条第6項에 規定된 相互間의 助力을 提供하기 為하여 豫備捜査의 着手時부터 特히 緊密한 協力을 継続 行하여야 한다。	3. (가) 合衆国 軍隊의 構成員, 軍屬 또는 家族이 大韓民国 안에서 大韓民国의 利益에 反하여 犯한 犯罪때문에 合衆国法院에 訴追되었을 境遇에는, 그 裁判은 大韓民国 안에서 行하여져야한다. (1) 다만, 合衆国의 法律이 달리 要求하는 境遇, 또는 (2) 軍事上 緊急事態의 境遇 또는 司法上의 利益을 為한 境遇에 合衆国 軍当局이 大韓民国 領域밖에서 裁判을 行할 意図가있는 境遇에는 除外된다. 이러한 境遇 合衆国 軍当局은 大韓民国 当局에 이러한 意図에 対한 意見을 陳述할수있는 機会를 適時에 賦与하여야하며 大韓民国 当局이 陳述하는 意見에 対하여 充分한 考慮를 하여야 한다. (나) 裁判이 大韓民国 領域밖에서 行하여질 境遇에는, 合衆国 軍 当局은 大韓民国 当局에 裁判의 場所와 日字를 通告하여야한다. 大韓民国 代表는 그裁判에 立会할 權利를 가진다. 合衆国当局은 判決과 訴訟의 最終 結果를 大韓民国 当局에 通告하여야한다. 4. 本条規定의 施行과 犯罪의 迅速한 處理를 為하여, 大韓民国 関係当局과 合衆国 軍当局은 約定을 締結할 수 (도) 있다。

— 3 —

0216

非 公 式 合 意 案	最 終 合 意 案
4. 本合意議事錄 第3項에 따라 大韓民国 関係当局이 特定事件에 対한 権利 抛棄를 撤回하고 이러한 境遇 関係当局間의 討議에서 諒解가 이루어지지 아니할 때에는, 合衆国政府는 外交経路를 通하여 大韓民国 政府에 異議를 提起할 수 있다. 大韓民国 政府는 大韓民国의 司法上의 利益과 合衆国의 利益을 充分히 考慮하여 外交分野에 있어서의 그의 権限을 行使하여 意見差異를 解決하여야 한다. 大韓民国 政府가 前記規定에 따라 意見差異를 解決함에 있어서 大韓民国 当局이 裁判権을 行使함이 不可避하다고 決定하는 境遇에는, 権利 抛棄의 撤回는 最終的이며 確定的이다. 5. 合衆国 軍 当局은, 大韓民国 関係当局의 同意를 얻어, 捜査審理 및 裁判을 為하여 合衆国이 裁判権을 가지는 特定刑事事件을 大韓民国의 法院이나 当局에 移送할 수 있다. 大韓民国 関係当局은, 合衆国 軍 当局의 同意를 얻어, 捜査, 審理 및 裁判을 為하여 大韓民国이 裁判権을 가지는 特定 刑事事件을 合衆国 軍当局에 移送할 수 있다.	合意議事錄 第3項(나)에 関한 諒解事項 1 1. "特히 重要"하다는 用語는 個個의 特定 事件의 慎重한 調査後 大韓民国이 裁判権을 行使함이 必須的이라고 思料되는 事件에 関係되며 또한 同 用語는 一般的으로 다음型態의 犯罪에 関係되나 制限的은 아니다. (가) 大韓民国의 安全에 関한 犯罪, (나) 사람을 죽음에 이르게 한 犯罪, 強盗罪 및 強姦罪, 다만, 그 犯罪가 合衆国 軍隊의 構成員, 軍属 또는 家族에 対하여 行하여진 境遇에는 그러하지 아니하다. 및 (다) 前記 各 犯罪의 未遂 또는 共犯, 2. 前項에 規定된 犯罪에 関하여, 関係 当局은 第22条 第6項에 規定된 相互間의 助力을 提供하기 為하여 準備 捜査의 着手時부터 特히 緊密한 協力을 継続 行하여야 한다.

0217

-4-

非公式合意案	最終合意案
6. (가) 合衆国 軍隊의 構成員, 軍属 또는 家族이 大韓民国 안에서 大韓民国의 利益에 反하여 犯한 犯罪 때문에 合衆国 法院에 訴追되었을 境遇에는, 그 裁判은 大韓民国 안에서 行하여져야 한다. (1) 다만, 合衆国의 法律이 달리 要求하는 境遇, 또는 (2) 軍事上 緊急事態의 境遇 또는 司法上의 利益을 為한 境遇에 合衆国 軍当局이 大韓民国 領域밖에서 裁判을 行할 意図가 있는 境遇에는 除外된다. 이러한 境遇 合衆国 軍 当局은 大韓民国 当局에 이러한 意図에 対한 意見을 陳述할 수 있는 機会를 適時에 賦与하여야 하며 大韓民国 当局이 陳述하는 意見에 対하여 充分한 考慮를 하여야 한다. (나) 裁判이 大韓民国 領域 밖에서 行하여질 境遇에는, 合衆国 軍当局은 大韓民国 当局에 裁判의 場所와 日字를 通告하여야 한다. 大韓民国 代表는 그裁判에 立会할 権利를 가진다. 合衆国 当局은 判決과 訴訟의 最終 結果를 大韓民国 当局에 通告하여야 한다. 7. 本条및 本合意議事録의 規定의 施行과 軽微한 犯罪의 迅速한 処理를 為하여, 大韓民国 関係当局과 合衆国 軍当局은 約定을 締結할수있다. 同 約定은 또한 通告없이	合意議事録 第3項(나)에関한 諒解事項 II 合衆国当局의 見地에서 事件이 特히 重要한 것이라는 決定에 関한 疑問이 提起된 境遇에는 合衆国 外交使節은 大韓民国의 関係当局과 相議할수있는 機会가 賦与된 権利를 保有하며 또한 그러한 機会가 賦与되기를 期待한다. 交換公文 親愛하는 大使 貴下 今日 大韓民国政府와 合衆国政府는 大韓民国과 合衆国政府間의 施設과 区域및 大韓民国에서의 合衆国軍隊의 地位에 関한 協定에 正式으로 署名하였읍니다. 同協定의 第22条및 同合意議事録은 大韓民国에 있는 合衆国軍隊 構成員, 軍属및 그들의 家族에 対한 裁判権行使를 規定하고 있읍니다. 이에 関聯하여, 大韓民国政府는 우리 両国家를 結束하는 相互 尊重과 友誼의 強인한 紐帯를 意識하고 또한 合衆国軍隊가 大韓民国의 防衛에 있어서 遂行하는 重大한 役割을 認定하여 (第3項(나)에関한 合意議事録) 第4項에 따른 節次上의 約定을 為하여 다음과 같은 諒解事項을 提議하는바입니다:

0218

非公式合意案	最終合意案
하는 處理와 本合意議事錄 第3項에 規定된 權利拋棄를 撤回할수있는 期間에도 미칠수있다.	相互 防衛目的을 爲하여, 大韓民國에 配置된 合衆國軍隊의 駐屯으로 말미아마 發生하는 事件의 處理를 迅速히 하기 爲하여, 第3項(나)에 關한 合意議事錄의 規定을 施行함에 있어서, 大韓民國政府는 合衆國 軍當局이 個個의 特定事件에 있어서 拋棄를 要請할것을 要求하지 아니하며 大韓民國 政府가 特定事件에 있어서 大韓民國當局이 裁判權을 行使함이 特히 重要하다고 決定하지 아니하는限 合衆國 軍當局은 裁判權을 가진다. 司法行政의 迅速化를 爲하여 大韓民國政府에 依한 그와 같은 決定은 大韓民國이 그의 第一次 裁判權에 屬하는 犯罪 發生을 通告받거나 또는 알게된後 15日內에 또는 第3項(나)에 關한 合意議事錄 第4項에 따라 相互 合意될수도 있는 그보다 短期間內에 法務部長官이 書面으로 合衆國의 關係軍當局에 通告하여야한다. 合衆國 軍當局은 15日 또는 달리 合意된 期間이 滿了되기 前에는 裁判權을 行使하여서는 아니된다. 本人은 上記 諒解事項에 對한 貴下의 確認을 感謝히 여기는 바입니다. 敬具

0219

第23条 請求權

非 公 式 合 意 案	最終合意案
合意議事録 1. 달리 規定하는 境遇를 除外하고는 (가) 本条의 第5項, 第6項, 第7項및 第8項의 規定은, 서울特別市의 地域에서 일어난 事件으로부터 発生한 請求權에 関하여는, 本協定의 効力発生日後 6個月만에 効力이 発生하게된다。 (나) 第5項, 第6項, 第7項및 第8項의 規定은 実行可能한 가장빠른 時日에, 合同委員会가 決定하는바에 따라, 大韓民国의 其他地域에 그適用을 拡大한다。	合意議事録 1. 달리 規定하는 境遇를 除外하고는, 本条의 第5項, 第6項, 第7項 및 第8項의 規定은, 서울特別市의 地域에서 일어난 事件으로 부터 発生한 請求權에 関하여는 本協定의 効力発生日後 6個月만에 그리고 大韓民国 안 다른 곳에서 発生한 請求權에 関하여는 本協定의 効力発生日後 1年만에, 効力이 発生하게된다。

0220

非公式合意案	最終合意案
4. (나) 合同委員会는, 合衆国軍隊雇傭員의 大韓民国防衛에 있어서의 役割과 大韓民国 法令의 関係規定을 考慮하여, 労動争議가 前記節次에 依하여 解決되지 아니하는 境遇에는 더以上 団体行動権을 行使하여서는 아니될 緊要한 雇傭員의 諸範疇를 決定한다。	4. (나) 雇傭員 또는 雇傭員団体는 労動争議가 前記節次에 依하여 解決되지 아니하는 境遇에는 継続 団体行動権을 가진다。 다만, 合同委員会가 이러한 行動이 大韓民国의 共同防衛를 為한 合衆国軍隊의 軍事作戦을 甚히 妨害한다고 決定하는 境遇에는 除外된다。
合同委員会에서 이 問題에 関하여 合意에 到達할 수 없을 境遇에는 그問題는 大韓民国政府의 関係官과 아메리카合衆国 外交使節間의 討議를 通한 再検討의 対象이 될 수 있다。	合同委員会에서 이 問題에 関하여 合意에 到達할 수 없을 境遇에는 그 問題는 大韓民国政府의 関係官과 아메리카合衆国 外交使節間의 討議를 通한 再検討의 対象이 될 수 있다。
合意議事録	合意議事録
4. 雇傭主가 合衆国軍隊의 軍事上 必要때문에 本条에 따라 適用되는 大韓民国 労動法令을 따를 수 없을 때에는, 그 問題는 可能한限 事前에 検討와 適当한 措置를 為하여 合同委員会에 回附되어야 한다。	4. 雇傭主가 合衆国軍隊의 軍事上 必要때문에 本条에 따라 適用되는 大韓民国 労動法令을 따를 수 없을 때에는, 그 問題는 事前에 検討와 適当한 措置를 為하여 合同委員会에 回附되어야 한다。
合同委員会에서 適当한 措置에 関하여 相互 合意가 이루어질 수 없을 境遇에는, 그 問題는 大韓民国政府의 関係官과 아메리카合衆国의 外交使節間의 討議를 通한 再検討의 対象이 될 수 있다。	合同委員会에서 適当한 措置에 関하여 相互合意가 이루어질 수 없을 境遇에는, 그 問題는 大韓民国政府의 関係官과 아메리카合衆国의 外交使節間의 討議를 通한 再検討의 対象이 될 수 있다。
諒解事項	諒解事項
韓国労動法令으로부터의 離脱은 合同委員会에의 回附가 軍	韓国労動法令으로부터의 離脱은 合同委員会에의 緊急時

0221

非公式合意案	最終合議案
軍事作戰을 甚히 妨害할 境遇에는 回附할 必要가 없는 것으로 諒解한다。	回附가 軍事作戰을 甚히 妨害할 境遇에는 回附할 必要가 없는 것으로 諒解한다。

0222

-9-

韓.美間 駐屯軍地位協定締結交涉

I. 刑事裁判管轄權

韓國側案	美國側案
가. 第一次管轄權의 拋棄 ① 韓國當局은 美軍當局이 要請하면 韓國當局이 管轄權을 行使함이 特히 重要하다고 決定하는境遇를 除外하고 第一次管轄權을 美軍當局에 拋棄한다. ② 韓國當局이 내리는決定에 關하여 異議가 提起된境遇 美國外交使節에 韓國當局과 協議할수있는 機會가 賦與된다. ③ 諒解事項 韓國이 管轄權을 行使함이 特히 重要하다고決定하는 事件의 範수에 該當하는 犯罪는 다음과같은 犯罪를 包含한다. 가) 韓國의安全에 關한犯罪 나) 사람을 죽음에 이르게한犯罪 다) 強간罪 라) 強盜罪	① 韓國政府는 韓國當局에 賦與된 第一次管轄權을 美國을 爲하여 拋棄한다. ② 韓國當局이 特定事件에 있어서 特殊한事情을 理由로. 韓國의 司法上의 重大한利益이 韓國의 管轄權行使를 不可避하게 한다는 意見을 가질境遇에는 美軍當局에 通告함으로서 權利拋棄를 撤回할수있다. 가) 特定事件의 愼重한檢討와 그結果에 따른것을 條件으로 特히 다음과 같은事件에 있어서 韓國의 司法上의 重大한利益이 韓國의管轄權行使를 不可避하게 할수 있는것으로 한다. 1) 韓國의安全에 關한 犯罪 2) 사람을 죽음에 이르게한 犯罪. 強간罪. 強盜罪 3.) 上記各犯罪의 未遂또는 共犯 ③ 美國當局이 特定事件에 對한 權利拋棄를 撤回하고 關係當局間의 諒解가 成立되지않을때에는 美國當局은 外交經路를

0223

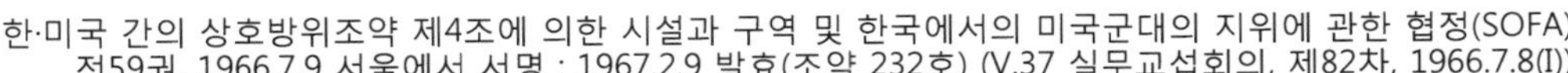

韓國側案	美國側案
마) 韓美兩國中 어느當局이 特히 重要하다고 認定하는 犯罪 바) 上記 各犯罪의 未遂또는共犯	通하여 韓國政府에 異議를 提起할수 있다. 韓國政府는 韓國의司法上의 利益과 美國의利益을 充分히 考慮하여 外交分野에 있어서의 그權限을 行使하여 意見差異를 解決하여야 한다.
나. 公務執行中 犯罪 ① 美軍法務官이 發行한 證明書는 管轄權決定을爲한 事實의充分한 證據가 된다. ② 韓國地方檢察廳 檢事長이 反證이 있다고 思慮하는 例外的인境遇 韓國關係官및 美國外交使節間에 再審되어야 한다. ③ 諒解事項 가) 證明書는 修正되지 않는한 確定的이다. 美軍當局은 韓國當局이 提示한異議에 對하여 正常한考慮를 해야한다. ④ 公務의定義는 1956年度의 美極東軍의 定義를 一部修正하여 合意議事錄에 規定한다.	① 美軍의權限있는 當局이 發行한 證明書는 管轄權決定을爲한 事實의充分한 證據가 된다. ② 韓國檢察總長이 反證이 있다고 思慮하는 例外的인境遇 韓國關係官및 美國外交使節間에 再審될수 있다. ③ 諒解事項 가) 證明書는 合意議事錄의 節次에 따라 修正되지 않는限 確定的이다 ④ 公務의 定義는 1956年度의 美極東軍의 定義대로 諒解事項으로 規定한다.

0224

韓國側案	美國側案
다. 被疑者의 裁判前身柄拘禁 ① 韓國當局이 拘禁할 正當한事由가없는限 모든司法節次가 끝나고 韓國當局이 要請할때까지 美國當局이 拘禁한다. ② 韓國의安全에關한 被疑者의 身柄은 韓國當局이 拘禁한다. ③ 韓國當局이 身柄의引渡를 要請하면 美國當局은 好意的考慮를 하여야한다.	① 모든司法節次가 끝나고 韓國當局이 要請할때까지 美國當局이 拘禁한다. ② 韓國의安全에關한 被疑者의 身柄은 韓國當局이 拘禁하되 拘禁事情의 適否에關한 兩國間의 合意가 있어야 한다. ③ 同

II. 民事請求權

韓國側案	美國側案
1. 公務執行中 第3者에 對한 損害 韓國法에 依據 韓國當局이 解決하여 賠償金을 支拂하고 其後 兩國政府가 그支拂된金額을 分擔하며 美國當局에게 全的으로 損害의 責任이 있을때에는 韓國15% 美國85%의 比率로 分擔하되 個個의 請求事件에 關한 分擔案에 對하여 美國當局이 受諾한事件에 限하여 美國政府는 韓國政府에 辨償한다.	韓國案과 同一한方法으로 解決하되 美國當局에게 全的으로 損害의責任이 있을때의 分擔率은 韓國25% 美國75%로하며 個個의 請求事件에 關한 分擔案 損害의責任限界및 賠償金額에 對하여 美國當局이 受諾한事件에 限하여 美國政府는 韓國政府에 辨償한다.

0225

韓國側案	美國側案
2. 請求權條項의 發効時期 第5項 公務執行中 第三者에對한 損害의 解決規定은 協定發効 6個月後부터 發効한다.	第5項 公務執行中 第三者에對한 損害 第6項 非公務執의 損害 第7項 非公務中의 車輛使用으로 發生하는損害및 第8項 公務執行與否에 關한 紛爭解決規定은 서울特別市에서 일어나는 事件에 限하여 協定發効6個月後부터 適用하며 其他地域에 對하여는 合同委員會의 決議에 따라 漸次的으로 適用토록 한다.
3. KSC의 行爲로 因한 損害 第5項 公務執行中 第三者에 對한 損害의 解決을 爲하여 KSC는 美軍의 雇傭員으로 看做한다.	本條의 規定을爲하여 KSC는 韓國軍의 雇傭員으로 看做한다.

III 勞務調達

韓國側案	美國側案
1. 雇傭主는 美國軍(非歲出機關包含) 雇傭人은 美軍屬이 아닌 韓國國籍을 가진 民間人으로 한다.	1. 雇傭主는 美國軍(非歲出機關包含)및 軍招請契約者 雇傭人은 美軍屬이 아닌 雇傭人(KSC및家事使用人은除外) 但 準軍事的인

0226

韓國側案	美國側案
2. 勞動條件은 本條規定에 相反되지 않거나 別途合意(合同委에서 事前에)되지않는限 韓國勞動法令을 遵守한다	2. 本條規定과 美軍의 軍事上 必要에 相反되지 않는限 韓國勞動法, 慣習慣例를 遵守한다. (必要時 可能한限 事前에 合同委에서 協議한다)
3. 罷業權은 合同委에서 同行使를 禁止當한者를 除外한 雇傭人에게 賦與되어야 한다. 紛爭解決期間中 特別委에 回附된날로부터 起算하여 冷却期間(勞動爭議法14條依據)이 經過하면 罷業權을 行使할수있다.	3. 罷業權은 韓國軍雇傭人과 同一한 法的規制를 받는다. 紛爭解決期間中에는 罷業을包含한 一切의 正常業務妨害行爲를 하지못한다.
4. 美軍業務에 不可缺한技術者에 對하여 事前에 要求하면 相互合意下에 戰時에 兵役義務를 延期한다.	4. 美軍業務에 不可缺한 技術者에 對하여 事前에 要求하면 戰時에 兵役義務를 延期하여야 한다.

보통문서로 재분류(1967. 12. 31.)

0227

외교문서 비밀해제: 주한미군지위협정(SOFA) 14
주한미군지위협정(SOFA) 서명 및 발효 14

초판인쇄 2024년 03월 15일
초판발행 2024년 03월 15일

지은이 한국학술정보(주)
펴낸이 채종준
펴낸곳 한국학술정보(주)
주 소 경기도 파주시 회동길 230(문발동)
전 화 031-908-3181(대표)
팩 스 031-908-3189
홈페이지 http://ebook.kstudy.com
E-mail 출판사업부 publish@kstudy.com
등 록 제일산-115호(2000. 6. 19)

ISBN 979-11-7217-025-7 94340
979-11-7217-011-0 94340 (set)

책에 대한 더 나은 생각, 끊임없는 고민, 독자를 생각하는 마음으로 보다 좋은 책을 만들어갑니다.